ROUTLEDGE LIBRARY EDITIONS:
DEVELOPMENT

CONFLICT AND INTERVENTION IN THE THIRD WORLD

CONFLICT AND INTERVENTION IN THE THIRD WORLD

Edited by
MOHAMMED AYOOB

Volume 86

Routledge
Taylor & Francis Group
LONDON AND NEW YORK

First published in 1980

This edition first published in 2014
by Routledge
2 Park Square, Milton Park, Abingdon, Oxfordshire OX14 4RN

Simultaneously published in the USA and Canada
by Routledge

711 Third Avenue, New York, NY 10017

First issued in paperback 2014

Routledge is an imprint of the Taylor and Francis Group, an informa business

British Library Cataloguing in Publication Data
A catalogue record for this book is available from the British Library

ISBN 978-0-415-58414-2 (Set)
ISBN 978-0-415-60179-5 (hbk) (Volume 86)
ISBN 978-1-138-86571-6 (pbk) (Volume 86)

Publisher's Note

The publisher has gone to great lengths to ensure the quality of this reprint but points out that some imperfections in the original copies may be apparent.

Disclaimer

The publisher has made every effort to trace copyright holders and welcomes correspondence from those they have been unable to contact.

CONFLICT AND INTERVENTION IN THE THIRD WORLD

Edited by

MOHAMMED AYOOB

CROOM HELM LONDON

Croom Helm Ltd, 2 – 10 St John's Road, London SW11

British Library Cataloguing in Publication Data

Conflict and intervention in the Third World.
1. Underdeveloped areas — Foreign relations—Case studies
2. World politics—1975-1985—Case studies
I. Ayoob, Mohammed
341.5'8 D849

ISBN 0-7099-0063-5

Contents

Acknowledgements

This book owes a great deal to the debate and discussion in the Department of International Relations, Australian National University, over the last two years, on and around the subject of great-power intervention in Third World conflicts. It was this debate both in the seminar rooms and the corridors of the department that first brought home to me the idea that such a volume needs to be written and produced as soon as possible in order to contribute, even if marginally, to the wider discussion on this very important concern in the field of late-twentieth-century international relations. It is, therefore, first of all the department as a whole—faculty and students—to whom I owe a debt of gratitude for providing the stimulus for the production of this volume.

However, there have been certain individuals in the department and its sister institution, the Strategic and Defence Studies Centre, who have been particularly helpful in this venture and to whom I owe a special word of thanks: J.D.B. Miller, not only for agreeing to write the Foreword but also for providing by his leadership an atmosphere very conducive to systematic research and dispassionate debate; T.B. Millar, both for writing the introductory essay and for his intelligent and sympathetic comments on almost everything that I have written over the last two years—even though there are a number of my conclusions with which he has heartily disagreed; R.J. O'Neill for his constant encouragement both in this venture and in my other academic (and non-academic) efforts and for performing for me the role of a sounding board on whom I could try out any and all of my ideas no matter how inconsequential or, sometimes, downright absurd; and J.L.S. Girling who has not only contributed a valuable chapter to this volume but also shared with me the sympathy and concern for problems of the Third World which motivated me to undertake this task.

To the contributors to this volume I owe a deep sense of gratitude both for meeting deadlines and for putting up with my rather exacting editorial standards. Without them, of course, the book would never have seen the light of day.

I am also very grateful to Robin Ward and Elizabeth Macfarlane who helped me in many ways to put the volume together, including the tedious task of checking footnotes and making them conform to the publisher's style. To Lise Christensen, Lynn McLeod, Shirley Steer and Bev Ricketts, who typed various parts of the manuscript and often struggled bravely to decipher my less than legible handwriting, I am particularly grateful. And last, but not the least, I owe a debt to my wife, Salma, who tried with a considerable amount of success to keep out of my way during those long evenings when I was either struggling with my own contributions to the volume or was busy trying to put the other contributions into final shape.

Mohammed Ayoob

Foreword

This book should be a rich source of fruitful discussion, since the conflicts with which it deals lend themselves to more than one interpretation. 'Great powers' and 'the Third World' are both groupings which excite controversy; while one can find much in common between the states which constitute each of them, there are still so many differences in behaviour between, say, the United States and China on the one hand, and India and Papua New Guinea on the other, that there can be endless argument about what the groupings mean in practice. None the less, both groupings are worth retaining, because we find it hard to do without them and to reduce all international behaviour to unilateral actions and bilateral relationships. The difficulties arise when one set of definitions confronts another.

Such difficulties would probably figure in any comprehensive discussion of the issues raised in this book. Drawing on my own experience over the years, I can see two attitudes emerging, each equipped with material from these essays.

On the one hand would be those to whom the case studies presented here confirm a picture of the Third World as harried and distressed, largely through the actions of great and near-great powers. From this standpoint, the dissensions plainly visible between Third World states (and within them, as in the case of Cyprus) are realities, but not realities of the same order as the activities of the major powers. These powers, so the attitude would maintain, not only exacerbated the dissensions in earlier periods (as suggested by S.D. Muni, Mohammed Ayoob and John Zarocostas), but also continue to manage them for their own purposes. By means of arms sales and selective intervention of various kinds, they keep the Third World countries hostile towards their neighbours, and perpetuate their own superiority through the processes of deprivation and dependence. People maintaining such an attitude would agree that there were exceptions, but would argue that, by and large, there is a deliberate tendency to perpetuate the inferiority of those already inferior, and to uplift those of the industrialised North who are already better off than they have a right to be.

On the other hand, a contrasting attitude would stress the relative autonomy of the Third World states. Never before have there been so many sovereign states, and never before so many weak ones. What were once tribal conflicts or their equivalent are now elevated to wars at the international level, and become occasions for dispute and opportunity amongst the major powers, instead of being settled by some imperial overlord. When these conflicts are of long standing (as some of them are, in Indo-China and elsewhere), there is bound to be disturbance over a wide area if they are fought out with modern weapons and if they involve resources of any magnitude; they become hard to ignore, whether the major powers want to ignore them or not. People holding the broad attitude described here will probably emphasise the thrusting nature of great powers, and use T.B. Millar's essay to assert that new states are no better, morally, than old ones, when the use of violence arises. They will derive some comfort, however, from Robert Springborg's demonstration of the difficulties that lie ahead of great powers when they try to control Third World countries over any long period.

Whichever of these attitudes one takes up, one is bound to be struck, in reading this book, by certain features of the various conflicts that are not often emphasised in press reports and other sensationalised accounts of international relations. One is the very *local* quality of what goes on: Cyprus is not Indo-China; India is certainly not Rhodesia. This local quality provides a basis for that nationalism which J.L.S. Girling finds so powerful in so many cases. Along with it goes the *persistence* of much local conflict, whether one thinks of it as arising directly from local circumstances, as I.R. Hancock does of Rhodesia, or as stimulated and exacerbated by deliberate external influences, as S.D. Muni and Mohammed Ayoob do. Turning to the intervenors (i.e. to the great and near-great powers), a reader will find fascinating, I think, the highly *intermittent and selective* quality of intervention by the superpowers, while appreciating also the *shrinking significance* of former imperial powers, especially Britain. Whether one could say quite the same of France is a question not dealt with here in any detail.

Thus, the book contains ample material for further argument—material in both the intertwined areas of fact and opinion. It is about one of the most important, yet most complicated, aspects of contemporary international relations. It deserves to be taken very seriously indeed.

J.D.B. Miller
Professor of International Relations
Research School of Pacific Studies
Australian National University

1 Conflict and Intervention

T.B. MILLAR

I

All conflict between states is intervention. You cannot fire bullets or rockets across a border without intervening, dramatically and damagingly, in the domestic affairs of that state. When we speak of intervening in a conflict we are speaking of intervening in an existing intervention.

Wars between neighbours are far more likely to occur, and are more convenient to prosecute when they do occur, than wars between non-neighbours. A common boundary gives opportunity for argument about where the line should rightly lie, for disagreements between the people who live on either side of the line under unequal jurisdictions, for attempts to reunite cultural, tribal or 'national' groups split by the division often arbitrarily drawn between them. And the logistics of prosecuting the conflict are almost always relatively easy compared with the problems of transporting armed forces to remote battlegrounds. Borders are so permeable, and so frequently permeated. Distant fields may be greener but they are harder to get to. Hence the fact that the great majority of wars are wars between neighbours, or begin that way. Conflict is primarily a regional manifestation.

But what is a region? Like beauty, the region tends to be in the mind of the beholder, or perhaps of the participant. For some purposes the Pacific, occupying one third of the surface of the globe, might be considered a region; for other purposes, it could be divided into a score or more of regions. 'The War in the Pacific', 1941-5, between Japan on the one side and the United States and the British Commonwealth on the other, ranged from the American Pacific coast to India. The connecting link was Japan, which from 1931 onwards, steadily took on by extension one enemy after another, sensibly omitting the Soviet Union but disastrously including the United States. We tend to think of a regional conflict as being a conflict between neighbours, and perhaps *their* neighbours. The intervention of powers geographically removed from the immediate neighbourhood of the combatants gives a new dimension to it, conceptually at least, and to some people provides an element of impropriety additional to what may have existed in the original conflict. There is a general notion that war is essentially the business of the primary combatants.

It is hard to write about war without bringing in moral judgements about right and wrong, defender and aggressor, good and evil, justice and injustice. Experience over sixty years with two international organisations—the League of Nations and the United Nations—has demonstrated how difficult and usually how unfruitful it is to define the nature of aggression, and who, in a conflict, is an aggressor. Not only is there a problem in determining who fired the first shot; it is equally difficult to discover the degree of provocation, if any, or the 'basic causes' of the conflict. And public judgements are also regrettably subject to considerations extraneous to the conflict under review. Mussolini gained a good deal of international support for his invasion of Ethiopia due to the (entirely erroneous) view, held by statesmen who should have known better, that Italy would stand up to Hitler's Germany. In Japan's attack on Manchuria in 1931—an act of war in which the government in Tokyo appeared to be manipulated by the military on the ground but cannot thereby be absolved from responsibility—propaganda won some observers to the view that it was the Chinese who were to blame. This was at least partly because Japan was bending its immense energies to establishing an empire in north-east Asia—an area which potential victims in other areas considered preferable to their own for such an enterprise. The degree of censure adopted in resolutions of international bodies such as the UN is not objectively determined but is a conscious political act for which the objective facts (assuming they can be determined) constitute only one, and often by no means the most important, consideration.[1]

In both these cases—Abyssinia and Manchuria—the major powers were in a weak moral position to condemn the successful aggressor states. Britain, France, Belgium, Portugal, the Soviet Union and the United States had all acquired their empires, except for a few colonies of settlement, by processes, directly comparable with those of Italy and Japan—by bloody conquest using superior military technology—as had two other ex-imperial powers, Spain and Germany. Britain, France and Italy had treated Abyssinia as less than sovereign since early in the century. Abyssinia itself had become an empire by military means. Whether or not these powers remembered or did not remember the sins of their youth, was irrelevant. Each new conflict provoked genuine concern because it was a real or potential new risk to world order, to their own peace and prosperity and national interests, to the institutions erected 'to maintain international peace and security', and to the lives and property of innocent people.

Notions of morality and justice have traditionally been largely irrelevant to decisions whether or not to engage in (i.e. initiate) conflict. Rather they have been part of the process of winning support for one's cause, or of analysing the conflict later. The concept of the 'just' war goes back at least to Roman times, but it was, as it still largely is, a justice based on defined formalities, on one's own or one's group sense of law, rather than on an inherent rightness or wrongness.

This is not to say that war is amoral, i.e. outside the canons of or on a different plane from morality, or that there are not degrees of right and wrong, justice or injustice, involved in war. There are indeed such degrees, as we all know. Rather it is to say that governments tend to use such arguments so far as these support their own national interests or their own domestic position, and to ignore them when they don't. Britain in 1914 went to the aid of 'brave little Belgium', but not to the aid of Luxembourg, though it had a treaty with both. In 1939 it threw Czechoslovakia to the wolves in the hope that the wolves would thereby be pacified, but went to war over Poland when it was clear that they were not. Governments subject themselves to what Charles Manning at the London School of Economics used to call the 'it's all right about X' syndrome. What is condemned in unfriendly country (or leader) Y is condoned in friendly country or leader X. And it's especially 'all right' about *us*. All the governments have blind spots about the morality of their own predations, and find ready justifications: civilising the natives, bringing them justice, order or religion, adjusting 'natural' boundaries. Nehru, a powerful critic of British imperialism for the soundest of reasons, had no qualms about taking over Hyderabad, Junagadh and Goa by *force majeure*, and, after occupying the vale of Kashmir, denying the Kashmiris a promised plebiscite. Indonesian nationalists successfully fought the Dutch for their independence, subsequently by bluster and a spurious 'act of free choice' extended their own empire to include West New Guinea, and then invaded East Timor in a bloody action justified on the grounds that the territory might otherwise go communist. I recall an American journalist in London running on at length to me about the iniquities of the British Empire. I reminded him of the Philippines, Cuba, Puerto Rico, Samoa, the American wars against Mexico and before all that the annexation of the continent. 'But there was no one there,' he protested, 'only Indians.'

II

Why do governments go to war? In fact, governments decide for war, perhaps declare war, but it is their citizens who actually *go* to war, do the fighting, suffer the casualties. This is not merely a piece of semantics. Governments require the support of the armed forces and much of the populace if they are going to wage war. Clausewitz told us that war is the continuation of politics by *other* means, i.e. the means take on a qualitative change. Although peace-war-peace is a continuum in important respects, there are few casualties in the diplomacy that leads into or out of armed conflict.

In his book *The Causes of War*[2] Geoffrey Blainey analyses the decision-making process in several scores of wars since 1700. He demonstrates that many wars are begun for irrational reasons, and that in most cases the decision-makers have a substantially inaccurate view of the comparative forces involved (including the state of their own), and the likely duration and outcome of the conflict. Most theories about the causes of war do not stand up to empirical investigation. War is never 'accidental'. It is not prevented by the flow of trade, of ideas, of 'understanding', nor by a common culture, religion or language. History does not show that an arms race will lead to war: it may well delay the outbreak of war, and although expensive, will still be much cheaper than war. History does not show that a balanced power grouping will preserve the peace, or that an unbalanced one will necessarily lead to conflict. Nor is war likely to be used to overcome internal dissent. Are pressures or ambitions the main causes of war? War is the test of comparative power, says Blainey, is fought for the purposes of power, and the aims of war are 'simple varieties of power' exercised by the power-seekers.

> The vanity of nationalism, the will to spread an ideology, the protection of kinsmen in an adjacent land, the desire for more territory or commerce, the avenging of a defeat or insult, the craving for greater national strength or independence, the wish

> to impress or cement alliances—all these represent power in different wrappings. The conflicting aims of rival nations are always conflicts of power. Not only is power the issue at stake, but the decision to resolve that issue by peaceful or warlike methods is largely determined by assessments of relative power.[3]

Yet disparities of power exist the world over, and usually do *not* provoke conflict, perhaps because of external or internal restraints, perhaps through lack of desire or incentive. And if the exercise or increase of power is frequently the objective, or *an* objective of conflict, it does not always supply the motive, nor the reason why war is preferred to diplomacy. The acquisition of territory, of resources, the improvement of commerce or the safeguarding of its channels have been the visible objectives of many governments in war. The existence of an oppressed or disaffected minority in country A with cultural links to country B may give an incentive for B to intervene in A, may create an opportunity, suggest a plausible *casus belli*. Disproportionate power is the means, but may only be part of the objective.

Strangely, perhaps, as Arthur Koestler points out, the motives of the *combatants* (at least those who think about it) or of the decision-makers are rarely selfish, personal, or a reflection of individual aggressiveness. Man as a political animal—leader or led—takes on qualities relevant to his political situation. 'If we did for ourselves what we do for our country, what scoundrels we would be,' said Cavour. Man's integrative tendencies, says Koestler, are incomparably more dangerous than his self-assertive tendencies. The gun needs a cause, and the cause loads the gun. Thus:

> the crimes of violence committed for selfish, personal motives are historically insignificant compared to those committed *ad majorem gloriam Dei*, out of a self-sacrificing devotion to a flag, a leader, a religious faith or a political conviction. Man has always been prepared not only to kill but to die for good, bad or completely futile causes. And what can be a more valid proof of the self-transcending urge than the readiness to die for an ideal? ... the tragedy of man is not his truculence but his proneness to delusions.[4]

Both leaders and led are prone to delusions, of manifold kinds: the delusions of the master race, the dominant tribe, the invincible leader, the one true religion, the only correct ideology; the delusion of wars in the name of the Prince of Peace, wars over a fine point of religious doctrine, wars to bring in the millenium, wars to pre-empt war, wars to end all war. Yet with the rarest of exceptions all such wars are wars about power, designed to change the power relationship, to put *us* in charge of *them*, make them defer to us. Inevitably, one nation or group of nations will end a war disadvantaged, with a sense of defeat and humiliation, with resentment at the losses incurred and perhaps a thirst for retribution—a thirst to change the power relationship once again.[5] International society tends to frown on such desires, preferring the status quo to further conflict, or preferring at least that change be by peaceful means. The United Nations Charter was founded on this principle, and the Organisation of African Unity, composed of states, many of which had borders drawn by imperial rulers without logic or equity, resolved to accept those borders in perpetuity, for good or ill.[6]

This resolve has largely held, in Africa as elsewhere, yet as the majority of states are former colonies or protectorates of a European power, so the majority of conflicts have elements of the imperial legacy, sometimes including direct military intervention by one or more imperial powers. This is not to support Lenin's thesis that war is as inevitable a by-product of imperialism as imperialism is of capitalism[7]—a thesis not borne out by World War I, of which he was writing, nor by most wars since then including the recent war between two communist powers, China and Vietnam. Wars evolve from the totality of history. Not only the boundaries of the former colonies were determined by their imperial masters, but also the educational systems, style of government, trading and investment patterns, military organisation and even international outlook.

All these began to change after independence, and some conflicts developed essentially or wholly from local causes. But it is not surprising that among what we call the Third World, which consists very largely of former colonies of European or American empires, conflict between them has often involved or engaged the interest of the former metropolitan great power or powers. During the post-World War II period, the 'First World' (Western, industrialised, non-communist states) and the 'Second World' (communist states) developed their own confrontation and competition for influence and power, and such confrontation and competition were also quickly translated to the Third World in its weakness, with or without invitation. Both sides were prepared to fish in troubled waters if it suited their national interests or ambitions. The term 'neo-colonialism' was invented to describe a situation where an ex-colonial state continued after independence to be strongly influenced by the policies of its former ruler. The suggestion is that the new nation—it may be 20 or 50 years old—from a weakness compounded by its colonial experience, invites or allows intervention by the imperial power, defers to its demands, if the imperial interest is threatened. By the logic of events, this term was extended to apply to other great power influence, pressure or intervention, i.e. other than the former imperial power, and notably by the Soviet Union or the United States seeking to manage and profit from the conflict.

Not all intervention has been selfish, predatory, maleficent or unsought. Not all has involved a disproportionate exercise of strength by the great power, although the disproportionate strength was usually in the background. Much of it has been reactive. An individual from Mars might find it difficult to distinguish between the motives of the intervening powers, motives which would include the protection of friendly governments, of political or economic investment, or of strategic advantage in the wider confrontation. But the Martian, if he had the advantage of a liberal education, might also on occasion distinguish between the ultimate desires of the intervening states on behalf of their clients, either to strengthen their independence, sovereignty and capacity for self-fulfilment, or to weaken them.

Whereas recently independent states broadly accept, at least in rhetoric, the morality of the existing international order, many have applied a different moral status to those countries with continuing colonial or colonial-type affiliations *across water* to European metropolitan powers. The use of force to end such a relationship has been broadly condoned: intervention was and is seen as a lesser evil, indeed a positive good, a liberating process. Yet the onus to do the liberating is not lightly undertaken. War is a costly business, in lives and treasure. Most new-nation contributions to overthrowing colonial-type governments have gone towards guerrilla operations less likely to invite national reprisal. Or, as in the case of Cuban forces in Africa, the interventions are professionally military, but everyone knows they are paid for by the Soviet Union. The Cubans are mercenaries in thin disguise; they represent the Soviet Union and act at its expense, with its weapons and logistics, in its interests.

III

'Every decision to wage war is influenced by predictions of how outside nations will affect the course of the war,' writes Blainey.[8] This is a reasonable, if unprovable, assumption. Some treaties are made in order to prevent or deter the intervention of a third or fourth party: the Anglo-Japanese alliance of 1902, for example, or the Sino-Soviet treaty of 1950, or the Indo-Soviet treaty of 1971. Vietnam's invasion of Kampuchea in late 1978 was presumably calculated on the basis that China would not intervene, and a treaty was signed with the Soviet Union as a form of insurance against such an event. China *did* intervene, presumably with the calculation that, her attack being on a limited scale, the Soviet Union would not react against her. The Chinese leader Deng Xiaoping (Teng Hsiaoping) went to Washington beforehand with a splash of publicity, as part of China's own pyschological insurance. The Soviet Union did not intervene and so the conflict was contained; but if it had intervened the United States would have been forced to consider whether it also should become involved. Because of superpower assumptions about the central balance of power, what began as a small, limited, local war could have expanded to unpredictable and frightening proportions, as has happened numbers of times during the past three hundred years. The shot at Sarajevo that brought so much of the world to a long and costly war has a surprising number of parallels.

It is rare to find any conflict in which someone other than the primary parties does not intervene. Intervention, as said at the beginning, is what all conflict is about. On that assumption, is there any qualitative difference between the initial decision to commence hostilities and the decision by third, fourth etc. parties to become involved? Although some academic writers, including Blainey, feel that it is invidious to allocate 'blame' in a war, and although in retrospect one may see a degree of provocation perhaps equal to the degree of aggression, the resort to force is a specific act, *sui generis*. Some nations, like some people, do behave badly. Diplomacy does not result in people getting killed; war does. One cannot equate the burglar with the householder, the murderer with his victim. Continuing this perhaps simplistic analogy, the act of going to the help of the murderer has features qualitatively different from the act of going to the help of the assailant.

International society is of course far more complex than that, and just as we may question the motives of someone who intervenes in a civil situation, so intervenors in international conflict may have a variety of motives. This book is, in fact, essentially, a book about *motives*, and about the effects of comparative size, and of geographical distance, on morality. It discusses, in the case studies, the extent to which the shifting pattern of local and regional conflict has drawn on or been used by the intervention or involvement of larger external powers. Is it more wrong, improper, or illegal, for the Soviet Union from a distance to help a friendly state than for, say, Zambia, nearby, to do so? Is it 'all right' for India to swallow Goa (small, surrounded, prosperous, colonial) but not all right for India to swallow Bangladesh (large, adjacent, poor, independent)? Is it all right for India to help Bangladesh against Pakistan, but not all right for the Soviet Union to do so? Is it all right for Cubans to help revolutionary forces in Angola, but not for Russians or Chinese or South Africans or the CIA? We tend to have peculiar standards on questions such as these. All kinds of factors affect our perspectives and our judgements, including considerations of race. An Indonesian general once suggested to me that the Indonesian army might usefully take over from the American army in south-east Asia. 'We would be more acceptable,' he said, 'we are the same colour.' One tends to think that a large power intervening at a distance must have selfish motives, and one is probably right. What about the motives of the country intervening from nearby? They could well be even more acquisitive. We all follow what we believe to be our national interests. We all object to being used by another power for its own purposes, and to have this result in war is to add injury to manipulation.

Whatever grounds there may be for intervention in a conflict between neighbours, there would seem to be fewer grounds for external intervention in or stimulation of a civil war, rebellion or insurgency. Yet throughout history there have been innumerable examples of this, on one side or the other. One of the great propaganda successes of Marxist politicians and publicists these past thirty years has been in promoting the notion that a rebellion by forces on the political left is by nature progressive, desirable, even inevitably successful. The fact is that the great majority of insurgencies during this period, including communist insurgencies, have failed. And except for the USSR, Yugoslavia, China and Vietnam, the communist governments that now exist were put there by an external power.

I once proposed a series of criteria for effective, legitimate intervention by a democracy in a conflict within another state—criteria which may apply also to conflict between two states:

1. Intervention, or military assistance, must be specifically requested of the potential intervenor by the government of the country under attack.

2. It must appear to the intervening government (I) that the requesting government (R) has the clear support of a majority of its population, and is itself acting with intelligence, vigour and humanity; the R government must be demonstrably more responsive to the needs of the people than is any revolutionary movement.

3. The attack, or insurgency, must unquestionably be substantially supported, if not directed or controlled, by an external power.

4. Intervention must have at least the acquiescence of the majority of the I electorate, and must be believed by the I government to promote I's national interest.

This proposal drew on the Vietnam war experience, and is perhaps a counsel of perfection—at best a rough guide and basis of judgement, and pointing also to the fact that every intervention, every conflict, is different. If we can discern a pattern in regional conflicts into which great powers intrude, it is probably a pattern of events, of sequences, rather than of principles. Intervention by a great power is not *ipso facto* more wrong than intervention by a smaller one: some small states survive, as they see it, under the protection of a great power. Intervention at a distance is not necessarily more improper than intervention at hand: it is just more difficult, and thus open to fewer states. There are many other considerations. Each case is a separate case.

Yet if we are concerned with principles, with morality and justice, we cannot simply bow to the difficulties of finding a scale of judgement, with clear extremes. International society is not a jungle, even though there are bits of jungle in it. It is governed by laws and conventions, of varying degrees of acceptability and enforceability. It is governed by the spirit in man, by values. If their codification is still very rough and not always ready, if their rules are imperfect and fragile, it is up to each generation to seek to refine them and to extend their sway, and so reduce the chaos, waste and misery caused by human conflict.

Notes

1. Being a political act, these decisions are subject to political change, even retrospectively. In modern times, the Russians and the Chinese have been well practised in the art of rewriting history. There is much less sympathy in the West now than there was in late 1950 for the view that China was an 'aggressor' in Korea. Recently when I was discussing with a member of the Chinese Foreign Office the possibility of a second attack by the Democratic People's Republic of (North) Korea on the South, he said with a broad smile, 'Of course *we say* that last time it was the South that attacked the North.' He was trying to tell me that this piece of history was undergoing revision, the facts having become more palatable.

The world-order tragedies of Manchuria and Abyssinia are told as from inside the League of Nations by Salvador de Madariaga, *Morning Without Noon: Memoirs* (Saxon House, Farnborough, 1974), Part III.

2. Geoffrey Blainey, *The Causes of War* (Macmillan, London, 1973).

3. Ibid., pp. 149-50.

4. Arthur Koestler, *The Ghost in the Machine* (Hutchinson, London, 1967), p. 234.

5. There is a story about a man who entered the grounds of a wealthy New England home and began to pick the flowers. The owner came out and objected. 'Who owns this land?' asked the intruder. 'I do,' replied the man. 'And who owned it before you did?' 'My father, and his father before him for a total of five generations.' 'How did your great-great-grandfather get the land?' 'He fought the Indians for it.' 'Well,' said the visitor, taking off his coat, 'I'll fight *you* for it.'

6. Not all government are so accommodating, and there are numbers of territorial disputes around the world. Exactly a hundred years ago, for example, Chile fought and defeated Bolivia and Peru, taking several thousand square miles of territory later found to be rich in minerals, and the port of Antofagasta. Bolivia, which through this war became a landlocked nation, is now seeking retribution. Chile also has a border dispute with Argentina. The Soviet Union has border disputes with Japan and China; China with Japan, Vietnam and India; Israel with its Arab neighbours, Algeria with Morocco, Ethiopia with Somalia, and so on.

7. V.I. Lenin, *Imperialism, the Highest Stage of Capitalism*, 1917, reproduced in V.I. Lenin, *Selected Works*, Vol. I, revised edn (Progress Publishers, Moscow, 1976), pp. 634-731.

8. Blainey, *The Causes of War*, p. 57.

2 Indo-China

J.L.S. GIRLING

I

The most unexpected—and fateful—development in a region which had only recently seen the end of a devastating war involving external powers was the violent struggle between Hanoi and the Pol Pot regime in Kampuchea (Cambodia) culminating in the Vietnamese-backed dissident takeover early in 1979. This was exacerbated by the bitter, related dispute between Vietnam and China, with all its overtones of Sino-Soviet rivalry.[1]

Although these hostilities and tensions form a relationship among communist states, they cannot easily be explained in Marxist terms. (See also the discussion at the end of this chapter.) A better understanding of the roots of conflict, the current form it takes, and its international implications, is provided by 'traditional' concepts in political science and international relations.

These concepts, on the domestic side, include historical experiences and nationalism, which arises out of those experiences, but is shaped by new social forces resulting from modern political and economic developments. On the external side, these explanatory concepts include geopolitics, balance of power and (great) power politics.

To give an idea of the importance of the latter—and this is a constant theme in international relations—it is sufficient to note the 'hierarchy of power' which characterises the present situation. Thus one superpower (the Soviet Union) uses its global political and diplomatic strength (and even the threat of military action in 1969) in an effort to change the policies of its weaker rival, China. China, a big regional power, in turn 'leans on' and then invades its smaller adversary Vietnam. Vietnam, the major military force in south-east Asia, in turn applies military, political and diplomatic pressure—finally resorting to all-out war—on its small neighbour Kampuchea, a country with about one-sixth the population of Vietnam. As for the former regime in Kampuchea, which was too vulnerable and crisis-ridden to pose a serious threat to its neighbours, it oppressed its own population instead.

Using the 'traditional' categories mentioned above—historic experiences and nationalism; geopolitics and balance of power—this chapter will analyse, first, the complex relationships between Vietnam and Kampuchea, and then the dispute between Vietnam and China. While the first continues to be expressed in violent form—by Vietnamese mopping-up operations against Pol Pot forces—the second arena of hostility, culminating in the Chinese attack on Vietnam, has even more serious implications.

This is because hostility between China and Vietnam, which is dangerous enough in itself, also reinforces the Soviet commitment to its ally Vietnam, thus intensifying the Sino-Soviet dispute in south-east Asia. Preoccupied with the fear of Soviet expansion throughout the world, the Chinese argue that Vietnam is merely an instrument of Soviet policy—'the Cuba of the East'. The Soviet Union and Vietnam, on the other hand, charge that China's attack on Vietnam marks the first stage in Peking's aim to dominate the rest of south-east Asia.[2]

II

The first step towards explaining the conflict between the revolutionary regimes in Vietnam and Kampuchea starts with a paradox. Whereas in a communist Vietnam a 'bloodbath' was confidently predicted (notably by the previous US administration), this has not happened. Conversely in Kampuchea, which for so long had been regarded as an oasis of peace, where the revolutionary leaders were Paris-trained intellectuals, and where the head of the national united front (Prince Sihanouk) was known for his pleasure-loving qualities, a compromise was equally confidently expected in the event of a revolutionary victory. While a 'bloodbath' may or may not have occurred in Pol Pot's Kampuchea, it is evident that many officials of the Lon Nol regime were executed, the urban population (swollen by refugees) driven into the countryside, and the mass of the people put to labour under harsh and primitive conditions.

In order to explain these very different outcomes one must first turn to the contrasting experiences of the Vietnamese and Kampuchean revolutionaries. The former have been steeled by thirty years of war. Strong party leadership, impressive self-discipline and a remarkable solidarity were needed simply to survive in the struggle against immensely more powerful enemies. Moreover, after so many years of violence and destruction, causing heavy casualties and the uprooting of large numbers of people, once victory was won, the party leadership responded to the need for policies of prudence, moderation and reconciliation. The demands of reconstruction and reunification were enormous, given the divergent economy of South Vietnam, stimulated by military concerns, and almost totally dependent on the United States both for its budget and to finance the massive imports of Hondas, water-pumps and supply of oil and fertilisers, which had kept it going. The task of integrating such disparate economic structures and political institutions within one country posed an immense problem which could best be solved, the party leadership argued, not by sweeping, immediate changes, but as a result of careful, patient and methodical preparation.

Admittedly, by 1978, the Vietnamese regime had intensified its economic and political controls, in comparison with the gradualness and moderation of its initial approach. But even the continuing detention (in 're-education' camps) of its former adversaries, and the current suspicion of or hostility towards Buddhists, neutralists and others who had been critical of the Saigon administration and sympathetic to the revolution—even the present grim 'tightening of the screws'—cannot seriously be compared in terms of violence and ruthlessness with, for example, the repression carried out by anti-communists like Diem (or with the massacres in Indonesia after October 1965).

In contrast with Vietnam, Kampuchea until 1970 had experienced more than a century of peace. Tranquillity, contentment, a cheerful and easy-going people, unburdened by severe land problems, carrying on a traditional way of life under the rule of a colourful and seemingly benevolent paternalism: such appeared to many observers the characteristic features of Kampuchea under Sihanouk. Then with the overthrow of Sihanouk in 1970 this comparatively peaceful land was engulfed in total war. The more hopeless and unviable the Lon Nol regime demonstrated itself to be, the more forcefully the United States tried to prevent its collapse. In 1973, with a precarious peace agreed upon in South Vietnam, the full intensity of US bombing shifted to Kampuchea (and after August 1973, with the ban on direct American involvement imposed by the US Congress, to Laos). All the horrors of modern warfare confronted the peasant soldiers of the 'Khmers rouges' as they closed in on Phnom Penh. The heavy losses they (and the surrounding population) suffered inflamed the hatred they felt for the United States, the Lon Nol regime, and for the urban population—supported by the US and sheltered from the worst effects of the war.

When the Kampuchean revolutionaries finally stormed Phnom Penh in 1975 they were determined to eradicate, along with the old regime, what they believed to be a corrupt, repressive, parasitical way of life, alien to the fundamental needs and values of Khmer (Kampuchean) society. This extreme radicalism, nurtured by the years of underground struggle against Sihanouk himself (until 1970), facing incessant harassment and persecution, and isolated from their revolutionary allies (for the interests of both the Vietnamese and the Chinese communists were in friendly relations with Sihanouk), had become increasingly bitter and intense. Reinforcing this ideology of radical extremism—to destroy, and then create a new society rooted in the soil—was the severe shortage of administrative staff, owing to heavy war losses and the exigencies of the revolutionary struggle, which necessitated reliance on young and inexperienced peasant soldiers to keep a large (and ideologically suspect) population under control. This combination of circumstances produced the harsh discipline, the ruthless punishment of minor infractions of rules, the constant purges, and the emphasis on coercion that were reported in a society without monetary exchange, virtually without trade, without schools beyond primary level, and with almost no form of nationwide communications—a country that had been transformed into one vast agricultural work camp.[3]

This is how one scholar, in an illuminating article, perceived the differences between the Vietnamese and Kampuchean revolutionary regimes.[4] The Vietnamese, he argued, benefited from the experience of running a state (in the North) and developing a bureaucratic routine. The Communist Party of Kampuchea's experience, however, had been one of intense and violent class struggle against the bureaucracy, whether headed by Sihanouk or by Lon Nol. Thus, after seizing power, the Communist Party led by Pol Pot 'relied on disruptive and even violent mass-based struggles to resolve social contradictions, including such fundamental ones as those between city and countryside and between mental and manual labour. The party's theory of socialist construction stresses the absolute primacy of mass mobilisation, subjective revolution and learning through practical work over technology and theoretical sophistication.'

The communist parties in Vietnam and Kampuchea thus experienced different revolutionary situations and, after coming to power, pursued different goals. These differences in party history and ideology are clearly one of the causes of the present conflict. But there are also underlying causes which explain, not so much the particular issues under dispute, as why they should have resulted in armed conflict, and why the struggle has been so bitter and protracted.

The immediate causes of conflict are disagreement over the land and off-shore frontiers between Vietnam and Kampuchea (a problem which goes back to the Sihanouk era, and earlier).[5] This, in turn, reflects the mixed populations of the border regions and within the two countries. There are about a million 'Khmers Krom' living in what was formerly part of the Khmer Empire, but which over the past two or three centuries had been infiltrated and occupied by Vietnamese soldiers and settlers: this is the Mekong Delta region, the heart of southern Vietnam. Similarly, from the time of the French protectorate over Kampuchea, Vietnamese had moved across the border to work in French rubber plantations, as clerks in the administration, as artisans and small shopkeepers, fishermen and so on. Unlike the Chinese minority in Kampuchea (around half a million people, slightly more than the Vietnamese), which was more readily assimilated, the Vietnamese retained a distinct ethnic identity.[6]

During the American campaign against the NLF in South Vietnam, the Khmers Krom in Vietnam were an important source of recruits for the US 'special forces' and later rallied to Lon Nol. The Vietnamese community in Kampuchea, on the other hand, had provided recruits and money for the Vietminh movement against the French; and they continued to be regarded with suspicion by Sihanouk and his administration after 1953, when the country became independent. In 1970, these Vietnamese, whether Catholics or communists, became victims of the pogrom following Lon Nol's seizure of power; and those who were left were harried and finally driven out of Kampuchea by the Khmer communists under Pol Pot.[7]

The underlying cause of conflict stems from this animosity, which in turn arises from the historic fear of the Khmers of being dominated by the Vietnamese and incorporated into Vietnam.* As

* This fear is reflected in the Pol Pot regime's accusation that the Vietnamese were trying to force the Khmers into an 'Indo-Chinese Federation' which would be con-

Heder puts it: 'Practically every analysis of Kampuchean history or commentary on modern Kampuchean politics written by a Kampuchean repeatedly and ominously raises the spectre of the disappearance of the Kampuchean race, culture and nation ... [The] combination of intense fear of racial and national extinction with Kampuchea's historically-based mythology of greatness in national construction [the achievements of the Khmer Empire] ... strongly emphasise national exclusiveness and self-reliance ...' The 'intense nationalism and radical self-reliance' of the Kampuchean communists reflected in an isolationist foreign policy, made it extremely difficult to negotiate—that is, to compromise—the differences between the two countries.[8]

The Pol Pot regime insisted that all Vietnamese must quit Kampuchean territory before negotiations on the border dispute could take place. (The Vietnamese had been entrenched along the frontier region since the mid-1960s, when the area became a 'sanctuary' for the revolutionaries in the war against the United States and Saigon.) The Vietnamese, on the contrary, called first for a mutual ceasefire with military withdrawals from a zone along the borders, which the Kampucheans rejected. Behind the problem of disputed frontiers—and of control of offshore resources of petroleum and natural gas—lay the Vietnamese need for security from Khmer frontier harassment, which started almost immediately after liberation in 1975. This, in turn, reflected the Khmers' rigid defence of their sovereignty, which they saw as the only way to maintain independence against the pressures of the Vietnamese.

Since neither side was prepared to back down, particularly after Pol Pot emerged triumphant from an internal power struggle and

---

trolled by the more populous and powerful Vietnamese. (There are currently some 7 to 8 million Khmers as against nearly 50 million Vietnamese.) From 1930, communist movements in Vietnam, Laos and Kampuchea were in fact joined in the Indo-Chinese Communist Party, in what was considered to be a common struggle against the French throughout Indo-China. In 1951, when separate communist parties were formed, it was agreed that an 'Indo China Federation' remained an objective, in the event of success, only 'if the nations so desire'. According to the Vietnamese, 'after the 1951 Congress of the Indochinese Communist Party, and following the Geneva Conference in particular, the "Indochinese Federation" question passed forever into history, as did French Indochina. Like Laos and Kampuchea, Vietnam has never referred to the Indochinese Federation question again ...'. 'Facts on the "Indochinese Federation" Question', document presented at Foreign Ministry press conference, Hanoi, 7 April 1978. However, the Vietnamese do emphasise their 'special relationship' with the revolutionary movements in Kampuchea and Laos; and this, under present circumstances, may well amount to a 'federation' in all but name.

received China's backing in the process (he visited Peking in September 1977), the Vietnamese evidently decided that further negotiations were fruitless. At first they may have calculated that a Vietnamese show of strength would be sufficient to render Pol Pot more amenable to compromise, or else would encourage dissidents within Kampuchea to assert themselves against the divisive policies of the present leadership.

However, Vietnam's first dry-season offensive—launched late in December 1977—did not attain either of these objectives. But it did give rise to the theory that Hanoi's aim was limited to occupying a zone along the frontiers, to serve both as a buffer against Khmer border attacks and as a means of stepping up the pressure on Pol Pot.[9] The Vietnamese did nothing to discourage this belief.[10] Indeed Prime Minister Pham Van Dong himself, visiting ASEAN countries in September and October 1978 on a goodwill mission, impressed his hosts as being more of a friendly (and even harassed) supplicant for their favours than as the representative of a powerful state.[11] This impression of reasonableness, and even weakness, may well have been designed to lull the suspicions of adversaries—in Kampuchea and China—and of outsiders, like the United States and Japan. If so, there are ample precedents in Vietnamese history for such a deceptive strategy—advocated incidentally by the classic Chinese strategists—as the 1968 Tet offensive also indicates.

There remained the 'political risk' of attempting the direct overthrow of the Pol Pot regime. This risk was evidently neutralised, in Hanoi's calculations, by five factors: the widespread condemnation outside Kampuchea, and particularly in the United States, of Pol Pot's violations of human rights; the consequent disaffection and alienation of a substantial part of the Kampuchean population (who, if they did not positively support a Vietnamese-backed force, would not oppose it either); related to this, the lack of enthusiasm shown by the Chinese leadership for Pol Pot (whose ideological affinities were closer to those of the 'Gang of Four') and its reluctance to be committed too strongly to such a divisive regime; a fourth reassurance for Hanoi was the friendship treaty signed with Moscow in November 1978, which safeguarded Vietnam's flanks from pressures by Peking. The final step was the formation early in December, under the leadership of a Khmer officer who had recently fled to Vietnam, of an anti-Pol Pot Kampuchean front.

The offensive launched on December 25 by Vietnamese forces backing the dissident Kampuchean 'National United Front for

National Salvation', which captured Phnom Penh and most cities early in January 1979, dramatically transformed the situation in south-east Asia. Peking's embarrassing ally—the Pol Pot regime—has been replaced by the Heng Samrin administration, dependent on Hanoi. And Kampuchea no longer serves as a buffer state between Thailand and Vietnam. The Vietnamese action in turn led to the Chinese invasion in February 1979. The implications of these changes will be discussed in a later section.

III

Behind the former regime in Kampuchea lay the power of China. From 1975 on, the Chinese leaders viewed friendly relations with Kampuchea and Thailand as a means of blocking the potential expansion of Vietnam, and with it the influence of Vietnam's ally, the Soviet Union. For a time, however, the Chinese maintained a dual policy. On the one hand, they kept up their assistance to Vietnam, especially a much-needed supply of rice and an important programme for economic reconstruction; this was done in order to retain the goodwill of the Vietnamese and to offset the influence of the Soviet Union. On the other hand, Peking pursued its balance of power policy in south-east Asia, with the aim both of rallying 'Third World' support against Soviet 'hegemony' and of isolating the Vietnamese. This dualism became increasingly unmanageable, however, as Kampuchea and Vietnam were drawn into conflict, and the Chinese were forced to make a choice. Early in 1978, therefore, with the aim both of weakening Vietnam and of distracting its attention from the hard-pressed Kampucheans, Peking cancelled its economic assistance programme to Vietnam (meanwhile protesting against Vietnam's treatment of its Chinese minority), and the two countries became locked in a bitter political and ideological dispute.[12]

The similarities in the relationship between Vietnam and China on the one hand and between Kampuchea and Vietnam on the other, are truly remarkable. Among the most important of these similarities are historical experiences, the contemporary struggle for independence, the use of aid as a political weapon, as well as the ethnic-economic role of the overseas Chinese.

Part of the first—the historical—relationship has already been mentioned: the Khmer fear of national extinction at the hands of the Vietnamese. (Ironically, the French colonial occupation of both countries in the nineteenth century helped to preserve Kampuchea as an independent entity.) But the Vietnamese share a parallel, if less anguishing, experience of external domination. This stems from the fact that the Vietnamese were considered part of the Chinese empire for a thousand years, only breaking away in an epic struggle in the tenth century AD. And in the course of the next thousand years the Chinese made several attempts to annex Vietnam—usually by intervening on behalf of one party in a disputed succession. Each time these attempts were repulsed: on occasions by a veritable 'people's war' of Vietnamese village soldiers encircling the Chinese-held towns and compelling the enemy to withdraw.

The second parallel between the two sets of relationships is the struggle for independence. In this struggle both Kampucheans and Vietnamese felt they were let down, at critical moments, by their more powerful allies. Thus the Vietnamese revolutionaries, having defeated the French in 1954 at the famous siege of Dien Bien Phu, were then obliged, under pressure from the Soviet Union and China at the Geneva Conference, to yield their claim to control all Vietnam. The Vietnamese had to be content with the northern zone—and the promise of nationwide elections in two years' time. The Soviet Union and China believed that this was the most they could extract from the West without risking the break-up of the conference and the intensification of international conflict, which did not suit their global and regional interests at the time.

The Kampuchean revolutionaries suffered the same disillusioning experience at the hands of their allies. Not only did they receive no recognition from the Geneva Conference—unlike even the Pathet Lao in Laos—but they were soon made to realise that North Vietnam (and China) set far greater store by good relations with Sihanouk than by support of a small band of hard-pressed revolutionaries. Indeed, as a result of Sihanouk's ruthless repression of the left, the latter came out in armed revolt (backing the peasant rebellions of 1967-8 in Western Kampuchea): this was at a time when the Vietnamese communists had developed ever-closer relations with the Kampuchean Head of State. The Vietnamese needed Sihanouk's assent to their use of 'sanctuaries' along the border in order to withstand the massive assaults then being launched by the Americans; meanwhile, Sihanouk believed that Kampuchea needed to accommodate to the 'wave of the future' represented by the revolution in Vietnam.

There are further significant parallels in the struggles of the two revolutionary movements. During the war of American intervention in Vietnam, for example, the Chinese leadership repeatedly urged the Vietnamese to 'fight to the end' to 'drive out the American imperialists'. But in 1971-2, as a result of the Chinese-American rapprochement, this line underwent a complete change. Peking's major concern was the threat from the Soviet Union, and the need to rally all possible support, including that of the United States, to meet this threat. The imperative of national survival, as the Chinese saw it, took precedence over the needs of the Vietnamese revolutionaries. The latter were left in the lurch to face Nixon's blockade of North Vietnam and the vicious bombing of Hanoi and other cities. But the Vietnamese could not be expected to forget this harsh lesson in *realpolitik*, which goes a long way towards explaining the bitterness of the dispute between the two countries.

The Kampuchean communists endured a similar, if less traumatic, experience. This stemmed from the trade-off between the Vietnamese revolutionaries and the US administration, which resulted in the peace agreement of 1973. Part of the bargain was apparently an understanding that the Vietnamese would persuade their allies in Kampuchea to agree to a similar type of compromise with Lon Nol. The Vietnamese went so far as to reduce their arms supply to the Khmers rouges in order to put pressure on them to conform. The latter strenuously resented this attempt to subordinate the Kampuchean revolution to the 'larger' interests of Vietnam. The Pol Pot* wing of the Kampuchean resistance was thereby strengthened in its determination to go it alone—and at the same time to eliminate the 'moderating' influence of Vietnam, and of the Sihanoukists too.[13]

The third and related parallel is the use of aid as a political weapon. In each case a more powerful country has blatantly put pressure on its weaker neighbour. Just as the Soviet Union cut off its technical and economic aid to China more than 15 years ago—causing tremendous economic dislocation in a country which had barely recovered from the ravages of years of war—so did China in July 1978 *vis-à-vis* the Vietnamese. Just as Soviet policy miscarried, since it failed either to make the Chinese change course or to bring the country to its knees, so is Chinese pressure unlikely to succeed.

* Pol Pot, after years of underground resistance to Sihanouk, became Secretary-General of the Communist Party of Kampuchea in 1963, joining the 1967-8 peasant revolts. Only with great reluctance was he persuaded by the Vietnamese in 1970 to join the exiled Sihanouk in a national united front against Lon Nol. Already by the early 1970s the Pol Pot wing was carrying out radical nationalist policies—against both Sihanoukists and Vietnamese.

To the contrary, such pressure reinforces Vietnamese national anti-pathy towards China, and also obliges the Vietnamese to place greater reliance on the Soviet Union—precisely the situation, one would have thought, that Peking had intended to avoid.

In the fourth place, relations between Vietnam and Kampuchea and between Vietnam and China are complicated by ethnic-economic factors: that is, the 'middle-man' role of the Vietnamese (and Chinese) in pre-revolutionary Kampuchea, and the similar role of the Chinese community in Vietnam. It is one of the ironies of this situation that Peking should have protested against Vietnamese government measures expropriating (largely Chinese) private enterprise in the South, even though these are an integral part of the socialist policies to which both countries subscribe,[14] while not uttering a word about the far harsher exactions that the Chinese in Kampuchea have suffered. For here, too, 'national interests' run contrary—or at least on different levels—to ideological precepts.

IV

The international implications of the conflict between China and Vietnam are fourfold. First of all, China's ambiguous relationship with the overseas Chinese communities (and with the various insurgent movements) in south-east Asia is highlighted by the drama in Vietnam. In the second place, however, Peking counter-attacks by drawing attention to Vietnam's 'expansionist' record and by accusing the Vietnamese of being an instrument of Soviet policy— 'the Cuba of Asia'. Thirdly, in their search for allies, both sides (as well as the Soviets in a belated conversion, the Americans, in a revival of their once-waning interest and the Japanese, endorsing 'heart to heart' relations) have come out in favour of ASEAN. Finally, China's armed attack on Vietnam, intended to 'teach a lesson' to the Vietnamese and to demonstrate China's mastery and 'resolve', has had no such conclusive effect. Without resolving the problems, China's action has exacerbated the antagonism between the two countries, thus seriously enlarging the potential for instability in the region.

Chinese Vice-Premier Deng Xiaoping's visit to Thailand, Malaysia and Singapore in November 1978 illustrates the complexity of the situation. Deng was warmly welcomed in Thailand, and the Thai government made little or no effort to tone down Deng's strictures against Soviet 'hegemonism'.[15] Moreover, Prime Minister Kriangsak seemed unworried by the Chinese leader's reassertion of the 'two levels' policy, i.e. the principle of revolutionary solidarity at the party level and of friendly relations with Third World governments (whatever their political complexion) at the state-to-state level.

In Malaysia, with its substantial Chinese community, however, Prime Minister Hussein Onn pointedly reminded his visitor that 'the destiny of Malaysia will only be decided by the people of Malaysia. Others cannot and will not be allowed to make that decision.' Unlike the Thais, the Malaysians are said to have prevailed on Deng not to make polemical statements about Soviet hegemony.[16] And, finally, the Prime Minister emphasised that he would have preferred Deng to have renounced support for the Communist Party of Malaya—as Vietnam's Prime Minister Pham Van Dong had pledged with regard to both Thai and Malaysian insurgents—but that Deng could not do so as an important point of principle.[17] The Chinese fear that if they publicly renounce support for the insurgents, the Soviet Union will get a great deal of political mileage out of this and might replace China as the patron of south-east Asian communism. On his last stop during the same trip the Chinese leader heard Singapore's Prime Minister underline the fact that Singaporeans and Chinese have different destinies, and that the people of Singapore 'are in the midst of ensuring a separate and durable future for themselves in south-east Asia'.[18]

The second international problem is revealed in Peking's warning that Vietnam is 'the Cuba of the East', as Deng Xiaoping put it in Bangkok. But this is as exaggerated as Vietnam's counter-accusation that Peking is interfering in the internal affairs of south-east Asian countries by supporting the overseas Chinese (although this does hold true for the situation in Vietnam). For the Chinese have repeatedly stated that overseas Chinese should abide by the laws, and respect the customs and ways of life, of their 'host' countries. As to the notion that Vietnam is an instrument of Soviet policy—an Asian Cuba—this can only be attributed to China's obsession with its Soviet rival (an obsession equally shared by the Soviet Union with regard to China). For the Vietnamese throughout their history, and not least during the darkest days of the war, have displayed the most striking evidence of their independence. Even now, although obliged to join COMECON (to help make up some of the vital economic projects abandoned by the Chinese) and to seek reinsurance through the Soviet-Vietnam Treaty of Friendship and Co-operation[19] (as the Indian government also did during a similarly critical period), the Vietnamese have demonstrated the desire to maintain, or resume, friendly relations with the West, and to resist being made instruments of external ambitions.

V

What, then, are the regional implications of the Vietnamese-backed dissident takeover in Kampuchea combined with the wider, international implications of the Sino-Vietnamese (and Sino-Soviet) disputes? On the first point it is important to recognise that certain key questions remain to be answered. For example, will a substantial number of Kampucheans, alienated by the excesses of the Pol Pot regime, rally to the new, moderately-oriented administration in Phnom Penh?[20] Alternatively will there be a sustained guerrilla resistance in the countryside, animated by fear and hatred of the Vietnamese? Perhaps most likely is an Angola-type situation in which Vietnamese forces maintain security until the authority of an autonomous Kampuchean regime is consolidated. This is similar to, though more precarious than, the situation in Laos. For it could more easily be upset by nationalist guerrilla resistance, bogging down the Vietnamese in a protracted war.

Still focusing on the change in Vietnam-Kampuchean relations (leaving aside, for the time being, discussion of China's intervention) the extension of Vietnam's authority throughout Indo-China has far-reaching implications. First, Vietnamese political decisiveness and military prowess have been demonstrated; second, the tactics of sponsoring other countries' dissident groups and acting on their behalf can be extended beyond Kampuchea; and thirdly, Soviet support is assured by the November 1978 treaty. As for the impact on ASEAN, it is above all the Thai government, an important partner in China's balance of power policy, whose situation has most deteriorated: the future cannot seem as reassuring as it did only a few months ago.[21] And, finally, the United States, so long strategically involved with Thailand and Indo-China, has confirmed by its inaction (despite verbal opposition to Vietnamese aggression[22]) that changes in mainland south-east Asia no longer provide a reason for intervention.

However, even without taking account of China's attempt to redress the balance, these gains are not all one way. Even if the Vietnamese are not embroiled in a protracted war in Kampuchea, they will be preoccupied in that country (as they are to a lesser degree in Laos) in seeking to maintain a delicate balance between satisfying Vietnamese interests and at the same time not provoking nationalist reactions. Moreover, internal problems in Vietnam, particularly the economic dislocation caused by the withdrawal of Chinese aid and the flight of skilled workers, managers and entrepreneurs from among the overseas Chinese, remain formidable.

In the second place, although the Soviet Union has gained in prestige from the success of its ally, Vietnam, these gains have occurred in a region which is not of vital importance to the Soviets. South-east Asia, in this respect, cannot compare with north-east Asia, the Indian subcontinent, or the Middle East. Moreover, the very increase in the Soviet presence in south-east Asia—through its military, political and economic involvement in Vietnam and Laos, and no doubt later in Kampuchea—tends to make the non-communist governments in the region more wary and distrustful of the Soviet advance. For while ASEAN governments are, or rather were, generally satisfied with the 'stabilising' effect of recent Chinese policies, they fear the destabilising consequences of a more active role by the Soviets—and the Vietnamese.

It is against this background that the significance of China's intervention must be judged. Before the Chinese launched their attack on Vietnam, it was widely believed that they would gain more by exercising restraint than by armed retaliation. For what Peking had 'lost', as a result of the overthrow of its embarrassing ally, Pol Pot, it would more than make up for, first of all by closer relations with ASEAN, facing what both parties consider to be a common danger; but above all, by the 'drawing together' (again, impelled by common interests and perceptions) of China, the United States and Japan. Peking's restraint, in other words, would be amply rewarded by the benefits of increased co-operation with the West. The military, industrial and technological strengthening of China envisaged in this process could only enhance its long-term impact on its neighbours to the south.

What then induced the Chinese leadership to turn away from this posture of moderation, pragmatism and 'predictability' (conforming with the modernisation programme and the opening to the West and to Japan) and by launching a massive assault on Vietnam to set at risk its well-earned constructive reputation?

The only answer seems to be the priority accorded by Peking to another kind of reputation—that 'reputation for action' which all great powers, or would-be great powers, feel the need at critical times to assert. From a standpoint remarkably similar to that of US governments in the 1950s and 1960s, the present Chinese leaders claim that Vietnamese 'regional hegemonism' (i.e. Vietnamese communism) is colluding with the Soviet Union in its 'strategy of world domination'. China, like the Americans in the Cold War, insists it faces the problem either of appeasing or opposing this strategy, wherever it occurs.[23] Vietnam must therefore be 'taught a lesson' that it cannot 'ride roughshod' over other countries—i.e. that it cannot continue to serve Soviet aims, or to defy China over Kampuchea—with impunity.

Fundamentally the Chinese, by invading Vietnam, have attempted to demonstrate two things: that China is not a paper tiger, and therefore cannot be pushed around; and that China, in the face of Western weakness or passivity (symbolised by detente), must itself set an example by resolutely standing up to the Soviet Union and its 'proxies'. (The Vietnamese border 'provocations', emphasised by the Chinese initially as the reason for launching their 'counter-attack', were the pretext rather than the cause of conflict.[24])

Such 'lessons' could most effectively be taught by a short, sharp military offensive, smashing Vietnamese regular units and thereby opening the country to occupation, followed by a unilateral Chinese withdrawal. This strategy, modelled on the spectacular campaign against India in 1962, would not only demonstrate China's military might and humiliate its adversary, but at the same time the withdrawal of forces at the point of success would attest to China's skill and prudence in waging a limited war with limited objectives.

But the situation of India in 1962 and of Vietnam in 1979 are different. To begin with, while the Nehru Government in 1962 was almost totally unprepared for the Chinese use of force, the Vietnamese had had ample warning of China's intentions. Above all, India was a non-aligned country without a military ally; it was only much later, in 1971, that a defensive arrangement with Moscow came into effect. Vietnam, on the contrary, had been receiving an increasing flow of Soviet arms and technical aid from the 1960s—support that was reinforced by the Treaty of Friendship and Co-operation signed in November 1978.

The difference between the two situations meant that *unless* the Chinese speedily and obviously defeated the well-prepared and experienced Vietnamese, and then withdrew 'mission accomplished', they would face the prospect that the more deeply they became engaged in war with Vietnam, the more risk they ran of Soviet retaliation. For the Soviet Union, too, would be placed in precisely the same situation of needing to demonstrate its 'reputation for action', to prove that it could be relied upon to honour its commitments.

After 17 days of fierce fighting, when the Chinese announced their decision to withdraw (having delivered 'sufficient punishment'), what had actually been accomplished? To put it concisely: while the Chinese invasion had achieved something it had solved nothing. Undeniably the Chinese leaders can record this achievement: they have shown a readiness to use force in pursuit of national interests—rather than as a matter of self-defence—which is the hallmark of the great power in world politics* But the Chinese attack has solved nothing. The Vietnamese, despite the loss of one or two frontier towns, have not evidently been defeated, nor did they sue for peace, nor have they shown any willingness (so far) to compromise on Kampuchea.[25] Vietnam's hostility towards China is more acute, and its reliance on the Soviet Union all the greater. Moreover, the situation in south-east Asia as a whole has become more complex and precarious: while some governments may tacitly approve of China's action in checking Vietnamese pretensions, others are fearful of the consequences of Sino-Vietnamese and Sino-Soviet rivalry for the region. Internationally, too, China's 'reputation for action' has been achieved, but this has compromised its reputation for peaceful constructive behaviour.

VI

To conclude: this study of regional conflict and its international implications raises three issues of major theoretical and practical importance. These are: the historic roots of such conflicts; the ambiguities of great-power involvement; and the vexed problem of communism and nationalism. I shall discuss each of them in turn.

It is evident, in the first place, that the post-1975 revolutionary regimes in Kampuchea and Vietnam were, to a remarkable degree, 'locked' into a collision course by their widely differing experiences of struggle (leading to divergent revolutionary goals), by historic national antagonisms, and—which also brings in China and the Soviet Union on opposite sides—by the exigencies of geopolitics. The tendencies towards conflict inherent in these three factors were previously kept in check only by the need to face a far more urgent common problem—the counter-revolutionary threat posed by

* All powers are ready to use force; but smaller countries are less likely to get away with it.

American intervention in support of right-wing regimes. Once this threat was removed—for China by the rapprochement with the United States in 1972 and for Vietnam and Kampuchea with the withdrawal of American forces and the collapse of the Thieu and Lon Nol regimes in 1975—these fissiparous tendencies became acute.

The conflict between the communist regimes in Vietnam and Kampuchea was not the result either of a premeditated scheme of Vietnamese aggrandisement (instead, for three years the Vietnamese sought to concentrate on their own pressing internal problems) or of a Soviet grand design of global expansion, as the Chinese allege. Rather, the conflict stemmed from the incompatible attitudes and policies of the two neighbouring regimes, inheritors of intractable problems. These were exacerbated beyond the bounds of reasonable solution by the overwhelming pressures of trying to cope with the internal upheavals of revolutionary transformation. Once negotiations became deadlocked, each side stepped up the use of force: Kampuchean forays across the border were met by Vietnamese retaliatory strikes. The conflict grew of its own momentum, dragging in China (which had at one stage sought to mediate between the two regimes) in support of Kampuchea, while the Soviet Union strengthened its economic and military ties with Vietnam.

Initially, none of the parties to the conflict—with the exception, perhaps, of the Soviet Union, which was least involved—had intended these consequences. The Pol Pot regime, presumably, had not sought to provoke a situation endangering its own survival; the Vietnamese, preoccupied with reconstruction and reunification, had no wish to divert scarce resources to waging war; and the Chinese had little to gain by driving the Vietnamese into the arms of their feared rival, the Soviet Union. Such, however, as with many international crises, was 'the logic of events'.

And yet, despite the dual impulse towards greater intensity of armed conflict and towards wider international involvement, the great powers involved have demonstrated considerable restraint, in order to prevent a 'local' conflict escalating out of control. This, rather than Brzezinski's notion of 'proxy war'—in which Peking and Moscow were believed to be instigating their respective clients to fight it out for their patrons' benefit—is what more accurately characterises the Indo-China situation.

Indeed, the ambiguity inherent in the rivalry of great powers in an unstable world environment—whereby each seeks to derive unilateral advantages, but not to the point of upsetting the overall framework of restraint—leads to the second issue of major theoretical and practical importance: great-power exploitation-cum-management of crises.

It is true that the *opportunities* for great-power involvement—military, political, economic and cultural—and even for armed intervention, are legion in a turbulent world of independent 'sovereign states': that is, of countries in varying degrees of dependence on, or usefulness to, the great industrial and military powers (capitalist and communist), all of which can be ranked domestically (according to dominant and subordinate structures) as well as internationally in a hierarchy of power. As a result of the link between internal and external structures, internal changes affecting the domestic hierarchy may also upset the regional or international hierarchy, and thus the balance, of power; this in turn elicits, often enough, pre-emptive or reactive great-power response.[26]

The opportunities for involvement, or intervention, are one thing; the *costs* of involvement, and still more so of intervention, are quite another. These costs depend, not just on the 'receptivity' or otherwise of the particular environment in which a great power operates (and the form in which it does so), but also on the aims and attitudes of rival powers, who may be expected to react to the extent that their interests (as perceived by them) are adversely affected. It is this action-reaction process, escalating the degree of conflict at each successive stage, which in an era of nuclear overkill *has* to be controlled ('managed') if both—and indeed all—parties are to survive.

Such then is the framework of mutual interest which, hopefully, limits and confines the vaulting ambitions (and opportunities) of great powers. Yet, as we know only too well, the very *intensity* of great-power rivalry throughout the world and the fear, anger and suspicion it engenders, militate against the *reasoned* (reconciling, co-operative) response to conflict that is required. Thus the situation in reality (as distinct from the aspiration) is not so much one of a 'stable structure of peace' which, as it were, encapsulates the dangerously emotional activities going on within; rather, 'stable structure' and 'unilateral advantage' (i.e. the action of one great power at the expense of another) are two sides of the same coin: two contradictory tendencies inherent in a world of (rival) states.[27]

Even if we observe the 'rules of the game' worked out by the superpowers, which are moves towards the formation of a stable international structure, we can discern the same contradictory tendencies. Certainly some of the rules, or understandings, make for co-operative international behaviour. Thus 'signals' are sent out in advance to indicate one power's interests and intentions in a particular issue or area, so that the other power can 'signal' back its acceptance at best, or intended counter-move at worst, before any irrevocable *action* is undertaken. Yet in a precisely similar situation other signals of quite a different character are designed to demonstrate unilaterally a nation's credibility to its allies, neutrals and adversaries; notably, its capacity and will to 'honour its commitments'. There is no co-operative intent to these signals, as far as the adversary is concerned. To the contrary, the signalling power is determined to demonstrate its 'reputation for action', that is, to prove that it will not back down (compromise) before the pressure or threats of the adversary. But the adversary is in a similar condition. He, too, has to 'make good' on his threats if he, in turn, is not to lose 'credibility'—with regard to his own allies, neutrals and adversaries. And so it goes.

VII

The final issue raised by this study is the vexed problem of Marxist theory (with its international connotations) and the realities of national conflicts, with the Sino-Soviet dispute as one major example, and the war between Vietnam and Kampuchea as another. The conclusion can hardly be avoided that there is an obvious inadequacy in orthodox Marxist interpretations;[28] and this in turn has serious implications for the study of domestic, and especially foreign, policy.

If, as Marx believed, the economic structure determines the political, legal and intellectual 'superstructure',[29] why is it that socialist states like China and Vietnam, with basically similar economies, are politically and ideologically in conflict with one another? And why is it that the Kampuchean and Vietnamese regimes, which at least share the principle of collective control of the economy, are actually at war? Both situations are the reverse of Marx's claim that 'as the antagonism between classes within the nation vanishes (because socialism has put an end to exploitation) the hostility of one nation to another will come to an end'.[30]

One explanation for the divergence between theory and reality is that the cosmopolitan outlook of Marx, Engels and other mid-nineteenth century European intellectuals made it difficult for them to consider nationalism, and hence national conflict, as other than a passing phase: that is, as the ideological expression of the rising capitalist bourgeoisie during its struggle against a continental alliance of feudalism and autocracy. It was not long, however (in Marx's view), before the triumph of capitalism on a world scale would transcend these national origins. At the same time the proletarian class, brought into being by capitalist modes of production, would also be 'stripped of every trace of national character'.

According to the *Manifesto of the Communist Party*:

> National differences and antagonisms between peoples are daily more and more vanishing, owing to the development of the bourgeoisie ... [and] the world market ... The supremacy of the proletariat will cause them [national differences] to vanish still faster ... In proportion as the exploitation of one individual by another is put an end to, the exploitation of one nation by another will also be put an end to. In proportion as the antagonism between classes within the nation vanishes, the hostility of one nation to another will come to an end.[31]

Marxist faith in 'proletarian internationalism' was put to a vital test during the events leading up to the First World War, when it was assumed that working-class and peasant soldiers would not fight for their imperialist or bourgeois masters, but would turn against them. 'Proletarians of all countries unite. You have nothing to lose but your chains!' The war of nations that followed was a shattering refutation of this universalist hypothesis. The class solidarity of those manning one side of the economic barricade against the other side—owners of the means of production—did not prevail over national solidarity in the First World War, except in semi-industrialised Russia;[32] and it still has not prevailed in the capitalist countries taking part in two world wars, and in the Cold War.

The continuing underestimation by Marxists of the force of nationalism stems from the basic incompatibility of the theory of class struggle as the motive force of history with the assumptions of social consensus implicit in the concept of nationalism: namely, that the national movement and the nation-state provide psychological and social fulfilment to their members which transcends—at least during certain periods—individual differences or class antagonisms. At such times, members of society believe that they are not merely isolated individuals, but instead gain satisfaction from belonging to a community, sharing a sense of common identity, and obtaining the order and security that a wider association may achieve against the dangers of an uncertain or hostile environment.

We call this phenomenon of group solidarity 'nationalism' when it embraces all (or most) of the members of a nation, or even when sectional interests are expressed in terms of the nation. In principle, the group-solidarity phenomenon applies to all levels of society: at the household and village level, at the level of religious affiliation, of occupation, age, sex, region and so on. Nor are these various levels of group solidarity necessarily mutually exclusive. A staunch member of the working class may also be a fervent nationalist—even if his perception of the 'nation' differs from that of other classes; although often, in its emotional content, it is much the same. (Surveys of supporters of the French Communist Party, for example, have shown that the majority would fight in defence of their country in the event of a Soviet attack.) In other words, class solidarity does not necessarily exclude national solidarity. What is important to realise in this context, however, is that the nation is still a meaningful form of expression for many people: it is one that they can identify with; and at times of international crisis it is perhaps the most meaningful of all.

Consider again the significance of the Kampuchean and Vietnamese revolutionary experience. The solidarity shown in their struggle against vastly superior enemies, internal and external, is of the same order as the nationalism described above (indeed both revolutions explicitly combined national and social objectives); and of course the solidarity of a class becomes the nationalism of the state once the revolutionaries come to power. Once this happens, as we have seen, the more the *external* pressures or threats increase, the greater the national content in the revolutionary state's response: thus the Kampuchean assertion of national identity against the Vietnamese; and the Vietnamese appeal to national traditions of resistance to the Chinese. Conversely, the greater the *internal* pressures, the more 'socialist' the response: the eradication of urban-based 'feudal' or monarchist survivals, and of state-capitalist beginnings, in Kampuchea; and the expropriation of private business enterprise, and tightening of party controls, in southern Vietnam. However, internal discontent may also be redirected against 'alien' or external enemies; such solidarity-making or diversionary moves are characteristic of most regimes, whether communist or non-communist.

To sum up thus far: class struggle is clearly a major (existing or latent) motive force *within* societies: it is the way in which the Khmer and Vietnamese revolutionaries came to power. Nationalism, on the other hand, while at times transcending social differences and at other times failing to prevail, is a major motive force in *international* relations: as the hostility between Vietnam and Kampuchea and the dispute between Vietnam and China, and between China and the Soviet Union, reveal. But neither class conflict nor national consensus is at all times *the* major motive force; nor do they necessarily operate in a distinct division of labour, as between the domestic and external spheres.

Thus, the experiences of the countries described above—in internal and foreign policies alike—raise two fundamental issues. The first is the relationship between economic and political structures within a country and among countries. And the second issue is the role of specific (especially national) factors in what Marxists believe to be a universal process. These issues are linked. For while there is a universal *economic* process—the development, as Marx pointed out, of the international capitalist system, resulting in the 'universal interdependence of nations' in place of the 'old local and national seclusion and self-sufficiency'—yet the *political* process, as the case of Vietnam and Kampuchea amply illustrates, still operates basically within a specific, national framework.* This applies also to international relations, whether this concerns the foreign policies of the superpowers, or of China versus the Soviet Union, or Vietnam versus China.

I am not suggesting that the economic system is irrelevant to international politics—although as a system it plays a comparatively unimportant role in the Sino-Soviet dispute, apart from propaganda accusations by both sides, and in the rift between Vietnam and China—but that, even where it is relevant, as in the case of American foreign policy, the economic structure cannot convincingly be

* The national framework of policy-making may of course be regarded by Marxists as a 'survival', lasting longer than expected, but eventually to be superseded by *international* perspectives corresponding to the world economic system ... But if the time-scale for this transformation has to be extended more or less indefinitely—and cannot be precisely correlated with economic change—then it is hard to see the explanatory power of such a theory.

said to 'determine' the political process. The relationship is an ambiguous one, and in certain vital areas—above all, security—politics is in command.

Notes

1. See also J.L.S. Girling, 'Southeast Asia in 1978: A Political Overview', *Southeast Asian Affairs 1979* (Institute of Southeast Asian Studies, Singapore, 1979).

2. Including members of the Association of South-East Asian Nations (ASEAN): Indonesia, Thailand, Malaysia, Singapore and the Philippines.

3. See the report of Yugoslav journalists visiting Kampuchea, published in the *Asian Wall Street Journal*, 9-10 May 1978.

4. Stephen R. Heder, 'Origins of the Conflict', *Southeast Asia Chronicle*, no. 64 (September-October 1978).

5. Milton Osborne, 'Kampuchea and Viet Nam: A Historical Perspective', *Pacific Community*, vol. 9, no. 3 (April 1978), pp. 249-63.

6. Francois Ponchaud, *Cambodia Year Zero* (Allen Lane, London, 1978), p. 92.

7. According to Hanoi in September 1978, there are some 150,000 refugees from Kampuchea in Vietnam; they include Vietnamese and Chinese as well as Khmers.

8. Heder, 'Origins of the Conflict'.

9. Even in December 1978, after the final Vietnamese offensive had started, official US analysts, drawing on a 'limited fund of information', still believed Hanoi's campaign was aimed at establishing a large, permanently-occupied area along the frontier to provide an alternative homeland for dissident Cambodians. US officials were sceptical about Hanoi's ability to crush the Cambodians, because of the higher morale of Khmer ground forces and the extent of rugged terrain. They doubted that the Vietnamese would take the political risk (although militarily there would be a good chance of success) of striking at Phnom Penh itself. David Binder reporting from Washington for the *New York Times*, reprinted *International Herald Tribune*, 27 December 1978.

10. Foreign Minister Nguyen Duy Trinh, visiting Tokyo in mid-December 1978 to negotiate further Japanese aid—the latter stating that this would depend on Vietnamese restraint over Kampuchea—appears to have satisfied his hosts on this score. *International Herald Tribune*, 16-17 December 1978. Nayan Chanda, writing in the *Far Eastern Economic Review*, 23 February 1979, reports that the Vietnamese decision to back the rebel Kampuchean movement with military strength had been taken at a Central Committee meeting of the party ten months before. The decision was taken after Pol Pot had rejected the Vietnamese peace proposals of February 1978.

11. ASEAN leaders viewed him, rather patronisingly it seems, not as the exporter of revolution or of military adventures (at least for the time being), but as the premier of a country in dire economic circumstances, facing serious problems with China, and an expensive military struggle with Cambodia. Rodney Tasker, reporting from Singapore, *Far Eastern Economic Review*, 8 December 1978.

12. See also David Marr on Vietnam-China relations in Malcolm Salmon (ed.), *The Vietnam-Cambodia-China Disputes: Motivations, Background, Significance* (Australian National University, Department of Political and Social Change, Canberra, 1979).

13. Heder, 'Origins of the Conflict'; also Carlyle Thayer on Vietnam-Kampuchea relations in Salmon, *The Vietnam-Cambodia-China Disputes*; William Shawcross, 'Cambodia', *Far Eastern Economic Review*, 14 April 1978; R.P. Paringaux, 'How Pol Pot Demolished the Indochinese Alliance', *Le Monde*, 31 March 1978; Ponchaud, *Cambodia Year Zero*, pp. 179, 189.

14. The Vietnamese government, after 1975, at first permitted private business to operate in the south. It was estimated that the economy there was in the hands of 3,000 large and 11,000 smaller businesses—90 per cent of which were owned by ethnic Chinese. From May 1975 to March 1978 the Vietnamese government tried without much success to persuade private businessmen to shift into new roles as investors and managers in the productive sector, or as members of marketing co-operatives. But as part of the plan to transform the economy into one of 'large-scale socialist production', starting with the 1976-80 Five Year Plan, the government in March 1978 closed down a large number of private wholesalers and retailers in the south; and it followed this up in May by introducing one unified currency for all Vietnam: information by David Marr; see also Nayan Chanda, 'Vietnam: A Question of Priorities', *Far Eastern Economic Review*, 4 August 1978.

15. Deng's press conference in Bangkok. *Bangkok Post*, 9 November 1978.

16. *The Sunday Times* (Singapore), 12 November 1978; and *Straits Times*, 13 November 1978.

17. Ibid. Pham Van Dong had pledged in Bangkok in September 1978 that Vietnam would not assist communist insurgents in Thailand; and he repeated that pledge with regard to the Malayan Communist Party on his visit to Kuala Lumpur.

18. Excerpts from Lee Kuan Yew's speech are given in *Straits Times*, 13 November 1978.

19. According to Article VI of the treaty, signed in Moscow on 3 November 1978: 'In case either party is attacked or threatened with attack, the two parties signatory to the treaty shall immediately consult each other with a view to eliminating that threat, and shall take appropriate and effective measures to safeguard peace and security of the two countries.'

20. The Kampuchean People's Revolutionary Council, set up on 8 January 1978, includes Heng Samrin, chairman; Penn Sovan, in charge of defence; Hun Sen, foreign affairs and Chea Sim, internal affairs. The 11-point programme of the National United Front for National Salvation (also led by Heng Samrin), announced on 3 December 1978, includes: general elections, organisation of 'people's democratic power at all levels' and a new constitution; creation of 'revolutionary mass organisations' affiliated to the Front, grouping various strata of the population; building a Kampuchean revolutionary army; realising the people's rights to real freedom and democracy, 'the right to return to their old native land, and to build their family life in happiness', and freedom of residence, movement, association, and religion; 'to restore the national economy ravaged by the Pol Pot-Ieng Sary [deputy Prime Minister and Foreign Minister under Pol Pot] regime ... It will be a planned economy with markets ... '; 'to establish banks, issue currency, restore and develop the circulation of goods'; to develop schools and universities; and to 'carry out a foreign policy of peace friendship and nonalignment'.

21. There are two problems: first, Kampuchea no longer provides a buffer to Vietnamese expansion; second, the consequent growth in Vietnamese power may appear a threat to Thai security, and thus jeopardise Prime Minister Kriangsak's moderate policy line of detente with communist countries, as well as internal detente (by giving a handle to his rivals on the extreme right).

22. It seems probable that the Carter administration, despite diplomatic denials, was soon after to condone what it thought would amount to a limited Chinese strike to punish Vietnam—and to warn off the Soviet Union from further adventures. This is certainly the impression Deng Xiaoping must have received

during his visit to the United States in late January and early February 1979, when the US administration expressed no opposition to his intention to 'punish' Vietnam.

23. Chinese policy was succinctly expounded by Mme Chen Muhua, a Vice-Premier, on a visit to Australia. *Canberra Times*, 7 March 1979.

24. The border, now openly disputed by the Chinese, had been defined by conventions in 1887 and 1895 between the French government, controlling Vietnam, and the Chinese imperial government. Although this border is subject to renegotiation, both the Chinese and Vietnamese governments agreed in 1957 and 1958 to maintain the status quo; until the present crisis the existing border demarcation had presented no problem. However there are competing claims over two groups of islands, the Paracels and Spratleys, in the South China Sea.

25. A tactical consideration in China's decision to attack Vietnam was no doubt the assumption that the Vietnamese would be obliged to withdraw some of their troops from Kampuchea—to defend the northern front—and thus relieve the pressure on Pol Pot's forces. In fact two Vietnamese divisions are said to have been withdrawn, although the bulk of the troops are still there. There remains the possibility of an international deal being worked out to achieve a compromise in Kampuchea. But such a deal is unlikely, for two reasons. First, it would be hard to find a compromise solution that satisfies both China and Vietnam. And second, such a compromise--for example, the return of Prince Sihanouk—would be even less acceptable to the revolutionary factions, whether led by Pol Pot or Heng Samrin or others, in Kampuchea. For if Sihanouk returned as a figurehead it would achieve nothing; but if he resumed some form of authority this would pose serious risks—to the revolutionaries—of a return to the old discredited order.

26. See J.L.S Girling, *America and the Third World: Revolution and Intervention* (Routledge and Kegan Paul, London, 1979).

27. *Why* should nations struggle for power and come into conflict with one another? Benjamin Cohen in *The Question of Imperialism* (Basic Books, New York, 1973) pp. 248-57, rejects the Marxist view that it is due to capitalist expansion and competitiveness; but his answer is that 'unfortunately, *no* satisfactory answer is possible here ... [It would require] the combined insights of sociology, anthropology, and psychology ... ' His conclusion is that 'separate nations are *a given fact*' [author's italics] of human nature, which itself requires a study.

28. There are two main reasons for discussing classical Marxism rather than neo-Marxist variations. The first reason is simple: 'official' Marxism is the ideology of the states whose conflicts I have been analysing. The second reason is more complicated. Briefly, I have not considered the modifications and shifts of emphasis introduced by neo-Marxists into the original schema—in an effort to reconcile theory with practice: when historical outcomes conflict with theoretical conclusions—because these are still *within* the 'great tradition' of economic determinism, i.e. broad stages of history corresponding to changes in the modes (and ownership) of production. It is Marx who founded that tradition and it is the range and penetration of his ideas that give them their emotional force and explanatory power—an explanatory power that, with all its inadequacies, has yet to be achieved by his successors ... The task of these successors, of course, is to overcome the inadequacies while still remaining faithful to the original schema. Yet it is the latter—the 'great tradition'—that I find deficient. The question of nationalism is one highly relevant instance. Thus if the *tradition* (economic determinism and its political implications) is deficient, why discuss the followers when one can deal directly with the chief?

29. Marx's 'proposition is: that in every historical epoch, the prevailing mode of economic production and exchange, and the social organisation necessarily following from it, form the basis upon which is built up, and from which alone can be explained, the political and intellectual history of that epoch; that consequently

the whole history of mankind ... has been a history of class struggles, contests between exploiting and exploited, ruling and oppressed classes'. Preface by Engels to the 1888 English edition of the *Manifesto of the Communist Party*.

30. Marx and Engels, *Manifesto of the Communist Party* (1848). The quotation is given more fully below.

31. Ibid.

32. Marx and Engels, in their preface to the 1882 Russian edition of the *Manifesto*, considered the possibility of 'the primeval common ownership of land' in Russia passing directly to 'the higher form of communist common ownership'. But their conclusion was qualified: 'If the Russian Revolution becomes the signal for a proletarian revolution in the West, so that both complement each other, the present Russian common ownership of land may serve as the starting point for a communist development.'

3 South Asia

S.D. MUNI

I

The Third World was not born as a free and fully autonomous entity. The process of colonial and imperial rule was in the nature of a big melting pot into which the Third World societies were sucked and moulded. They emerged out of this melting pot with hybrid structures and distorted personalities. But this was not all. The colonial metropolis, while granting independence to a particular Third World country or region, did not completely sever its umbilical cord. It sought to preserve and nurse its basic economic and strategic stakes in that country or region. The post-colonial behaviour of a Third World country or region, therefore, cannot be understood except in the context of this melting-pot process. The continuing involvement of the great powers in the Third World stemmed out of this process as a massive and, perhaps, inevitable legacy.

The conflict in South Asia is no exception to this rule. It has witnessed a whole range of manifestations from informally expressed diplomatic displeasure to full-scale war. The expressed issues in such interstate conflicts in the region have included territorial disputes, economic issues, threat to political stability and national security, communal disharmony and danger to the very survival of one participant or the other. The most acrimonious relationship has, however, been between India and Pakistan who have gone to war with each other four times in the past thirty years. And all these wars have brought out in bold relief the extent and intensity of the great powers' involvement in the region. This is not to imply that the great powers have simply exported to and imposed upon the subcontinent conflicts created outside the region. Local roots of conflict in the region have, of course, existed, but these local roots were largely the creation of the historical melting-pot process, colonial rule, and the great powers have linked their stakes and strategies with these roots in order to activise and inflate them much beyond their inherent proportions. Before we take up the various aspects of the great powers' involvement in the Indo-Pakistan conflict, the regional roots of conflict in the subcontinent must be identified and analysed.

II

South Asia as a region has two important characteristics. First, it is Indo-centric in character. Both geographically, and in terms of socio-cultural continuities and economic infrastructure, India occupies a central place. The other countries of the region, like Pakistan, Nepal, Bangladesh, Bhutan and Sri Lanka have individually and separately more in common with India than with each other. The second characteristic of the region is its asymmetric and hierarchical power structure. India occupies a dominant power position. In population, economic resource-base and growth potential, military strength and viability of constitutional, political and administrative structures, India is far superior to any one of its neighbours, or even to all of them put together. These two characteristics in conjunction, make India the proverbial Big Brother in South Asia with all its negative connotations. It generates legitimate and understandable, although often exaggerated, apprehensions among India's neighbours *vis-à-vis* New Delhi. It makes the former feel insecure and uncomfortable in the company of such a giant neighbour. Interstate tensions have often been generated as a result of such feeling. It should, however, be kept in mind that this very fact of India's centrality and dominant position underlines its deep stakes in the stability of the region. Instability is not inherent in a situation of natural hierarchy of power. On the contrary, endeavours to impose an artificial balance in such a situation may bring about instability and strife. It has seldom been realised by scholars as well as statesmen, particularly of the Western world, that South Asia is a region where such a dynamic situation prevails. Developments in the region since 1947 have repeatedly demonstrated that conflict has resulted from the efforts to blur and distort the natural power-hierarchy in the subcontinent. We shall take up this point in detail later.

The regional roots of conflict in South Asia can be classified into two broad categories not completely unrelated to each other. They are: (i) the legacies of colonial rule and (ii) the post-independence strategies and processes of nation and state-building. In the first category, three of the colonial legacies stand out prominently, namely, the creation of an unnatural and absurd state system;

incomplete demarcation of state boundaries; and the unresolved question of the status of ethnic and religious minorities of one country of origin present in another.

With regard to the India-Pakistan conflict, the partition of 1947 embodied the worst of these three legacies in several respects. Pakistan was a geographical absurdity which ultimately led to the creation of Bangladesh. The British knew that this was not a viable structure and the last viceroy, Lord Mountbatten, had predicted that East Bengal would break away from Pakistan in a quarter of a century.[1] What he did not, or could not, predict was that this separation, which came in 1971, would be preceded by an extremely tortuous process including a full-scale war between India and Pakistan. In addition, to this, the British indecision, conscious or otherwise, regarding the status of the princely States of Hyderabad, Junagadh and Kashmir added significantly to the conflict potential inherent in the Indo-Pakistan relationship. Kashmir continues to remain a bone of contention between them even after three major wars. Apart from it, the actual territorial award finalised by Sir Cyril Radcliffe was an extremely hurried exercise. Both India and Pakistan resented the final outcome. In 1965, territorial disputes about Dahgram in the east and Kutch in the west brought the two countries to war. Boundary disputes continued to plague Indo-Pakistan relations for two decades after partition. The concern expressed about peace in the subcontinent after the partition by Harold Macmillan from the opposition benches in the British Parliament on 10 July 1947 clearly indicated that the British were not unaware of the consequences of their final act.

While partition was sought for and granted on the basis of what came to be called the 'two-nation' theory and while subsequent Hindu-Muslim communal tensions in India and Pakistan have been cited in support of this theory and have been used by interested parties both within and outside the subcontinent to vitiate and embitter bilateral relations between the two countries, in reality, the 'two-nation' theory was the name given by Jinnah to the 'two-states' theory. The Muslim League leadership was too ambitious and adamant on having a state to itself over which it could preside unchallenged. In particular, Jinnah's impatience and idiosyncracies were allowed to play a larger-than-life role by the British. This has now been documented.[2] The support provided to Jinnah by the Muslim officers in the British Indian Army and administration, who naturally had vested interests in reaching the heights of their careers in a new and separate Muslim State, still remains to be fully assessed and accounted for.[3] The seeds of partition lay not so much in the so-called communal antagonism but in the narrow and selfish political interests of the Hindu and the Muslim power-seeking elites. The communal factor was emphasised by them in this power game which they were asked to play through political parties and electoral exercises. This input of the British political culture, viz. political parties and electoral exercises, gradually resulted in communal and religious polarities in the pre-independence Indian political scene which were deftly escalated and exploited by the British rulers for the imperial governance of India. The British introduction of legislative measures, communal representation, administrative and educational policies, and the art of dealing with the freedom movement—all that has been aptly described as the British strategy of 'divide and rule'—made no insignificant contribution in making the partition finally inevitable. This communal malady did not subside with the creation of India and Pakistan and the withdrawal of British rule. It got transformed into Indo-Pakistan rivalries and conflict and became an excuse for the great powers' continued intervention in the subcontinent.

The second category of the local roots of regional conflict in South Asia lay in the post-independence processes of nation and state-building in the individual South Asian countries and the collective impact that they had in the region as a whole. It is true that the paths and strategies of social, economic and political developments pursued in each of the South Asian countries were, in a general way, a continuation of the pre-independence 'inheritance'.[4] The socio-cultural identities which were characterised by the factors of continuity and overlap defied the territorial boundaries of the new states. The economies were characterised by the simultaneous existence of dominant feudal and pre-feudal sorts of modes of production along with a marginal and, in some cases, entirely dependent modern sector. These economies were also fraught with strong tendencies of mutual competition and incompatibility owing to their differing growth potentials and directions of development. Politically, the British transferred power to broadly similar sets of elites but soon the varying socio-economic infrastructures in each of the respective countries started asserting themselves and determining, to a large extent, the respective forms of polity and styles of politics in the various countries. This brought about significant changes in the composition of ruling elites and political forces and, consequently, in the structure and dynamics of the political systems. The breakdown of the parliamentary experiment in Pakistan and the emergence of a competitive party system in Sri Lanka, as against the long innings of one-party dominance in India, illustrate the point vividly.

It was inherent in the very composition of the freedom-seeking groups/movements which succeeded in India, Sri Lanka and Pakistan during 1947-8 that their respective paths and strategies of nation-building would diverge significantly in several respects. There emerged in the South Asian countries a clearer emphasis on particularistic, religious, ethnic and linguistic components of their respective social fabrics than on the secular and universalistic goals and tendencies in the nation-building processes. The emphasis has been on Islam and Urdu in Pakistan, on Buddhism and Sinhalese in Sri Lanka, on Hinduism in Nepal, on the different sects and varieties of Buddhism in Burma and Bhutan and on Islam and Bengali in Bangladesh. In India also, under the professed goal of secularism, sectarian (communal, regional and linguistic) forces have gradually become powerful in the political processes. As a consequence of these divergent developments, the politics of nation-building in each of these countries has got entangled with the minority-majority dilemma. And owing to the socio-cultural continuities in the region, the resulting tensions and complexities have found easy and, at times, magnified reverberations across national boundaries. Intra-regional relations have naturally been affected by such reverberations.[5]

III

The linkages between internal political processes and external conflictual behaviour of states offer interesting insights in the study of international conflicts.[6] In the case of Indo-Pakistani relations, many scholars have traced the roots of hostilities between the two countries to their respective problems of political development, particularly of national integration and stability in Pakistan.[7] Such linkages, however, need to be investigated and identified carefully.

Take, for instance, the question of national integration. There is enough evidence to show that the conflict between India and Pakistan occasionally helped the respective governments to suppress, avert or deal with a particular crisis of integration. Pakistan made use of the 'Indian threat' in order to suppress dissent in East Pakistan for two decades as well as to contain dissidence in the smaller provinces of West Pakistan. In India's case, the agitation and the self-immolation threat by the Sikh leaders on their demand for a separate state (Punjabi Suba) was withdrawn as a result of the outbreak of conflict with Pakistan on the Kashmir question in September 1965.

As against this set of evidences, there is also evidence to show that India and Pakistan have displayed considerable propensity to complicate and exploit the fragile process of national integration in each other's country. India's unconcealed sympathies for the then East Pakistan and also the Pakhtunistan demand of the NWFP and tribal areas on the one hand, and Pakistan's support for the dissidents in Kashmir and its lip-sympathies for Indian Muslims in general, as also the reported material and moral support for the Nagas in north-east tribal areas on the other, are too well known to be documented here. India's involvement in the Bangladesh crisis in 1971, like the Pakistani intrusion into Kashmir in 1947-8 and 1965, of course provide the most direct evidence in this respect, though these were more complex sets of developments, to be understood simply as one country's intervention into the other with a view to complicate the process of national integration. It must, however, be clearly borne in mind that each country exploited the other's internal tensions and weaknesses through propaganda and other means mainly because they were locked in a conflict relationship and not the other way around. For, after 1972, when the process of Indo-Pakistani detente got underway, the two governments committed themselves to, and to a large extent observed, strict non-interference in each other's internal affairs. The relationship between Bhutto's Pakistan and Mrs Gandhi's India between 1974-6 was particularly marked by such mutual undertakings. While there is no conclusive evidence available so far to the effect that either of the countries launched an armed conflict with the other mainly because of an internal crisis of national integration, this does not deny the fact that the ruling elites in Pakistan found 'anti-Indianism' a convenient, although not always an equally effective, substitute for a more viable and meaningful symbol of national identity.

Like the integration crisis, political stability also does not show any definitive and direct relationship with armed conflict in the case of the India-Pakistan interaction. Except in the 1971 conflict which was preceded by the worst type of systemic crisis and threat to regime-stability in Pakistan, on no previous occasion when armed hostilities took place, in 1947-8, April 1965 and August-

September 1965, did either system or government face a crisis of legitimacy or stability.[8] The Indian system and regime have been stable throughout the period under study. In the case of Pakistan the years of real instability, i.e. between 1952 and 1958, failed to precipitate a conflict with India. This, however, is not intended to create the impression that domestic instability has no implications for interstate conflict. It is only to indicate that the implications are only indirect and partial.

For instance, instability delays and inhibits the success of steps taken towards resolving or reducing conflict. Regarding India's outstanding problems with Pakistan the former British Prime Minister, Harold Macmillan, quoted Nehru as having said in 1958:

> It was impossible to deal with the Pakistan Government—they never stayed in office for more than a few months; they had no sound democratic system; there was nobody who could settle any agreement—in fact he (Nehru) was not at all hopeful.[9]

Instability also makes it impossible for the political leadership and the negotiators to adopt an accommodative give-and-take approach. This was clearly evident during the Indo-Pakistani negotiations between Bhutto and Swaran Singh in 1963, since the position of the Nehru Government in India had been greatly weakened as a result of the military humiliation inflicted by China. Similarly in January 1966, at the Tashkent summit, India was in no position to make any concession on Kashmir because Shastri's government would not have survived such an agreement.[10]

Political instability contributed to the India-Pakistan conflict in another way also. The weakness and the ultimate breakdown of civilian political order in Pakistan resulted in strengthening the army's role within the political system. It was an unfortunate coincidence that, as a result of partition, Pakistan was carved out of areas which had a strong feudal base that sustained the role of the Pakistani army in the subsequent years. This, in turn, thwarted democratic impulses and the development of representative institutions.[11] Thus, the militarisation of politics led to the continuous emphasis on external (in this case Indian) threat and conflict, for that was the reflection of the new system's ethos and its search for legitimacy. No wonder President Ayub Khan stressed the 'threat from India' theme in his 1965 election campaign.[12] The Pakistani military's vested interests in its own expansion and strength and its socialisation process also kept alive the hostility towards India and, on occasions, precipitated armed conflicts with that country.[13] A notable aspect of the Pakistani military's dominant role in the political system and in Pakistan's policy towards India was the fact that the military machine received support and sustenance in a big way from the US military assistance programme to Pakistan. In view of these historical experiences, it would not be an exaggeration to say that a civilian regime in Pakistan, preferably with democratic inclinations, is an important precondition for peace and stability in India-Pakistan relations.

Finally, political instability, when viewed in the context of competition, rivalry and conflict among and within the ruling elites in India and Pakistan, offers further interesting and valuable insights into their conflict relationship. It was the continuous conflict between the political, bureaucratic and military elites in Pakistan which, after Jinnah's death, adversely affected the evolution of a mature foreign policy including the policy towards India. In the early years several well-meaning attempts to reduce the salience of the Indo-Pakistani conflict were frustrated owing to this internal tug-of-war. Since the beginning of the 1960s the undercurrent of rivalry between Bhutto on the one hand and Pakistani leaders like President Ayub, Sheikh Mujibur Rahman and even Yahya Khan, on the other, drove Pakistan to the brink of war as well as into armed conflict with India several times. It is now known, for instance, that Bhutto, since 1962, had been advocating a war with India as against a much more cautious approach adopted by Ayub. The former was also not happy with the ceasefire of 1965 and the Tashkent agreement of 1966 which formalised this ceasefire.[14] Even the British attempt at mediation during the Kutch conflict (April-May 1965) was delayed and complicated by Bhutto's intransigence.[15] Recent writings have also indicated that Bhutto had a vested interest in the 1971 India-Pakistan war and the eventual separation of Bangladesh from West Pakistan.[16] The result was that Pakistani decision-makers were almost driven to the state where that conflict became inevitable. The same Bhutto, after becoming the Prime Minister of the new Pakistan in 1972, also became the main architect of a policy of detente with India. However, Bhutto's hawkish approach to Indo-Pakistani relations before the emergence of Bangladesh should not be understood as a purely individual and personal exercise. He was representing and articulating the approach of certain powerful political interests in Pakistan, be they some sections in the military or bureaucracy or even external influences.

Intra-elite conflicts and competition in India were also not devoid of important implications for a policy towards Pakistan. In the initial period, Sardar Patel was the spokesman for a hardline policy towards Pakistan as against Nehru's approach of greater accommodation. One of Patel's secretaries has written:

> Temperamentally, on matters of dispute with Pakistan Sardar was firm and unyielding though he did not, except in matters of vital importance, trouble himself with details on which Panditji and Gopalaswamy had their way without interference from him. There is also no doubt that there was an undercurrent of militancy in Sardar's approach; militancy was, however, not synonymous with bellicosity or war-mongering but arose from a realisation that that was the only language which Pakistan understood.[17]

Fortunately for Nehru, Sardar Patel did not live long enough to influence policy towards Pakistan. Amongst the political parties, the Jana Sangh advocated a strong Indian posture towards Pakistan. The same Jana Sangh leadership, when in power in India after March 1977 as a constituent of the Janata Party, claimed to be the champions of peaceful and friendly relations with Pakistan. There were also a number of hawkish elements in the Congress but until Nehru's death they could not have their way easily. They did, however, put pressure on Nehru's successor, Lal Bahadur Shastri, particularly between April and December 1965, to deal with Pakistan firmly. They also opposed the payment of the Indian contribution to Pakistan falling due in 1965 under the terms of the Indus-Water Treaty.[18] However, as compared to the Pakistani situation, politics in India have had a much wider base and more varied issues for intra-elite conflict. Accordingly, the intensity of India as an issue in Pakistan's domestic politics was much greater than was the case in India *vis-à-vis* the Pakistan issue.[19]

The foregoing discussion clearly indicates that the problems of nation-building and political instability contributed a great deal in building up and perpetuating the environment of conflict between India and Pakistan. But it would be a big mistake to consider them the only or even the most powerful determining factors in pushing the two countries towards armed conflict. For had this been so, there were several other countries in India's neighbourhood who, beset by the same problems, would have entered into a conflict relationship with India on the same dimensions as was the case with Pakistan. Since this did not happen, we must look for additional regional and external sources of Indo-Pakistani conflict.

IV

The factor of status-inconsistency in international relations has not been adequately emphasised and properly investigated, particularly with reference to interstate conflict.[20] This factor has played a crucial role in the India-Pakistan conflict. The Indian and Pakistani perceptions and self-images of their power-status *vis-à-vis* each other in the regional as well as the global contexts were so mutually incompatible that their drives to achieve these self-perceived status-positions brought them into armed clashes with each other. The supporting and aggregating impulses and implications of the processes of state and nation-building, as also of the historical evolution of the two states, converged and were intricately enmeshed with the question of status-incompatibility. This incompatibility has further determined their respective security and strategic requirements in general and their security postures towards each other in particular. As a result it has conditioned and shaped the totality of their approaches towards each other. It can be easily described as the main propelling force behind the Indo-Pakistani conflict and their respective foreign policy behaviours.

The Indian ruling elite inherited the perception that, like British India, independent India was also destined to play a major role in Asian and world affairs commensurate with its geographical placement, historical experience and power-potential. Nehru, articulating this perception, told the Constituent Assembly of India on 8 March 1949 that 'the emergence of India in world affairs is something of major consequence in world history ... it has been given to us to work at a time when India is growing into a great giant again'.[21] Explaining the basis of this perception on another occasion he declared:

> India is very curiously placed in Asia and her history has been governed a great deal by geographical factors plus other factors. Whichever problem in Asia you may take up somehow or other India comes into the picture ... Whether it is a problem of defence or trade or industry or economic policy, India cannot be

> ignored. She cannot be ignored because as I said, her geographical position is a compelling reason. She cannot be ignored also because of her actual or potential power and resources. Whatever her actual strength may or may not be, India is potentially a very powerful country ... there can be no doubt in anyone's mind that India's potential wealth will become actual and that in not too distant a future.[22]

While, in this context, Nehru clearly stated that 'He cannot relate our foreign policy just to a few countries around us .. our foreign policy cannot limit itself to the nearby countries',[23] yet, even within this limit, the neighbouring region occupied a very significant place, particularly in strategic terms. The Nehruvian model of foreign policy envisaged very close and co-operative relations in all vital matters between India and its immediate neighbours. Nehru had even talked of forging a 'closer union', 'confederation ... of independent States with common defence and economic possibility' in South Asia.[25] India wanted Pakistan to be a friendly and co-operative member of this community, as a sovereign independent state.[26] India, for itself, envisaged, naturally, a central place in this community as was evident from its treaties with Nepal, Bhutan and Sikkim immediately after independence, and also its role in these countries and in Burma during the late 1940s and the early 1950s. According to this model, a stable and favourable regional environment in South Asia was necessary for India to play a leading and constructive role in the larger Asian and world arena. The underlying assumption of this foreign policy approach was that India's natural place in the power-hierarchy of the subcontinent must be asserted by it and acknowledged by others, both within the region as well as outside, particularly by the great powers.

The main motivation behind the foreign policy of independent Pakistan was derived from the ideology and the psyche of the pre-partition Muslim League. Accordingly, the two nation theory, which formed the ideological basis for the partition of 1947, had as its corollary a built-in assumption that after independence India and Pakistan would possess not only juridical equality but also equality in power terms and that this should be recognised by the world at large and particularly by the dominant powers. The 'two nation' theory was thus transformed into independent Pakistan's drive to achieve and enjoy power-parity with India. A perceptive Western scholar of Pakistan affairs has stated:

> In large measure, Pakistani feeling towards India has been a continuation of the political struggle before partition ... Mr Jinnah had never agreed to constitutional formulae which would have denoted lesser status for the Muslim league. India contained two nations; one sovereign nation is the equal of any other sovereign nation ... Many political leaders and most of the articulate section of the population have reacted with emotional intensity to any suggestion of Indian superiority in any field.[27]

Pakistan's President Ayub, almost verifying this, wrote:

> The world today is fighting for equality—equality amongst individuals as among nations, regardless of whether they are big or small. This requires an unequivocal recognition by the world that every nation is entitled to equal rights and opportunities. The degree of a country's sovereignty and self-respect is not determined by the size of its territory or its resources. This sounds simple enough ... yet there are no means to enforce it. It is a world of the Big Two, Big Three or four or more. It is they who preside over the destinies of the world and determine its direction. The smaller countries, particularly those in the early stages of industrial development, belong to a lower stratum of existence ... We too have to establish our identity and fight for a position of equality and honour.

He continued in the same vein:

> The cause of our major problem is India's inability to reconcile herself to our existence as a sovereign independent nation ... At the back of it all was India's ambition to absorb Pakistan or turn her into a satellite.[28]

Obviously then, Pakistan did not accept the Indian framework of building co-operative relations in South Asia, for that would ascribe her a status lower than India. And for India, Pakistan's drive for parity with her was anathema for, in New Delhi's perception, it was aimed at distorting the natural power-hierarchy in the subcontinent and India's pre-eminent position in that hierarchy —a position which India was keen to demonstrate and consolidate. Since the power-balance existing in the subcontinent was in conformity with the Indian approach, and since India wanted to preserve and protect this status quo, Pakistan was as keen to disturb and change it. In doing so, Pakistan, as the smaller power, and the Pakistani ruling elite, always conscious of their regional inferiority, have sought external assistance to change the regional power-balance. India, on the other hand, has consistently cherished the goal of keeping the subcontinent free, as far as possible, from external influence. One must hasten to add here that this was so only in the context of Indo-Pakistani relations. Once India had its difficulties with China, it also became receptive to offers of external support in order to balance its position *vis-à-vis* China. For Pakistan, this was hypocritical and contradictory behaviour on India's part. These mutually antagonistic approaches explain India's consistent offer of a 'no war' pact to Pakistan and the latter's consistent refusal to accept the offer. India wanted the arms race within the subcontinent to stop, thereby legitimising the status quo which favoured India. This was antithetical to Pakistan's perception of regional balance. Bhutto wrote in 1967:

> After two decades of independence, Indo-Pakistan relations have remained static. None of the animosities have been removed, none of the causes of partition remedied. In the prevailing conditions a reduction in the armed forces of India and Pakistan would freeze the disputes for ever and benefit India. It would amount to *de facto* recognition of India's supremacy in the subcontinent and, for all intents and purposes, legalise its usurpation of Pakistan's economic and territorial rights ... Bilateral disarmament between adversaries is a negation of sovereignty and an admission of defeat by one of them.[29]

Pakistani leaders viewed the acceptance of a lower status *vis-à-vis* India, in terms of the subcontinental balance of power, as the very negation of Pakistan's independent existence. This constituted a source of threat and insecurity to them. The Indian leaders, on the other hand, saw any disturbance of the regional power hierarchy, by way of Pakistan's alliance first with the Western bloc and then with China, as a source of grave danger to peace, security and stability in the subcontinent. Thus, the question of status-incongruence between the two states was intricately mixed-up with their respective perceptions of peace and security. What caused partition continued to cause conflict between India and Pakistan.

Curiously enough, this status-incongruence was also deeply identified with, and intensely expressed in terms of, the Kashmir issue. In other words, the acquisition of Kashmir, besides other things, became a status symbol and a component of the power struggle between India and Pakistan. It is interesting to note that while partition was being negotiated both the sides rather readily acquiesced in leaving Kashmir as an independent state, whatever might be their ultimate and long-term intentions. There were two other states left independent likewise, Hyderabad and Junagadh, with Hindu majorities and Muslim rulers. India promptly integrated these states in the teeth of opposition from Pakistan. The latter failed to do anything in either case, owing to the very location of these states in the Indian heartland and because of the effectiveness of Indian moves. Pakistan had also failed to woo other border states like Jodhpur to its side. This heightened the Pakistani leaders' sense of frustration arising out of the already mentioned Radcliffe award which had delimited the boundaries between India and Pakistan. Since the Kashmir issue had certain similarities with Hyderabad and Junagadh, Pakistan apparently believed that in the light of Indian action in the two latter cases, its claim on Kashmir was legitimate and natural because of its predominantly Muslim population. Because of Kashmir's geographical contiguity to Pakistan, unlike Hyderabad and Junagadh, the Pakistani leaders were also in a much better position to do something more than exert only diplomatic pressure and encourage internal trouble to back up their claim. They therefore physically involved Pakistan in the Kashmir affair under the cover of tribal raiders.[30] In addition, it could also be viewed as a part of the overall strategy to put pressure on India in relation to Hyderabad and Junagadh as well as other disputes. Just when the tribal invasion of Kashmir had almost succeeded in capturing Srinagar, the capital of Kashmir, and translating Pakistan's claim into a concrete reality, India intervened. The effectiveness of the Indian intervention, which prevented the fall of Srinagar and was able to drive the raiders out of most of the valley, inflicted a sense of defeat and weakness on Pakistan which further complicated its status problem *vis-à-vis* India.

For India, Kashmir was of comparatively lower priority as against Hyderabad and Junagadh immediately after independence. Kashmir's Muslim character and the Maharaja's antipathy towards a section of Congress leaders, particularly Nehru, were important factors in India's calculations at that time. Although Nehru had a deep emotional attachment to Kashmir, the Indian leaders, at least ostensibly, were prepared to let Kashmir opt for Pakistan if the Maharaja so desired. Because of this comparatively low priority India was almost taken unawares by the swift Pakistani moves in that state. Yet, subsequently, having intervened and established itself, it was thought politically undesirable to move out of the state or even concede or accommodate Pakistani claims in any manner. Pakistan's direct involvement, which was a prelude to the involvement on the part of various external powers in Kashmir, also led India to treat Kashmir as a question of prestige and status for itself. Nehru once remarked that 'The Kashmir issue would have been solved long ago but for Western help to Pakistan.'[31] However, he did not explain how this could happen. We will take up the question of external powers' involvement in Kashmir later.

Kashmir's strategic location was, of course, central to the interests of both the parties to the conflict. Initially for Pakistan and later for India, Kashmir also held some economic attraction. Accordingly, Kashmir occupied a place of its own in the balance of power between India and Pakistan. Bhutto's statement was revealing in this respect when he said:

> Why does India want Jammu and Kashmir? She holds them because the Valley is the handsome head of the body of Pakistan. Its possession enables her to cripple the economy of West Pakistan, and militarily to dominate the country. India retains Jammu and Kashmir because she wants to increase her strategic importance by having common borders with the Soviet Union and China and correspondingly denying Pakistan these frontiers.

Explaining Pakistan's stakes, he continued:

> If a Muslim majority area can remain a part of India, then the *raison d'être* of Pakistan collapses ... For the same reason (as for India) Pakistan must continue unremittingly her struggle for the right of self-determination of the subject people. Pakistan is incomplete without Jammu and Kashmir both territorially and ideologically. Recovering them she should recover her head and be made whole, stronger, and more viable ... If, however, we settle for tranquil relations with India without an equitable resolution of disputes, it would be the first major step in establishing Indian leadership in our parts, with Pakistan and other neighbouring States becoming Indian satellites.[32]

The identification of the Kashmir issue with the whole issue of status-incongruence and its importance as the major source of conflict between India and Pakistan could not have been put more eloquently.

Before we come to the question of great-power involvement, the thrust of the foregoing arguments needs to be further substantiated. Even at the risk of repetition, it may be stated that in three of the four armed conflicts between India and Pakistan, the Kashmir front was one of the main theatres of war. The exception was the Kutch conflict in April 1965 but even at that time the situation in Kashmir was extremely tense and unstable. Further, two of the four wars (1947-8 and September 1965) were fought solely over the Kashmir issue. As far as the initiation of conflicts is concerned, the responsibility in large measure rested with Pakistan for the first three wars. In the Bangladesh war of 1971 responsibility for the outbreak of hostilities was shared by both parties to some extent. This can be understood in the light of what has been stated earlier, namely, that India as the pre-eminent power in the subcontinent was basically interested in preserving and perpetuating the status quo and stability in the subcontinent. Pakistan, on the other hand, had deep stakes in upsetting the status quo. It was only in the Bangladesh crisis of 1971 that India was interested in altering the status quo. This was made all the more urgent because of the mounting problem of refugees from East Bengal. The situation in 1971 was also viewed by the ruling elite in India as 'an opportunity of the century' which had all the factors present in it to legitimise India's action (if it was a successful one, as it turned out to be) in cutting Pakistan down to size and thus eliminating for a long time to come Pakistan's chances to distort the natural power-hierarchy in the subcontinent in which India occupied the dominant place.[33] A sense of urgency was injected into India's thinking in this context by the then rapidly emerging rapprochement in Sino-American relations. This process, if allowed to continue without an urgent resolution of the Bangladesh crisis, would have favoured Pakistan and would have had very adverse implications for India.

It is interesting to note further that, whereas status-incongruence locked India and Pakistan into a conflict relationship, the outbreak of armed hostilities coincided with periods of near power-parity between them, either actual or so perceived. The status of near equality, in terms of relative strength or weakness, between India and Pakistan at the time of the first Kashmir conflict was inherent in the confusion and disorder generated by the very act of partition. In 1965, India was still limping as a result of the 1962 Sino-Indian conflict and the subsequent internal political changes. It was not unreasonable for the Pakistani ruling elite to interpret India's weakness as Pakistan's strength. The *White Paper on Kashmir* issued by Bhutto's Government in 1977 strongly resented the fact that Pakistan did not intervene in Kashmir at the time of the Sino-Indian conflict of 1962. It also resented the fact that Pakistan did nothing 'when Kashmir simmered throughout 1964 and the first half of 1965' with internal 'uprising' and frequent border clashes. On 12 May 1965, i.e. midway between the Kutch and the Kashmir conflicts of 1965, Bhutto, then Pakistan's Foreign Minister, addressed a letter to President Ayub in which he stated:

> India at present is in no position to risk a general war of unlimited duration for the annihilation of Pakistan ... Moreover, from what I have been able to gather from authoritative sources, there is for the present at least, the relative superiority of the military forces of Pakistan in terms of quality and equipment ... This does not mean that there can be a general war of unlimited duration ... The morale of our nameless soldier on the front line is high. He has poignant choice to react now if India chooses to retaliate. This is our hour of decision and may God guide us on the right path.[34]

This was a clear statement, asking the President to open hostilities against India. It was no coincidence, therefore, that the conflict broke out in August 1965. An additional but equally important consideration in Pakistani thinking was that the then existing, favourable power-balance with India might not continue to remain so for long in view of Western arms assistance to India since the 1962 Sino-Indian conflict. Pakistani leaders had launched a strong campaign of protest against such assistance to India. Their diplomatic pressures, however, had failed to dissuade the United States from aiding India. The US was not willing to go beyond assuring Pakistan that India would not be allowed to harm Pakistan from this additional strength and they had secretly renewed in 1964 the US-Pakistan bilateral agreement.[35] Pakistan, therefore, felt compelled to disturb the growing trend in Indo-US relations.

In 1971 India had reached an appreciable level of military and economic competence. Politically, Mrs Gandhi's regime had firmly established itself as a result of the national elections held in February-March 1971. India was almost itching to demonstrate its regained confidence and correct the distortion in the power-hierarchy in the region that had crept in as a result of the conflicts with China and Pakistan during 1962-5. The indication of this restlessness was evident in a small way in a couple of border skirmishes with China in 1966-7 and 1969 in the Nathula and Thagla regions. India, by then, had also overcome the sense of isolation in the region and the world suffered during the early sixties. Pakistan, on the other hand, was caught in serious internal strife in Bangladesh although its military regime was confident of resolving the problem militarily. Externally, the Nixon administration's unqualified support to Pakistan coupled with China's continued support to that country and the implications for the South Asian region of the recently initiated process of Sino-US rapprochement, with Pakistan acting as a link, were clearly sources of reassurance for Pakistan that it would not be let down by its powerful friends. As a result of these almost parallel perceptions on the part of the two countries, it would have been difficult to avoid an India-Pakistan conflict at that stage on the question of Bangladesh. This is not to ignore or underestimate the nationalist aspirations of Bangladesh, or the tremendous pressure created by the Bangladeshi refugees on Indian administrative and political structures and economic resources, or the theoretical question of Pakistan's territorial integrity and sovereignty. All these questions were inextricably entangled and should be viewed as parts of the whole situation.

V

Even without further effort one can easily state that the role of the great powers in the regional conflict in South Asia has been both vital to and inseparable from the regional roots of the conflict. Whereas the regional roots lay in the history of the evolution of India and Pakistan as independent entities, in the status-incongruence in the subcontinent, in the Kashmir dispute, etc., the two parties to the conflict received the confidence and actual capacity to enter into hostilities with each other from their respective allies and supporters amongst the great powers. The great powers, on the other hand, found the South Asian conflict an essential regional component of their own conflict as signified in the Cold War, the Sino-Soviet rivalry and the redefined Cold War, that exists as a part of the complex process of superpower detente. They, therefore, found it irresistible to feed and reinforce the regional roots of the South Asian conflict. The great-power involvement was so deep and pervasive that one is even led to believe that the great powers in pursuance of their global and regional objectives would have invented a conflict in South Asia if none had existed.

The three great powers that were of major consequence in South Asia, as perhaps in other Third World regions, were the United States, the Soviet Union and China. Of these, the United States was clearly an intrusive power which intervened in South Asia mainly in pursuance of its global strategy. It had no intrinsic stakes in the region as such in terms of basic irreducible minimum interests, except in the context of its post-Second World War global role and strategy. It is necessary to mention here that the US role, or, for that matter, the role of any other great power, in the region cannot be understood without reference to the British role. Britain, as the former colonial power, had substantial and vital residual economic and strategic interests in the area. The US was introduced into the region by Britain and was requested to collaborate with the latter in the protection of those residual colonial interests in addition to the wider global considerations of the United States. For the Soviet Union and China, on the other hand, there were strong historical and geographical factors which determined the nature of their stakes in the subcontinent. What had prompted them earlier to interact with and intervene in the British-ruled region, also prompted them to confront the US during the early years and each other later on. The story of their respective involvements is a chronology of their responses to Anglo-American moves, at times friendly, at times otherwise. There were also significant implications of the role of extra-regional powers like Iran in South Asia, but that falls beyond the scope of this paper.

The subject of the great powers' relations with the South Asian adversaries, India and Pakistan, is rather well researched. What one can do here is to put the broad facts into proper perspective in order to understand the great powers' contribution to the regional conflict.[36] The great powers' policies in this regard operated simultaneously at two levels: the central or the global balance and the regional South Asian balance. The US, in its overall global strategy, had vital stakes in the Indian economic and political system and would have preferred Indian co-operation in its military and strategic moves against the 'communist threat'. The latter proposition did not have much appeal for India. Not that Indian decision-makers had any serious quarrel with the goals of Anglo-American policy; but being conscious of India's potential and having been socialised through the British strategic and geopolitical thinking, they did not want to foreclose any option and wanted to play the game of world politics in an Indian style with an Asian flavour. They wanted India to be an active actor, and not a passive follower, in the central strategic balance and in the new correlation of global forces that were emerging in the post-Second World War era. The principal disagreement between India and the West lay in their respective perspectives on Asia and its place in this new emerging order.

Accordingly, whereas India signed a Mutual Assistance Agreement with the US in December 1950, it vehemently differed with the US approach to the Korean question and the Japanese Peace Treaty; whereas India continued to relish the Commonwealth defence and economic links and even acquiesced in the continuation of the British naval base in Sri Lanka, it condemned the British military intervention in the Suez crisis of 1956 and rejected the rationale and basis of military blocs and alliances. While Nehru agreed that communism was not a desirable economic and political system, he did not accept the argument that the Soviet Union and/or China were too horrific and scary to do business with and treat them as untouchables. Learning his lessons from the British strategy of balance of power, he was even inclined to lean a bit towards the then weaker forces, the Soviet Union and China, largely as a defensive posture and to increase his leverage with the West, but not to the extent of harming the basic interests of the West. Since the United States had committed itself to a policy of 'containment', mainly through military alliances, it chose, however hesitatingly but perhaps unavoidably, Pakistan as an ally. Long before the military pact was concluded between the US and Pakistan, the US Assistant Secretary of State declared in 1951:

> We do however have a great incentive to help Pakistan for the reason that Pakistan is very co-operative with U.S. and the Western countries. Pakistan has a very forthright attitude with respect to the basic cold war issues. Pakistan did not send troops to Korea but Pakistan has in other ways demonstrated her willingness to participate with us.[37]

The fact that Pakistan's love for Western alliances emanated not from the concern for Cold War issues but from the search for a favourable balance with India did not really come into conflict with US policy. Herein lay the convergence of the two levels: the global and the regional.

What drove the US away from India and closer to Pakistan pushed the Soviet Union closer to India and made it indifferent, in fact occasionally hostile, towards Pakistani aspirations. Explanations for Indo-Soviet friendship have been sought in Nehru's radicalism, the geographic proximity of the two countries, India's anti-West posture and what not. But they were all secondary to the basic question of the convergence of the strategic and foreign policy objectives of India and the USSR in the post-war world. It was a new and challenging world. India wanted to play a major role in a new and resurgent Asia which was slowly but definitely releasing itself from Western political dominance. This Indian assertion, which was viewed by the West as defiance, howsoever mild, suited Soviet objectives. For India, the Western alliance system was a new form of dominance; it was checkmating the process of Asian resurgence. Its Pakistani component was particularly repugnant to India's vital interests. In such a situation India found in the Soviet Union an imperfect but none the less a powerful and acceptable supporter. The early Soviet initiatives in South Asia were essentially reactive. Later, the China factor gave them an intrusive and independent content. As a result, the frontiers of Indo-Soviet co-operation were gradually extended and diversified.

VI

Thus the two superpowers in their mutual rivalry came to select one of the two South Asian adversaries as their local favourites. These linkages have since then been fairly consistent in character. Since the regional balance has been subordinate to the central balance, i.e. to the nature of the relationship between the US and the USSR, the intensity of the latter has determined the intensity of the former. This was convincingly demonstrated during the 1960s, particularly since the intensification of the Sino-Indian conflict on the one hand and the Sino-Soviet rivalry on the other. Developments in Sino-Indian relations heightened the Western powers' concern about the Chinese threat to South Asia. They, therefore, stepped up their efforts to bring about a rapprochement between India and Pakistan in order to deal more effectively with what they thought was a common danger.

Pakistan viewed this move as a most undesirable development

since in this also lay the rationale for the subsequent strengthening of India through Western assistance. More important, in the Sino-Indian conflict Pakistan found a new option opening up for its policy goals *vis-à-vis* India. This was also the time when, on the one hand, the Sino-Soviet rivalry was surfacing and, on the other, the superpower detente was in the offing (particularly after the Cuban crisis of 1962). In the regional context the Soviet Union also found it advisable to woo both India and Pakistan simultaneously in order to keep Pakistan away from and India safe from China, as also to match the Western efforts to keep China out of South Asia. The relaxation of superpower tension at the global level and the emergence of a new and, what was considered to be, an aggressive great power in the vicinity of South Asia, blurred the initially established linkages between the superpowers and the regional contestants. Soviet mediation in the Indo-Pakistan conflict of 1965 at Tashkent with Anglo-American support could be possible only under such circumstances. This situation was radically altered by the dramatic development of the Sino-American rapprochement in 1971. US rethinking on China in this respect had been induced mainly by considerations that had very little to do with South Asia. The stalemate in Vietnam, the changing strategic balance *vis-à-vis* the Soviet Union, which was slowly but definitely eroding American superiority, and domestic pressures for opening new economic avenues abroad contributed to this opening towards China. As against this, India's significance to the US had started to decline.[38] As a result of this sudden shift in great power equations, the initial pattern of linkages between the superpowers and the regional actors was restored with China weighing in on the side of the US and Pakistan. The major consequences of this shift were the Indo-Soviet treaty and the subsequent emergence of Bangladesh following the Indo-Pakistan war of 1971. Henry Kissinger, the then US Secretary of State, was right when he said that Bangladesh was not merely a local conflict, but an expression of a particular correlation of global forces.[39]

A pertinent question arises here as to how one can explain the two Indo-Pakistani conflicts of 1965 which ran contrary to the implications of the superpower detente and also particularly the Western powers' efforts to bring about rapprochement and co-operation between the regional adversaries. A part of the answer has been given earlier, while explaining Pakistan's self-perceived sense of parity tending towards superiority in relation to India which had resulted from the combination of two factors: (i) the continuous Western military and political support since 1947 and (ii) India's military humiliation and weakness demonstrated by the Sino-Indian conflict. It has also been noted that Pakistan wanted to disturb the gradually strengthening trend of Western military and political support for India against China which it believed would be at its cost.[40] Pakistan's President Ayub, just a day after his election in 1965, told a press conference:

> U.S. policy in this part of the world has changed in a fashion that has imperilled our security ... I know the U.S. had its commitment and I do not blame the Americans in a sense for the global attitude, but arming India does not make sense to me and I feel very strongly about that ... China is not going to attack India. India will use these American weapons against smaller nations and continue trying to intimidate us as she has for the past 17 years. India is not going to act in a fashion that would further U.S. policy.[41]

Within a few months of this statement hostilities broke out in the Kutch sector. As is indicated in the President's statement, the other part of the explanation for the 1965 Indo-Pakistani wars lies in China's role which will be discussed below.

Before we come to the China factor in the subcontinent, it is both relevant and important to keep in mind the slight but significant difference in the US and the British perceptions of the Chinese threat to the subcontinent and its effect on the regional balance. These two Western powers have been co-ordinating their policies in the subcontinent since 1947, and continue to do so in the seventies. However, for the US the central balance was more important than anything else while for the UK its perceptions of South Asia and China were rooted in its long colonial history. The US treated the Chinese threat to South Asia as real and long-term. The British on the other hand, believed that Peking had more limited objectives. The British, therefore, did not want the Western powers to rush arms into India after the 1962 debacle, since that would upset the regional balance with which they, unlike the Americans, were primarily concerned. On the other hand, they wanted to utilise this occasion to put pressure on India to grant some concessions to Pakistan on Kashmir and other questions. The British Prime Minister, Harold Macmillan, also managed to persuade US President

John F. Kennedy, at their summit at Nassau in December 1962, to adopt a go-slow approach to arms supplies to India and to link a solution of the Kashmir issue to the question of arms supply. This was the real purpose behind the efforts of the US-UK team led by Duncan Sandys, the British Commonwealth Secretary, and Averell Harriman, the US Under Secretary of State, which attempted to mediate between India and Pakistan following the Sino-Indian border war of 1962.[42] Harold Macmillan, recalling the incident later, wrote:

> Looking back on this episode, it is curious to compare British scepticism with American alarm. Our advisers rightly believed that the Chinese forces would not advance beyond the line which it suited them to hold. They had made a *raid* in order to obtain, in these mountain areas, a more convenient frontier. They would not embark upon wholesale invasion ... but Washington was more nervous than London, for Chinese expansionist policies were believed to be responsible for all the troubles in South-east Asia ... We, with our longer experience, felt convinced that while it would be Chinese policy to take advantage of any troubles or difficulties in any adjacent area, they would not themselves advance on an adventurous policy. All through we were concerned in trying our best to bring about some solution in the underlying tragedy which followed independence in the Indian subcontinent. The chief risk seemed to us not the invasion and occupation of India by vast Chinese hordes. The real danger lay in the breaking up in disorder of the fragile structure which we had left behind when we retired so hurriedly in 1947—the partition of India. Subsequent events have logically confirmed our judgement.[43]

Obviously, the UK was more concerned with its long-standing stakes in perpetuating the Indo-Pakistani balance in South Asia. For the British, the central balance between the superpowers was not to be allowed to completely undermine the importance of the regional balance. This divergence in the approaches between Britain and the US became explicit at the time of the second Kashmir war in 1965. The UK openly accused India of aggression.[44] The US, on the other hand, considered Pakistan primarily responsible for the conflict. It put pressure on Pakistan to accept the UN ceasefire proposals and the Secretary of State, Dean Rusk, reacted to Pakistan's demand for help by stating that his country 'was being invited in on the crash landing without being in on the take off'.[45] This divergence was also the reason behind the then Pakistani Foreign Minister Bhutto's appreciation of the British stand while he was attacking the US for its arms supplies to India during the period preceding the 1965 conflict.

Like the British, the Chinese had basic interests in the regional Indo-Pakistani balance. For them this balance was a vital component of their policy towards the superpowers and the central balance. They have accordingly been very consistent in giving all possible support—military, economic, political and diplomatic—to Pakistan, irrespective of the fluctuations in the latter's relations with the superpowers. Even during the heyday of Sino-Indian friendship, China maintained an ambiguous position on the Kashmir issue and did not unduly criticise Pakistan for its association with Western military pacts. Pakistan and China had their first direct contact at the highest level when their Prime Ministers, Mohammed Ali of Bogra and Chou En-Lai, met during the Bandung Conference in 1955 and reached an understanding on matters of 'collective peace and co-operation'. China's support for Pakistan picked up momentum in the wake of the intensification of Sino-Indian tensions. This was so for obvious reasons. The process was further strengthened with the convergence of Soviet-American interests, particularly in the subcontinent, in favour of India. Both China and Pakistan resented this convergence and were keen to halt, if not reverse, the direction of developments. This mutuality of interests was a vital factor behind the 1965 Indo-Pakistani conflicts. China strongly disapproved of the Kutch ceasefire accord between India and Pakistan.[46] It also condemned the Tashkent accord as a manifestation of US-Soviet-Indian collusion against China. Pakistan's acceptance of Soviet mediation was naturally not liked by China.[47] China's subsequent support to Pakistan, including its ultimatums to India both during the 1965 and 1971 Indo-Pakistan conflicts, are too well known and well acknowledged to need any detailed discussion here.

VII

The implications of great-power alignments and their equations with India and Pakistan for the conflict in South Asia were all too clear. They set off a substantial arms race between the regional adversaries, the impact of which on their fighting capabilities was crucial. The arms race was nearly monopolised by the Western powers, the US and the UK in particular, until the beginning of the 1960s. The Indo-Soviet deal on the supply of MIG-21 aircraft concluded in August 1962 was the first step towards diversification of sources for major weapons supply to the subcontinent. Subsequently, however, the Soviet Union joined the Western powers as a principal arms supplier to India and China did the same in relation to Pakistan.[48] Arms thus supplied by the great powers, in addition to the overall support by them to one side or the other, helped to inflate and complicate the factor of status-incongruence, the major cause of conflict in South Asia. One wonders if the wars of 1965 and 1971 would have taken place at all in the absence of the great powers' involvement and the arms race generated by such involvement in the region.

It has been mentioned earlier that military aid encouraged and strengthened imbalances and distortions in the domestic political systems in the region, eg. by strengthening the military in Pakistan. This is not to ignore economic assistance that flowed into the region as a result of the various great power connections. In Pakistan the external economic input could not have corrected the adverse impact of external military input, since the two were supposed to be complementary to each other, aimed at serving the strategic objectives of the donor power. Both in India and Pakistan, Western economic assistance did not enter those sectors which could help build up a viable economic structure. US reservations on assistance to India for the Bokaro steel plant may be recalled here. Western economic aid went to sectors like communication, food aid and community development, where it made the recipient economy dependent and lethargic and enabled the donor to facilitate its presence in these societies. The idea of 'Small is Beautiful' was being practised in the subcontinent long before it was preached and articulated in the West. Soviet and Chinese assistance has been comparatively more advantageous and purposeful, especially in sectors like steel and petroleum industries, roads and power generation. However, this too was not devoid of strategic and political goals. Besides immediate strategic considerations, the ground was being prepared, as through oil exploration, to ultimately weaken the hold in South Asia of the economic vehicles of Western political influence, the multinationals.

The factor of status-incongruence is intertwined with the Kashmir dispute in Indo-Pakistani relations. This has been discussed earlier. The great powers, besides complicating and enhancing the status-incongruence as noted above, also had direct interests in the Kashmir dispute. This was so not only because the dispute was a crucial factor in the regional balance, but also, and perhaps more important, because the area was of utmost significance to their own competition and rivalries. The Soviet Union and China had long-standing geopolitical interests in the area. It was a meeting point of vast territorial expanses, cultural influences, economic interests and political empires: of the subcontinent, Russia, China and Afghanistan. It served as the most important land route for the pre-British invaders of India. China and Russia had come into contact with parts of Kashmir on various occasions in the past, either motivated by defensive policies—to keep inimical influences at a safe distance from their respective Central Asian peripheries—or propelled by ambitions of adventure and expansion. China, until recently, claimed sovereignty over Hunza, and the Russians never relished British efforts, more or less successful, to establish and entrench themselves in Gilgit, two principalities which are now in Pakistan-held Kashmir.

Kashmir was a vital security and strategic outpost for the British Empire. Lord Curzon had clearly underlined its significance in his articulation of the defence requirements for British India's north-western regions. The British did not seem to be willing to relinquish these strategic interests even while withdrawing from the subcontinent in 1947. There were some clear indications which pointed towards such a conclusion. Gilgit had been adminstered as a British agency because of its strategic location and there were plans to integrate it with the North-West Frontier region of the post-1947 Pakistan. However, just before granting independence to India and Pakistan, and when it became clear that Kashmir was going to join neither dominion, the British restored Gilgit to Kashmir. This was a deft political decision. On the one hand, it denied the strategic post to both India and Pakistan and made it possible that the British could continue to enjoy vital strategic privileges if Kashmir was to remain independent at all. On the other, it made Kashmir internally fragile and potentially a cause of conflict between India and Pakistan. The first Indo-Pakistan conflict in Kashmir perhaps came sooner than expected for the real British intentions to unfold. Soon after the breakout of a Pakistani-supported tribal invasion of Kashmir, the Gilgit Scouts, under a British commander, declared their accession to Pakistan.[49]

When the seriousness of the tribal invasion of Kashmir was realised in Kashmir and India, the then Govenor-General of India, Lord Mountbatten, otherwise acclaimed as India's friend, insisted on legal formalities of accession, at the cost of the loss of two crucial days, before India could respond to the call for military help from Kashmir's ruler. Mountbatten's subsequent role was, however, more important. He persuaded India to accept the accession only as a temporary measure and subject to the outcome of a plebiscite to be held in the state. The Maharaja and Kashmiri leaders like Sheikh Abdullah had not asked for such a plebiscite at all. Indian leaders, including Mountbatten's friend Nehru, had very strong reservations on this plebiscite condition. Further, this was done despite Mountbatten's clear assessment which he wrote to his King on 7 December 1947: 'I am convinced that a population containing such a high proportion of Moslems would certainly vote to join Pakistan.'[50] He, of course, must have had the minimum political sense to realise that once accession had taken place, no government in India would allow it to be undone irrespective of other commitments. In that case what was he aiming at? Perhaps to keep Kashmir a disputed territory between India and Pakistan. By allowing accession and India's military action (against the advice and objections of the British commanders of India's army and air force), he denied Kashmir to Pakistan and by adding the condition of plebiscite to the accession, he attempted to deny it to India as well. It was unfortunate that Nehru played into his hands, little realising that Mountbatten's pro-India image was expected to serve British interests. Mountbatten persuaded Nehru to commit India to a plebiscite 'under international auspices like the United Nations'.[51] This was an astute move to make Kashmir a bone of contention between India and Pakistan and thus keep the subcontinent divided and also to turn Kashmir into a fertile ground for international forces, particularly the Western powers, to intervene. The subsequent Anglo-American stand on the Kashmir issue in the UN, that 'distressed' Nehru, substantiated this suspicion about Mountbatten's role and British policy. Later, during 1962-4, while the US and the UK were putting pressure on India and Pakistan to effect a rapprochement, they had hardly any doubt that the Kashmir problem would continue to remain intractable.[52]

In this context one begins to wonder if the resolution of the Kashmir dispute was at all an objective in the Western powers' strategy towards the subcontinent. Recent disclosures have shed further light on the possibility of US collaboration with Sheikh Abdullah during 1950-3 in making Kashmir independent.[53] This adds a new dimension to Sheikh Abdullah's deposition and his arrest in August 1953. One of the charges levelled against him was 'dangerous foreign contacts'. Some hints of the identity of such 'foreign' powers were given by Bakhshi Gulam Mohammed who succeeded Sheikh Abdullah as Prime Minister of Kashmir. On the day of Sheikh Abdullah's arrest, Bakhshi declared that the Sheikh was thinking

> in terms of carving out a portion of the State from the wreckage as an independent State. These moves have naturally the connivance and support of interested foreign powers who have all along been resisting the exercise of the rights of the people of the State to freedom and self-determination. The present situation threatens to open up explosive possibilities for the future of the people of Jammu and Kashmir unless the designs of these forces and their foreign supporters are foiled in time ... The slogan of independence is highly misleading and there should be no doubt as to the motive of sponsoring such an idea in the context of international developments in Asia and other parts of the world. An independent Kashmir under the influence of an imperialist power will be a grave threat to the freedom and independence of the Indian and Pakistani people ... Another Korea may be staged here.[54]

Although Nehru described the developments around the Sheikh's arrest as totally internal to the Kashmir State, he endorsed Bakhshi's statement fully. He also disclosed about a month later that he wanted to discuss some matters with the Sheikh but the latter avoided him.[55] The international context at this time was one of Cold War and the attempted establishment of US-led military alliances in Asia. This was also the time when US-Pakistani negotiations on a military pact were at an advanced stage. Nehru, therefore, tried and succeeded in getting Pakistan to agree to the change of the UN-appointed Plebiscite Administrator for Kashmir, Admiral Chester Nimitz, a US citizen. Nehru's main argument was that the association of great powers must be avoided in any form since they could not be 'neutralist and impartial'.[56] This gave Nehru enough reason to gradually drop the plebiscite condition from Kashmir's accession and also to become disinterested in approaching the US on Indo-Pakistani questions.

Western moves in relation to Kashmir also encouraged and renewed Soviet and Chinese interests in the dispute. This explains the consistently pro-Indian position taken by the Soviet Union on Kashmir since both India and the Soviet Union were interested in keeping the area free from the influence of the Western powers or their ally, Pakistan. The Soviet delegate, Jacob Malik, reacting to the Western position on Kashmir in the UN stated on 10 January 1952:

> The United States of America and the United Kingdom are continuing as before to interfere in the settlement of the Kashmir question, putting forward one plan after another ... the purpose of these plans is interference ... in the internal affairs of Kashmir, the prolongation of the dispute between India and Pakistan on the question of Kashmir and the conversion of Kashmir into a protectorate of the United States of America and the United Kingdom under the pretext of sending assistance through the United Nations.

If this was true, Soviet interests were directly involved owing to the proximity of the area to the region of Soviet Central Asia. Soviet suspicions were perhaps not wholly baseless. The US, from its base in the vicinity of Pakistan-held Kashmir, conducted reconnaissance flights over the Soviet Union that became public knowledge through the U-2 incident in May 1960. Subsequently, Soviet as well as Chinese interests in the area have also been dictated by their mutual hostility. The Chinese face Soviet divisions in the Sinkiang area which is contiguous to Kashmir. They have constructed roads linking Sinkiang with Pakistan through Pakistan-held Kashmir. Peking has also shown active interest in the Hunza area since 1949-50. The traditional Chinese claim of sovereignty over Hunza did not allow them to take a precise stand on the Kashmir dispute between India and Pakistan, at least until the conclusion of the Sino-Pakistan boundary agreement in 1963. One of the important factors in Sino-Pakistani friendship is that China does not want Pakistan either to allow hostile external influence on its side of Kashmir or reach any settlement with India that ignores China's interests. In this connection, we have noted earlier China's displeasure with the Tashkent-type rapprochement between India and Pakistan.

In view of all that has been stated above, there remains very little doubt that Kashmir's strategic location was an independent temptation by itself for the great powers to involve themselves in the subcontinent. As a consequence of this involvement the dispute has been simmering perpetually, occasionally bursting out into full fires. India and Pakistan, while fighting over Kashmir, have seldom realised that they have been willingly or otherwise serving a cause that lies beyond the parameters of subcontinental politics.

VIII

The great powers have played a decisive role in subcontinental conflicts. By linking their specific interests with the local roots of conflict they have involved themselves in the region both as actors and managers in these conflicts. Over the years, their involvement has grown in depth and intensity, although the style of their intervention has displayed a variety of forms. Particularly notable in this respect is the fact that the Western powers, besides involving themselves directly like the Soviet Union and China, have also consistently preferred to make use of the United Nations. They have done this not because they had greater faith in the UN but because their control over the world organisation during the 1950s and well into the 1960s was adequate and firm. This also enabled them to deal with both the regional adversaries with relatively greater ease. Nevertheless, the goals and styles of the great powers' policies towards the subcontinent have been dictated by their respective strategic and economic interests. Their concern for the rights and wrongs in a given crisis-situation or for the consequences of such a situation for the short and long-term interests of the subcontinental actors has been negligible and incidental.

What are then the prospects of peace in the subcontinent? Surely in the post-Bangladesh restructured subcontinent, the rationale and impulses for status-incongruence stand invalidated. The assertion of the natural power-hierarchy in the region has also encouraged more meaningful moves towards bilateralism. This offers reduced prospects for the external forces to manipulate subcontinental dynamics to their advantage. But this has in no way convinced them that conflict is dysfunctional to their interests. Much as the road to peace in the subcontinent may lie in the minimum involvement of the great powers, this is a situation nearly impossible to obtain. The dynamics of international politics are too complex and the frontiers of the great powers' policies too vast for the regional powers to achieve this objective *if* they cherish such an objective. But this itself is a very big if.

Notes

1. Larry Collins and Dominique Lapierre, *Freedom at Midnight* (Simon and Schuster, New York, 1975), p. 162. The Cabinet Mission in its Report in May 1946 had also very clearly stated the vulnerability of the then proposed two parts of Pakistan. Text in *Parliamentary Papers* 1945-6; XIX CmD. 6821, 2-6, 8-9.

2. See for instance, Collins and Lapierre, *Freedom at Midnight*, pp. 115-23.

3. Mohammed Ayoob and K. Subrahmanyam, *The Liberation War* (S. Chand, New Delhi, 1972), p. 144.

4. The term 'inheritance' has been borrowed from Robertson and Nettle as used by them in *International Systems and Modernization of Societies*. It means the cumulative stage of development at a certain point of history of a particular nation.

5. For further elucidation see W. Connor, 'Ethnology and the Peace in South Asia', *World Politics,* vol. 22, no. 1 (October 1969), pp. 51-86; Lloyd Jensen, 'Levels of Political Development and Inter-state Conflict in South Asia' in Richard Butwell (ed.), *Foreign Policy and the Developing Nation* (University of Kentucky Press, Lexington, 1969), p. 205; and Urmila Phadnis 'Infra-structural Linkages in Sri Lanka-India Relations', *Economic and Political Weekly,* vol. 7, nos. 31-3 (August 1972), pp. 1493-1501.

6. Quincey Wright's *A Study of War,* 2nd edn (University of Chicago Press, Chicago, 1965) was of course one of the pioneering works on the subject. Some of the recent studies include Ivo. K. and Rosalind L. Feierabend, 'Levels of Development and International Behaviour' in Butwell, pp. 135-88; contributions of Michael Haas and Leo A. Hazlewood (Chs. 6 and 7) in Jonathan Wilkenfeld (ed.), *Conflict Behaviour and Linkage Politics* (D. McKay, New York, 1973); Manua I. Midlarsky and Staffor T. Thomas, 'Domestic Social Structure and International Warfare' in Martin A. Nettleship, R. Dalegivens and Anderson Nettleship (eds.), *War, Its Causes and Correlates* (Mouton, The Hague, 1975), pp. 531-48; Rudolph R. Rummel and Raymond Tanty, 'Dimensions of Conflict Behaviour Within and Between Nations 1958-60', *Journal of Conflict Resolution,* vol. 10 (March 1966), pp. 41-64.

7. Mohammed Ayoob, 'India and Pakistan: Prospects for Detente', *Pacific Community,* vol. 8, no. 1 (October 1976), pp. 149-69.

8. Jensen, 'Political Development', pp. 191-208. Jensen has identified even the election year as being an indicator of instability. Elections may change a government in theory but in the specific cases of elections in India during 1957 and 1962 and Pakistan in 1965 (Ayub's election), there was hardly any real danger to the stability of the system or the regime. It is also misleading to give high weightage to domestic disturbances and economic difficulties as signs of instability.

9. Harold Macmillan, *Riding the Storm 1956-1959* (Macmillan, London 1971), p. 386.

10. *White Paper on Kashmir,* brought out by Bhutto's Government in January 1977, disclosed that the Soviet Union in 1965 and the Western powers during 1962-3 had impressed upon Pakistan that India, on these occasions, was not in a position to make territorial concessions in Kashmir and so should not be pressed to do so. Text of the White Paper in *Pakistan Times,* 16 and 17 January 1977.

11. For theoretical and class explanation of this point see Barrington Moore Jr, *Social Bases of Dictatorship and Democracy* (Beacon Press, Boston, 1966).

12. See K.P. Misra, M.V. Lakhi and Virendra Narain, *Pakistan's Search for Constitutional Consensus* (Impex India, New Delhi, 1967), pp. 164-75.

13. For the military's role in Pakistan's politics and its policy towards India see Mohammed Ayoob 'The Military in Pakistan's Political Development' in S.P. Varma and Virendra Narain (eds.), *Pakistan Political System in Crisis* (South Asia Studies Centre, Jaipur, 1972); also his 'India and Pakistan: Prospects for Detente' and Ayoob and Subrahmanyam, *Liberation War,* pp. 144-50; Khalid B. Sayeed, 'The Role of Military in Pakistan' in Jacques Van Doorn (ed.), *Armed Forces and Society* (Mouton, The Hague, 1968), p. 274-97. For a general work on the subject see Morris Janowitz, *The Military in Political Development of New Nations* (University of Chicago Press, Chicago, 1964).

14. *White Paper;* G.W. Chowdhry, *India, Pakistan, Bangladesh and the Major Powers* (Free Press, New York, 1975). See particularly Chs. 3 and 5. See also Z.A. Bhutto, *The Myth of Independence* (Oxford University Press, Karachi, 1969).

15. *White Paper;* Chowdhry, *Major Powers;* Bhutto, *Independence; Dawn,* 1 May 1965; *Times of India,* 14 August 1965.

16. See *Bangladesh Documents,* vol. II (Ministry of External Affairs, New Delhi, 1975), Chs. III and IV. Some Pakistani writers like Chowdhry, *Major Powers,* p. 213, have also alleged that Bhutto misrepresented the Chinese stand on the Bangladesh issue after his special mission to Peking in November 1971. There is, however, no doubt about China's support to Pakistan against India as was evident in Chou En-Lai's letter of 11 April 1971 to President Yahya and other statements. As regards their advice of caution regarding a political solution of the Bangladesh issue, it can still be a matter of debate. See Ayoob and Subrahmanyam, *Liberation War* pp. 205-6, 217, 269.

17. V. Shankar, *My Reminiscences of Sardar Patel,* vol. I (2 vols., Macmillan, New Delhi, 1974/5) p. 158.

18. See *Times of India,* 5 and 10 November 1965.

19. M.S. Rajan, 'India and Pakistan as Factors in Each Others Foreign Policy and Relations', *International Studies,* vol. 3 (April 1962), p. 391.

20. For some theoretical propositions on the subject see M.I. Midlarsky, *On War: Political Violence in the International System* (The Free Press, New York, 1975); M.D. Wallace, 'Status, Formal Organisation and Arms Levels as Factors leading to the Onset of War, 1820-1964', paper delivered at the Annual Meeting of the American Political Science Association, 1970, Los Angeles, California.

21. Jawaharlal Nehru, *Independence and After* (The Publications Division, Government of India, New Delhi, 1949), p. 232.

22. Ibid., p. 248.

23. Ibid., p. 246.

24. Sisir Gupta, *India and Regional Integration in Asia* (Asia Publishing House, Bombay, 1964); Werner Levi, *Free India in Asia* (University of Minnesota Press, Minneapolis, 1952).

25. S.D. Muni, 'India and Regionalism in South Asia', a paper submitted at a seminar on 'Continuity and Change in Indian Foreign Policy' held at New Delhi, May 1978.

26. *Jawaharlal Nehru's Speeches 1946-49* (Publications Division, Government of India, New Delhi, 1958), pp. 338-9.

27. Keith Callard, *Pakistan: A Political Study* (Institute of Pacific Relations, London, 1957), p. 304.

28. Mohammad Ayub Khan, *Friends Not Masters* (Oxford University Press, New York, 1967) p. 115; also see Bhutto, *Independence,* and Zulfikar Ali Bhutto, *Foreign Policy of Pakistan* (Pakistan Institute of International Affairs, Karachi, 1964), Ch. II.

29. Bhutto, *Independence,* p. 97.

30. For details see Collins and Lapierre, *Freedom at Midnight*, pp. 401-13; Sisir Gupta, *Kashmir: A Study in India Pakistan Relations* (Asia Publishing House, Bombay, 1966), pp. 110-38.

31. Speech in Lok Sabba on 13 April 1964. This was just over a month before his death.

32. Bhutto, *Independence*, p. 180.

33. This comes out clearly in many statements made in India during the Bangladesh crisis. For an intelligent and suave articulation of such opinion see Ayoob and Subrahmanyam, *Liberation War*.

34. Text of White Paper in *Pakistan Times*, 16 and 17 January 1977.

35. Chowdhry, *Major Powers*, p. 121; on the issue of US arms to India see ibid., pp. 108-26; also Bhutto, *Independence;* Ayub Khan, *Friends Not Masters*.

36. Some of the important studies on the subject include: Chowdhry, *Major Powers;* William Barnds, *India Pakistan and the Great Powers* (Pall Mall Press, London, 1972); Russel Brines, *The Indo-Pakistan Conflict* (Pall Mall Press, London, 1968); S.M. Burke, *Pakistan's Foreign Policy: An Historical Analysis* (Oxford University Press, London, 1973); K. Neelkant, *Partners in Peace: A Study in Indo-Soviet Relations* (Vikas, New Delhi, 1972); Norman D. Palmer, *South Asia and United States* (Houghton Mifflin, Boston, 1966); Arthur Stein, *India and the Soviet Union: The Nehru Era* (University of Chicago Press, Chicago, 1969); Anwar Hussain Syed, *China and Pakistan* (University of Massachusetts Press, Amherst, 1974); J.A. Naik, *India, Russia, China and Bangladesh* (S. Chand, New Delhi, 1972); Baldev Raj Nayar, *American Geopolitics and India* (Manohar, New Delhi, 1976).

37. As quoted in Nayar, *Geopolitics*, p. 62.

38. US intelligence had learnt by 1965 that China had only 60,000 troops in Tibet and the Chinese pressure on India had declined; *Times of India*, 8 May 1965. This assumption was strengthened later by Chinese failure to translate their ultimatum to India during the September 1965 Indo-Pakistani war into active involvement.

39. This was revealed in Anderson's disclosures, *Times of India* 16 January 1972; *New York Times*, 15 January 1972.

40. Pakistan succeeded in this objective at least partially when the US put a ban on its arms supplies both to India and Pakistan. Explaining this ban to the Pakistani Ambassador, an important White House aide, Rostow, said that the US wanted India to be strong in the context of its policy of containment of China, but America did not seek to make India the most dominant power in Asia. The US had no intention of depending upon India alone; it must carry Pakistan with it too. Quoted in Chowdhry, *Major Powers*, p. 132. The US ban should also be viewed in the light of Note 38 above.

41. *Times of India*, 4 January 1965.

42. Harold Macmillan, *At the End of the Day 1961-63* (Macmillan, London, 1973), pp. 231-2. For the Pakistani appreciation of the mission see *White Paper, Pakistan Times*, 16 January 1977, also see Nayar, *Geopolitics*, and Chowdhry, *Major Powers*.

43. Macmillan, *End of the Day*, p. 235, italics added.

44. The British Prime Minister made a statement to the effect on 6 September 1965. Later, however, he apologised to India's Prime Minister, Mrs Gandhi, for having done so by mistake since he was ill advised by the Foreign Office bureaucrats. This was obviously an excuse.

45. Chowdhry, *Major Powers*, p. 121; also *White Paper, Pakistan Times*, 16 January 1977; *Baltimore Sun*, 'Analysis' by Philip Potter, 3 September 1965.

46. *Times of India*, 19 July 1965. The Chinese disapproval prompted the Pakistani government to send an official to Peking to explain Pakistan's position.

47. This was despite the fact that President Ayub had secretly visited China before accepting the ceasefire in September 1965. Chowdhry, *Major Powers*, pp. 189-94.

48. Mohammed Ayoob, 'The Indian Ocean Littoral: Intra-Regional Conflicts and Weapons Proliferation' in Robert O'Neill (ed.), *Insecurity: The Spread of Weapons in the Indian and Pacific Oceans* (ANU Press, Canberra, 1978), pp. 188-98; Ian Clark, 'Autonomy and Dependence in Recent Indo-Soviet Relations', *Australian Outlook*, vol. 31, no. 1 (April 1977).

49. Gupta, *Kashmir*, pp. 108-9; B.L. Kak, *The Fall of Gilgit* (Light and Life, New Delhi, 1977), pp. 147-62.

50. Collins and Lapierre, *Freedom at Midnight*, p. 410.

51. Nehru's radio broadcast from New Delhi, 2 November 1947; Nehru, *After Independence*, p. 59; also see Shanker, *Sardar Patel*, vol. I, p. 133, for how Sardar Patel failed in getting the expression 'UN auspices' to be dropped from the text of the broadcast.

52. Macmillan, *End of the Day*, p. 232.

53. According to the release of some classified papers by the State Department, in a secret telegram dated 29 September 1950 the then US Ambassador to India, Mr L.W. Henderson reported that the Sheikh, the then Prime Minister of Kashmir, wanted US help in making his state independent. The Sheikh has, however, denied the truth of Henderson's telegram; *Hindustan Times* (overseas weekly), 28 September 1978. Also see *Far Eastern Economic Review*, vol. 102. no. 43 (27 October 1978), pp. 29-30; Vijay Kumar, *Anglo-American Plot Against Kashmir* (Peoples Publishing House, Bombay, 1954); H.S. Surjeet, *Kashmir and Its Future* (Peoples Publishing House, New Delhi, 1955).

54. As quoted in Gupta, *Kashmir*, p. 266.

55. Ibid., p. 267.

56. Nehru's letter to Pakistani Prime Minister on 28 August 1953, quoted in ibid., p. 272.

4 The Middle East*

ROBERT SPRINGBORG

I

In the eye of many a Middle Eastern beholder, superpower influence is both ubiquitous and far from beautiful. To countless Arabs, Israel is little more than an imperialist extension into the region; a latter-day Jewish crusader stronghold, tied paradoxically by an umbilical lifeline to the Christian world. For their part, Israelis have been just as ready to view their Arab opponents as puppets dangling on Russian strings, with the puppeteers in the Kremlin pulling those strings in accordance with the strategy of neo-Tsarist expansionism and abiding Russian anti-semitism. The Lebanese civil war, involving as it has interventions of virtually all sorts, overt and covert, by regional and extra-regional actors, has possibly eclipsed even the Arab-Israeli conflict in terms of the prevalence of conspiracy theorists who seek to explain political decay and violence exclusively or largely in terms of superpower machinations. Even domestic squabbles in the *Dar al Islam* are not free from charges and counter-charges of imperialist, neo-imperialist, and/or socialist-imperialist lackeys, as the ideological cacophony flying between Damascus and Baghdad and other Arab capitals suggests. Middle Easterners then, perhaps more than other members of the Third World, see superpowers lurking behind, and indeed propping up, their local enemies. Hence many political strategies are devised on the assumption that it is not only one's regional opponents, but at least as importantly, their superpower patron, that is seeking to trim one down to size or even to annihilate one completely. Much in the tradition of psychoanalysis, the key question is whether the manifest anxiety over alleged cloak-and-dagger operations is a reasonable fear based on the reality of superpower behaviour in the region, or whether it is a paranoid delusion caused by deficiencies in the local cultures, economic and political systems, or even

**Author's Note.* This was written before the Israeli-Egyptian treaty; however, this event does not change the conclusions reached in the chapter.

psyches, or, more rationally, by the inevitable lag which must occur as perceptions slowly adjust to a changing reality.

Seeking the kernel of truth underlying these possibly paranoid delusions may be likened to a search for the Holy Grail, for interactions between superpower patrons and regional clients, be they sovereign states or aspiring national liberation movements, are usually shrouded in intentional ambiguity, presumably because neither partner is particularly proud of the clientelistic relationship. So, for example, because none of the parties really wants to put its cards on the table even at this late date, the cataclysmic June 1967 war continues to stimulate the imaginations of conspiracy theorists, the latest from the Arab side asserting that the quadripartite axis of Washington-Riyadh-Amman-Tel Aviv planned at least part of the affair, leaving its execution to the latter partner.[1] Many an Israeli is convinced of the veracity of a counter-conspiracy theory which implicates Moscow as the main bogeyman, alleging that it fed information to Nasser calculated to egg him on into a war with Israel. And so it goes on. The Sherlock Holmes approach to unravelling such mysteries by peering intently through a magnifying glass in search of tell-tale clues is, moreover, because of the mutual desires for cover-ups, probably a hopelessly frustrating approach. Reconstructing the decision-making process in those sovereign and non-sovereign entities involved in such conflicts as the June war and the Lebanese civil war is almost impossible. Instead one has to employ the second-best strategy of examining contextual variables, assuming that their linkage to behaviour is more or less straightforward and that entirely perverse decisions and actions are the exception rather than the rule. This may not be altogether warranted by the facts, and trends discernible one step removed from the 'nitty gritty' of political interaction in the area may, on subsequent and closer scrutiny, appear to be but the sandcastles of naive and uninvolved onlookers. Bearing this in mind and aware that events may eventually prove the speculations here to be ill-founded, we shall nevertheless stumble forward into the thicket guided by the proposition that superpower influence in the heartland of the Middle East region is now on the decline and will continue to recede in the foreseeable future.

Emotional nationalist rhetoric notwithstanding, neo-imperialism, be it thought of in terms of control over weapons supply, economic dependency, thinly veiled threats of coercive action, or even clandestine support for irredentist forces or ambitious colonels, is much less capable of orchestrating the politics of the region than was its forerunner. Under direct colonial rule the provision of military equipment was totally under the control of the imperialist power; the economy of the colony was run for and by the colonialists; coercive action was accepted as legitimate in the last resort; and manipulation of domestic political forces, legitimate and illegitimate, was *de rigeur*. Much as the neo-imperialists may like to imitate their predecessors, they are simply not in a position to do so. Attempting to control behaviour by alternating rewards and sanctions from a distance is far less effective than methods made available by sheer physical presence. While neo-imperialism is far from benign, it is nevertheless not the malignancy that colonialism certainly was.

Moreover, just as the sun eventually set on colonial empires, so is it setting on neo-imperialist domains. Neither of the superpowers is now in a position consistently to wield the big stick in the area, not only because each is partially neutralised by the other, but also because regional actors have amassed considerable military and other resources, rendering gunboat operations risky and such far-fetched notions as invasions of oil fields little short of ludicrous. While in 1958 a few boatloads of marines could put the cap on a civil war in Lebanon, in 1975-6 Lebanon could possibly have turned into a Vietnam-style quagmire had the Americans gone wading in, which they wisely did not. Lest it be countered that the Nixon doctrine (i.e. the reliance on local gendarmes to police various areas of the globe) has made direct intervention from Fort Bragg unnecessary, or the evolving Havana doctrine (i.e. the use by Moscow of Cuban troops in Africa and possibly the Middle East[2]) has made Soviet bush-fire war brigades redundant, one should pause and reflect for a moment on the nature of those patron-client relationships. Paradoxically, many of the same individuals who argue that the 1967 war was planned by President Johnson, King Faisal, King Hussein and Prime Minister Golda Meir, and that the latter then duped her partners by exceeding the battle plan and grabbing the Sinai Peninsula, Golan Heights and West Bank after having sunk the USS *Liberty*, also claim, illogically, that Israel is nothing more than a US running dog whose policies are a reflex action to Washington stimuli.[3] Whether or not this particular conspiracy theory is true or not, it is the case that the Israelis are considerably more than the tail to the American dog, or, to stay with the metaphor, that in this case the tail at least occasionally wags the dog.[4] The Russians have also found that reliable clients are hard to come by, as the Egyptian, Sudanese and now possibly even the Iraqi experiences suggest, and while the Cubans continue to prowl African jungles in the name of proletarian internationalism, the last chapter of that story is far from written. In short, the old maxim that if you want something done right, do it yourself, applies as much to the superpowers as it does to us as individuals fighting the complexities of the so-called post-industrial society, or more to the point, one where shoddy goods and incompetent service prevail. But since neither the Russians nor the Americans are in a position to be home handymen and fix all the leaks in their neo-imperialist systems, like it or not they have to call in help which necessarily has far less of a commitment to careful repair and restoration than does the system's owner. The Nixon doctrine is an attempt to gloss over declining American power, not a sign of its increasing omnipotence.

II

It is not tautological to observe that the decline of superpower influence in the Middle East is accompanied by increasing multipolarity. For while the power of the US and the USSR to control events in the area is weakening, on the one hand the capabilities of regional actors to shape their own destinies are improving, and on the other, increasing multipolarity in global politics, reflecting the growing economic importance and political self-confidence of Europe and Japan, as well as the emergence of impressive industrial capacities in various Asian countries from India to Taiwan and in Brazil, make new and mutually beneficial international economic and political liaisons possible. Looking at this second factor first, there can be little doubt that diversification of sources of supply and markets, especially for the oil exporters, has greatly reduced the significance of the US and the USSR to the economies of the region. Within the oil-exporting countries for example, and especially Saudi Arabia, South Korean construction firms have virtually cornered the market for commercial buildings. In the booming automobile market in the region it is Fiat, Peugeot, Mercedes, Nissan and Toyota, more than General Motors, Ford, Chrysler or Volga that are flooding the streets with their products. Arab economies formerly tied tightly to the East bloc by barter agreements have, either by direct and abrupt abrogation of contracts, as in the case of Egypt, or by adding innumerable contracts with Western governments and private firms for supply of goods and services in both directions, as in the case of Syria and Iraq, much reduced the ratio of East bloc goods and services in their total package of imports and exports. In agricultural sectors, generally overlooked by ambitious radical nationalist modernisers of an earlier era, like Nasser and the original Baathists of Syria and Iraq, and also, at least at the outset, by the beneficiaries of the oil price rises of 1974, there are real groundswells of activity as decision-makers from Morocco to Iran realise that agricultural development is essential not only to protect the balance of payments in this era of high food costs, but also to gainfully employ the masses in the traditional sector. As a result there is a scramble for agricultural expertise and equipment from abroad. Whereas in the 1950s and 1960s it was mainly the Americans or the Soviets who assisted in reclamation projects, built model farms and advised on specialised agricultural topics, at present the farming areas of many countries in the region are virtual mini-United Nations, with Dutch, Italian, German (East and West), Austrian, Yugoslav, Australian, New Zealand and other experts trying to impart their knowledge of agricultural science and methods as well as to sell the accoutrements of agricultural production. To add in passing that it is Japan and Europe, and not the United States or the Soviet Union, that take the bulk of Middle Eastern oil, underlines the fact that market forces are leading to an internationalisation and not to a binationalisation of the area. Even the production of oil, formerly the preserve of the seven sisters, those ugly step-daughters of American, British and Dutch capitalism, is now facilitated not only by the independent oil companies incorporated in countries as far afield as Brazil and Indonesia, and including various East bloc concerns not the least of which are Rumanian, but is in several locations entirely the monopoly of national oil companies. The Iraqi and Algerian national petroleum companies, for example, not only play key roles in the search for and development of oil fields, but have also taken over the marketing of their products including the construction of ambitious pipelines (under the Mediterranean in the case of Algeria and across Turkey in the case of Iraq) linking them to European markets.

Growing economic multipolarity not only provides alternative markets and suppliers for those with something to buy and sell, but it also works to the advantage of the region's pauperised states which now have the possibility of stitching together aid from a variety of sources into a patchwork-quilt national development programme. Thus in Egypt the Japanese are dredging the Suez Canal, the Germans are toying with the idea of the Qattara Depression scheme, the French are studying the possibility of rationalising Cairo traffic by tunnelling a subway under it, the Soviets, East Germans, Poles, etc., continue to back a variety of technical projects with cash and expertise, and the Gulf oil-producers and the Americans are underwriting numerous projects as well as providing general balance of payment support. This is a far cry from the days when there were either Soviets or Americans in an Arab country, but not both, and very few other foreign nationals at all. As a result even the poorer states are not under the thumb of a single donor and, while beggars cannot afford to be too choosy, they can be moderately discriminating if there are a sufficient number of potential contributors.[5]

Multipolarity is not only an economic, but also a political phenomenon. While the development of political power in world affairs appears to lag behind the accumulation of balance of payment surpluses, as the cases of Japan and West Germany suggest, there is nevertheless a correlation between the two. There is a short distance between Chancellor Schmidt lecturing the Americans on how to run their economy and how much oil to consume and Germany exerting much greater political independence than she has since World War II. Moreover, business and politics mix in the sense that those countries desirous of doing business in the Middle East, particularly in the Arab world, feel compelled to tailor their political strategies appropriately, a tactic which neither of the superpowers, each for their different reasons, is able to adopt. Thus the Americans seem doomed to cut off their nose to spite their face by imposing tougher anti-boycott conditions on US firms and by taxing US nationals abroad, thereby undermining US competitiveness and aggravating balance of payment problems, which in turn can be expected to further erode America's political clout. The Soviets, having less to buy and sell in the region, are not caught up in quite such a dilemma, but the fact that they are simply frozen out of the oil bonanza on the Arabian Peninsula must rankle, since, as yet, they have been unable to overcome the disadvantage of being perceived as a menacing superpower, and a godless one as well.

Heretofore the growing political independence of European countries, both East and West, and of various other countries around the globe, has been evidenced by the relatively unimportant phenomena of UN voting, overtures by members of one camp to those of the other (e.g. France to the USSR, Rumania to Great Britain), and by increasingly divergent foreign policies generally, such as those *vis-à-vis* the Middle East. In future it can be expected that political multipolarity will increase, thereby providing yet greater opportunities for 'divide and not be ruled' strategies by Third World countries in their dealings with the great and superpowers.[6]

The rebuttal to the argument of erosion of superpower influence through the emergence of competitive centres of economic power usually takes the form of positing that since, in the final analysis, it is only the military that counts, and since the superpowers are clearly super in this respect, talk of multipolarity is only the idle speculation of those soft-headed enough not to appreciate the implications of modern military technology. While there is little doubt that the Americans and the Russians have the military capabilities to destroy more life than even several of the smaller powers combined, the point is that total war is not a contingency which dominates the thinking of many policy-makers outside Washington and Moscow. Instead, the lesser powers are more inclined to devote their energies and resources to the far more likely occurrence of small-scale regional conflicts or interventions by the powers.

The essential stategy for guaranteeing territorial integrity in the face of threats by extra-regional actors is simply to raise the potential cost of intervention so high that no rational commander-in-chief of a great or superpower would consider the cost worth the potential benefit. Just as Sweden maintains its neutrality through impressive military power, given its size and resource base, so do almost all countries of the Middle East now make very uninviting targets for military escapades from the outside. The Israelis, for example, after taking delivery of aircraft currently on order, will have the third most powerful air force in the world, while the Iranians, at least until the latest crisis erupted, were not far behind. The arsenals of the leading Arab countries are likewise truly prodigious, while even the desert states of Libya, Saudi Arabia and Kuwait have enough hardware at their disposal to make gunboat, or even 82nd airborne, diplomacy a highly problematic affair. Thus the urgent talk of the early 1970s to the effect that Russian development of a sizable Mediterranean fleet would challenge American superiority there has died down, not because the Sixth Fleet has converted the Mediterranean into an American lake once again, but because neither fleet is in a position to call the shots in the area as the Americans once did. There are, moreover, no absolutely dependable bases in the region for either power, as for example, the Wheelus base was prior to Ghaddafi's rise to power. The Russians' hold on facilities in South Yemen is probably about as tenuous as the Americans' on Mesirah Island and while both enjoy considerable access to the military installations of those countries with which they are closely allied, that access is not available at will or for any and all purposes which the superpower might conceive. Added to the fact that regional actors now have considerable military punch simply by importing highly sophisticated equipment, is the equally important fact that the two superpowers are now more evenly balanced militarily in the area. This is yet another factor which provides room for manoeuvre to the countries of the region, a situation which did not prevail until the Soviet Union had substantially increased its military capacity in the area thereby ending total Western hegemony in the Middle East.

The relevance of the multipolarity argument is also evident in the military sphere, for not only do various European countries produce weapons more or less on a par with those coming off assembly lines in the US and the USSR, but in the case of several of the Arab states and Iran, these weapons can be bought in virtually unlimited quantities. Arms embargoes are a thing of the past and if neither of the superpowers cares to deliver the latest and the fastest, then, for some at least, there are the French and the British who are more than happy to do so. In every instance when the Americans are approached to sell Phantoms, F-15s and F-16s, there is the mutual knowledge between potential buyer and seller that there are Mirages, Jaguars, Hunters and even Swedish and Italian planes for sale on the other side of the Atlantic. King Hussein went so far as to fly to Moscow to negotiate the possible purchase of an air defence system to pry twelve batteries of Hawks out of American hands. In the relatively freewheeling arms procurement situation that now prevails, no supplier is in a position to impose rigorous constraints on his customers. Cash and carry is the order of the day and when Libyan Mirages piloted by Egyptians turned up over Sinai battlefields in 1973, no one was terribly surprised. In general then, just as political and economic bipolarity is dissolving into multipolarity, so is there very considerable diversification of sources of military supplies and a concomitant erosion of the dominant position of the superpowers in the region.

While the superpowers are confronted with the fact that economically, politically and even militarily, various countries are catching up with them, at least as regards influence in the Middle East is concerned, they are also confronted by the fact that the human, physical, financial and industrial resources of the area are developing very quickly, in many cases at growth rates far in excess of those that prevail in the US or the USSR. When the superpowers began their respective involvements in the area, for the most part in the wake of World War II, the level of development in the Middle East was low, possibly more or less similar to that which prevails in much of Africa today. Regimes were just emerging from colonial rule and were predictably unstable; military establishments resembled marching bands; educational, health, transport and other human and physical infrastructural facilities were grossly inadequate; bureaucracies in some cases had still to rely on European expertise; and so on. Throwing their weight around in such relatively primitive conditions was not a terribly demanding task; so, for example, the CIA could, with a minimum of fuss, oust distasteful regimes in Syria and Iran, while the Soviets were able, with a few boatloads of Czech arms, to buy Egyptian support. It should not come as a surprise, therefore, that superpower rivalry has now shifted to Africa, for that continent in the late 1970s closely resembles the Middle East of an earlier generation. Unable to orchestrate events at will in the Middle East because of that area's rapid development and increasing political institutionalisation, the Americans and the Soviets, sensing that they can still play the tough guy role in Africa and that real spoils are to be had there in addition to the usual geopolitical advantages, have come to the realisation that their resources for winning friends and undermining enemies could better be invested further to the south. Thus Middle Easterners, by virtue of their impressive development, have carved out a considerable independence for their region and are now in a position better to take advantage of the global system of multipolarity that is gradually evolving.

III

Soviet penetration of the Middle East in the 1950s and 1960s depended even more heavily on the relative underdevelopment of the area than did American involvement in the region. As a result, Soviet influence in the 1970s has receded faster than its American counterpart as the region has rapidly developed its economic, military and political resources. The economic element in the Soviet attraction for the Syrians, Iraqis, Egyptians and others in the turbulent Nasser era lay in Moscow's willingness to provide long-term credits, frequently repayable by barter, for construction of heavy and light industries and infrastructural projects. Even then many Arabs were highly dubious of Soviet technology, but since there were few or no alternatives, something appeared to be better than nothing.[7] Now, however, the Iraqis, sitting on oil reserves probably second only to those of Saudi Arabia, are in a position to buy the best, and even die-hard Baathist leftists are more enamoured of Western than of Soviet technology. The Syrians, while lacking large oil deposits, have benefited from the flow-on of petro-dollars, especially from Saudi Arabia, and from expanding agricultural production and favourable prices for agricultural commodities, so they too have sought goods and services from higher priced suppliers in the West. Egypt, least able of the three states to muster the cash necessary for Western technology, has become, with Saudi Arabia, the most virulently anti-Soviet of the Arab governments, for political reasons. So, whatever the attraction of Soviet barter deals, Sadat prefers to go further in debt by concluding agreements with the West rather than deal with Moscow. What is true of these three Arab states also applies elsewhere. In Algeria, for example, after some initial economic successes following independence, the Soviets have lost ground to a variety of competitors, not the least of whom is the USA. The Libyans, perfectly happy to purchase Soviet arms in large quantities, are much more reluctant to commit themselves to non-military transactions with the Soviets, apparently preferring to recruit the manpower and technology for their modernisation drive from widely disparate sources, Australia very much included.[8] The Arab oil-producing states of the Peninsula have not bought so much as a rouble's worth of non-military goods from the USSR and although the Iranians, seeking a little political insurance, have signed some fairly impressive deals with their northern neighbour, including the natural gas for iron and steel mill barter agreement, the Shah, intent on Iran becoming one of the world's great industrial powers by the year 2000, did not stake much of his country's manufacturing future on Soviet technology. In general, Middle Easterners, having had need of Soviet economic assistance some years ago, took it, and of course by accepting it also became entangled in the attached political strings. But currently, luxuriating in their newly found wealth, or having become completely exasperated with the Soviets, they see little reason to direct much economic attention to Moscow. Therefore, now that the Soviets have a great deal of excess capacity in the form of technicians with long years of service in the Middle East and the accompanying industrial capability, it should come as no great surprise when Soviet technicians start showing up in large numbers in Africa, and when barter deals on the once Dark Continent proliferate.

What is true of economic relations between the Middle East and the Soviet Union is also true of military entanglements. The October war notwithstanding, Soviet hardware, for whatever reason, has not demonstrated a winning capability. Almost everyone in the region with ready cash, possibly recalling the comparison of the Phantom with the MIG-21, is now scrambling after F-15s and F-16s, not MIG-25s, or, as in the case of Iraq, is supplementing its predominantly Soviet-supplied arsenal with equipment purchased from France.[9] Diversification of sources of military supply may be even more detrimental to Soviet influence in the region than is the proliferation of economic contacts between the Middle East and the West. In the future very few states of the region will have exclusively Soviet-supplied arsenals. Consequently, the Arab officer corps, which in many cases have for more than a decade been exposed exclusively to Soviet equipment and training, either at home or in Moscow, can now look forward to fraternising with French officers in Paris or British officers in London. Since the military does not seem likely to return to the barracks from presidential palaces in the foreseeable future, this exposure to the West on the part of increasing numbers of Arab officers may become an important political factor.

Last, but by no means least, are several interrelated political developments that are working to the detriment of Soviet influence in the region. In the first instance, the wave of radical nationalism that swept through the Arab world in the immediate post-independence era has now receded, leaving in its wake a number of hard-headed managerial, rather than revolutionary, elites.[10] These elites, moreover, have seemingly consolidated their hold on power, as the long-lived Baathist regimes in Damascus and Baghdad and as Boumedienne and his successors in Algiers, Numeiry in Khartoum and Sadat in Cairo, have demonstrated. The Soviets had skilfully exploited anti-US sentiment in the region in the 1950s and 1960s but in a curious way their very success in this enterprise turned out to be their undoing. As the Americans were bounced out of one Arab country after another, or were forced to assume very low profiles, they made increasingly less-visible targets for anti-imperialist campaigns. On the other hand, the Soviets, who had moved into the area in a big way, became susceptible to the counter charge of socialist-imperialism and the obvious butt of anti-foreign sentiment. In addition, superpower detente has called into question the very credibility of Moscow's anti-US and anti-imperialist posturings and such suspicion has been reinforced among many Arabs by apparent Soviet prevarications on the Arab-Israeli dispute.

Coupled with the maturation of many countries in the region from newly independent and highly unstable political entities into relatively well-institutionalised authoritarian regimes, has been a Soviet failure to fully apprehend that change and formulate an appropriate policy to cope with that transformation. The Soviets have continued to use the rhetoric of anti-Americanism long after it had demonstrated its insufficiency as the instrument with which one could win friends and influence people in the Middle East. Also, actions speak louder than words; while American *protégés* in the area have undoubtedly benefited from their patron's backing, as the sheer increase in the geographical size of Israel demonstrates, many Arab leaders must be asking themselves, as Sadat has done publicly, just how useful the Soviet connection actually was for its Arab friends. Either out of fear of US retaliation, policy differences with the Arabs as regards the best way to deal with Israel, or distrust of the so-called nationalist progressive (or *petit bourgeois*) regimes that control many of the Arab states, the Soviets failed to develop and implement a truly convincing policy (that is, convincing to the Arabs) on the Arab-Israeli conflict. Soviet prevarication in its Middle East policy has not gone unnoticed, causing many observers to wonder whether it is in fact the succession crisis and Brezhnev's prolonged last stand that has immobilised Russian policy towards the Arab heartland of Egypt and the Fertile Crescent. Certainly the personal animosity between Sadat and the current gerontocratic elite of the USSR is unlikely to melt away unless one or the other disappears from the scene. Although no other Arab state has so far followed Egypt's example in washing the dirty linen of its relations with the USSR in public, this should not be taken as an indication that everything has been and is clean and tidy in the bonds tying Moscow to Damascus, Tripoli or Baghdad. Indeed, in the case of Soviet-Iraqi relations, recent executions of communists in Iraq, coupled with muffled accusations of indirect Russian assistance to Jalal Talabani's Kurdish partisans in the

Patriotic Union of Kurdistan, indicate that all is far from well and that a crisis point may be at hand.

It is precisely because the Soviets have suffered setbacks in those states which they had brought into their orbit after successfully jumping over the Northern Tier states of the Baghdad Pact (later renamed CENTO), that they are now forced to look further afield, indeed, to the virtual 'boondocks' of the Arab world, to find potential supporters. The Sadat theory of encirclement, apparently believed by many US decision-makers and possibly even by Brezhnev and Co. to convince their Kremlin critics of the wisdom of their rapidly disintegrating Middle East policy, is not at all persuasive, as the limited engagement between Egyptian and Libyan forces in July 1977 demonstrated. The Soviets are in Libya because they cannot be in Egypt. Similarly, their success in South Yemen, as the recent overthrow of the Riyadh and Peking-leaning Salem Rubaya Ali by the Moscow-oriented Abdul Fattah Ismail suggests, should be seen less as part of the Soviet plan to gain hegemony over the Horn, and more as a reflection of the failure of the Russians to retain firmer footholds further to the north in the Arab world. While Russian successes in 1978 in South Yemen and in Afghanistan merit attention by concerned decision-makers, they should not be taken as signs that the Soviets are on the march in the Middle Eastern region. Rather they suggest that Moscow, unable to achieve more than a few successes in the major Middle Eastern countries since 1973 and increasingly aware that its policy in the Arab heartland has been ineffective, has gone even further afield to find truly underdeveloped polities on the periphery of the Middle East in which it can call the shots, at least for a while.

There are two problems for the Soviets entailed in this second leapfrogging of Middle Eastern states. First, by becoming heavily entangled in South Yemen, Ethiopia and Afghanistan, they have caused the inevitable adverse reaction in neighbouring states. North Yemen, one time playground for the Soviet proxy army of Egypt, is now more or less in the Saudi orbit, while Oman has fended off what are probably the final blows of the Popular Front for the Liberation of Oman. On the other side of the Red Sea, Egypt, Sudan and, to a lesser extent, Somalia, far from being encircled by the Soviets, are, in combination with their friends in Riyadh, backed in turn by Washington, in the driver's seat. It is South Yemen and Ethiopia that are isolated, not the bordering Arab states. Furthermore, transporting the socialist revolution across these borders has not succeeded in the past as the collapse of the Popular Front for the Liberation of the Occupied Arab Gulf indicates, and there is no reason to believe it will in the future. Similarly the overthrow of President Daud in Kabul has put the Iranians and Pakistanis on the alert and it is rather difficult to conceive of the Afghans, even backed by the USSR, somehow orchestrating destabilisation of either of their much more impressive neighbours. The turmoil in Iran and the instability in Pakistan is almost exclusively the result of domestic factors over which the Afghans, or for that matter the Soviets, have little or no control. In short, Soviet involvement on the periphery of the Middle East is causing a backlash, and not only among those states in the closest proximity to areas of greatest Soviet involvement. The Iraqis and Syrians, for example, cannot take too much heart from events in South Yemen and Afghanistan, and in fact both probably view with special alarm the reports that Cuban troops are alleged to have played a role in the Aden *coup d'état*. Charges of socialist-imperialism have much more resonance when the shock troops speak Spanish rather than Arabic. Also, Syrian and Iraqi sympathies and support for the Eritreans and the Somalis run counter to Soviet commitments on the Horn. The recent attempts at federating Iraq and Syria, if successful, will, in the long term, probably work more to the detriment of Soviet interests than to those of the Western powers.

The second problem faced by Moscow as a result of the Soviet move towards the geographical periphery of the Middle Eastern area is even more serious in that it may be a harbinger of the long-term decline of Soviet influence, not just in the Middle East, but in the Third World generally. If the appeal of Soviet barter agreements, military equipment and political ideology is conditional upon the absence of economic, military and political development, as it appears to be in the Middle East region, then the long-term prospects for Russian influence in the Third World cannot be encouraging for Soviet strategists. If previous patterns are a reliable indicator of future trends, then Soviet hegemony in South Yemen can be expected to persist until that country develops the material and human resources to begin to play the international field more confidently, seeking assistance from a variety of sources rather than placing all its eggs in the Soviet basket. While the USSR may delay this trend by manipulating local political forces, previous experience in the Arab East and along the Nile suggests that Moscow is not overly adept at mapping and then utilising the Byzantine byways of Arab elite politics. More in the tradition of colonialism, the Soviets prefer to let the locals come to them; however, as their predecessors learned, pulling strings from the sitting rooms of embassies has its limits.[11] Not even the British, with their systematic, in-depth analyses of Egyptian and Iraqi politics, could prevent the overthrow of their hireling monarchs in Cairo and Baghdad. The Soviets, probably because of the inherent provincialism of totalitarian rule, lack a truly sophisticated political-bureaucratic structure to oversee and guide local political developments. Therefore, their status in Arab countries remains highly ambivalent even when they appear to be as well dug in as they were in Cairo in the last years of the Nasser era. There is little reason to expect that their encore performance on the fringe of the Arab world, or for that matter, in Africa, will prove to be substantially different from their earlier productions in the Arab heartland.

IV

The malaise that has come over the United States since the termination of the disastrous Vietnam war, and which is summed up as 'Watergate', is more than just the result of a bunch of crooks having taken control of the White House. Unravelling the interwoven complex of issues that add up to the most serious crisis faced by the US since World War II is not easy, but one loose end with which to begin is the American economic performance. The US economy is traditionally not foreign-oriented as the relatively low ratio of imports and exports to GNP, as compared to all European countries, indicates. Self-sufficiency has become, however, a non-viable economic strategy, at least until some substitute can be found for imported oil. The American economy, traditionally inward rather than outward-looking, has not responded well in the face of the demand to increase exports and as a result balance of payment deficits have become truly staggering even for an economy the size of America's. With respect to the Middle East, for example, American exports of arms and agricultural commodities vastly exceed those of all other competitors, but in other fields, such as the export of consumer durables, automobiles, machine tools, turnkey factories and other buildings, and technical expertise generally, the US does not fare nearly so well. The Europeans and Japanese, perhaps because they know they are number two, have tried harder and as a result, more often than not, they have outdone the Americans in the race for contracts in the lucrative Middle East markets. What is true in the Middle East is not necessarily true everywhere else in the world, but it nevertheless remains a fact that American industry has not proven itself capable of producing internationally desirable goods at competitive prices. The US is in an economic tailspin largely as a result of the sudden need to import high-priced oil; and for a variety of reasons neither the businessmen nor the politicians have thus far demonstrated their ability to pull the country out of this morass.

The political legacy of the Vietnam war and Watergate is not a happy one and it has a direct bearing on American involvement in the Middle East. In the first instance, Australia and New Zealand notwithstanding, America waged war single-handedly in Vietnam, and having been out on a limb alone in Indo-China for more than a decade, it found itself exposed once again during the October 1973 war. Originally the breach with NATO allies was not sufficient to give pause to President Johnson or even to Nixon, but worrisome doubts over Vietnam did nag American foreign-policy makers and the articulate public as a whole, doubts which were rekindled by the October war. In short, the advisability of adopting the role of the world's policeman while the Europeans profitably tended to their own affairs, has been increasingly called into question. In Africa and in the Middle East Americans have become much more willing to tolerate Soviet provocations than they were before LBJ's 'lone ranger' foreign policy began to erode their confidence in internationalist strategies.

The second level at which American self-doubts have taken on political form in the wake of Vietnam and Watergate is that of national level decision-making, where struggles between the legislative and executive branches, and within the executive itself, have increasingly led to deadlocks and inaction. To gain some perspective on the degree to which American foreign policy making has become subject to combat between disparate political forces and therefore truly tortuous, one need only compare the despatch with which the CIA restored the Shah to power in 1953 following the Mossadeq interval, or the haste with which Eisenhower in 1958 ordered the marines into Beirut, to the incredibly protracted wrangle over arms deals with the Saudis, the Egyptians and even the Jordanians. The US Congress, having gained access over a wide front to foreign policy decision-making, and itself in turn being penetrated by innumerable special interest groups, such as the Zionist lobby, is analogous to the proverbial 'bull in the china shop'. Skilled diplomacy requires the subtlety of those with sufficient depth of perspective and international exposure to appreciate nuances, not the plodding provincialism of favourite sons keen to protect constituents' interests. Unfortunately, the executive branch of government, having thoroughly tarnished its image as a competent architect of foreign policy by throwing away 50,000 lives and a Fort Knox of gold reserves in Vietnam, can make few prior claims to sole legitimacy. Moreover, the current administration, unlike its predecessor, seems to have evolved a pluralistic structure for the making of foreign policy, with United Nations Representative Andrew Young, National Security Adviser Zbigniew Brzezinski, Secretary of State Cyrus Vance and President Carter himself all putting in their two cents' worth. As both Sadat and Mohamed Hassanein Heikal have remarked in their memoirs, the fact that Henry Kissinger was the man responsible for American policy in the Middle East, particularly after the October war, greatly facilitated their dealings with the US, dealings which had earlier in the Nixon administration been very frustrating for the Egyptians because too many State Department cooks were spoiling the broth.[12] One can only wonder what various Middle Eastern heads of state and foreign ministers make of the present set-up in Washington and how they decide which of the many heads of the Washington hydra to approach, a problem made particularly vexing no doubt by virtue of the fact that Young, Brzezinski, Vance, Carter and innumerable senators and congressmen all have their own priorities and pet schemes as regards the Middle East. In this wide-open situation it is natural that pressure groups concerned with American policy towards the Middle East have found easy access to decision-making.

The economic and political weakness of the US is reflected curiously enough in the many arms deals with countries ranging geographically from Morocco to Pakistan. It is hard for the opponents of arms sales to counter the argument that were it not for such transactions the American balance of payment deficit, not to mention unemployment figures, would be totally unacceptable. In other words, the US is keeping its economy limping along with the crutch of foreign currency earnings from weapons sales, a fact which hardly testifies to the good health of the economy. The face-saving argument put up by those who benefit from the profligate spreading of advanced armaments throughout a volatile region is that this in turn gives the US control over the military and even political strategies of recipient countries, for, according to this point of view, in the absence of US back-up support, protracted military operations are impossible. While this is true for some countries, the most obvious of which is Saudi Arabia, it is of only limited applicability to others, the most notable among them being Israel. A lot of damage can be done before a squadron of fighter bombers needs overhauling, a capability which is anyway being developed fairly rapidly in Israel, Iran, Egypt and other countries.[13] Finally, the growing competition between recipients of American weapons for dominant roles in the Middle Eastern subsystem, the most dangerous example being that between Iran and Saudi Arabia,[14] can bode only ill for the provider of arms, as the conflict between Greece and Turkey suggests. The Americans then, ailing economically and approaching political paralysis, have tried to pull the fat out of the fire by delivering arms to virtually all sides of the various Middle Eastern conflicts, a strategy from which very negative rewards may be reaped.

In conclusion, the superpowers are now not the Big Brothers that conspiracy theorists would have us believe, or that they actually were some time previously, except for one crucial exception, namely, the patron-client relationship between the US and Israel. It is this connection which, despite fluctuations in its intensity and degree of control by the patron of the client, has persisted through the thick and thin of recent Middle Eastern history. As *the* permanent feature of the Middle Eastern political landscape it has finally arrived at the front and centre of the calculations of all interested parties, or, to use Mohamed Hassanein Heikal's colourful terminology, the conclusion has become inescapable that the Americans, because of their almost unlimited backing of Israel, 'hold 99% of the cards in the Middle East conflict'. This is why Sadat, a bitter enemy of Heikal, nevertheless predicates his peace strategy on Heikal's axiom, while those Arabs who are in the Rejection Front have diverted what energies they have left after various internecine struggles in Lebanon and elsewhere to subverting Sadat's strategy of using the US-Israel connection to his benefit, thereby attesting to the fact that the Sadat strategy is based on a firm, and to the Rejectionists a threatening, foundation. The paradox of America arriving alone at centre stage in Middle East politics precisely at the moment when its economic and political houses are least in order has, of course, serious implications for the current round of peace negotiations, but before those consequences are investigated we shall comment on the regional subsystem and then speculate briefly on the likely strategies of the concerned parties.

V

As is the case globally, multipolarity is rapidly replacing bipolarity in Middle Eastern regional politics. While Israel remains as one firm pole in the region, in that it can attract no regional supporters, it is more properly likened to a garrison state than to a regional actor with the capability of developing a following. The other pole of the 1950s and even 1960s, Egypt, has simply lost its pre-eminence, so that now Syria is a military near-equal to Egypt and Iran, if and when it emerges out of its present turmoil, more than an equal; the Saudis have sufficient cash to pay the piper and call the tunes; and even Nasserite ideology has taken a back seat to Palestinian nationalism. Concomitant with the relative decline of Egypt and of the eastern Mediterranean area as the central foci of Middle Eastern affairs, has been an increase in the importance of formerly outlying areas, such as Libya and the Arabian Peninsula. This redirection of geographical interest has had the consequence on the one hand of reducing the salience of the conflict with Israel as the sole Arab political preoccupation, and on the other of causing many of the area's neighbouring states to fall out with one another over various and sundry issues. The bones of contention are several and normally include a heavy overlay of related concerns, so that it would be incorrect to assert that the conflict with Israel is altogether absent from other territorial disputes, e.g. in the Sahara between Algeria, Morocco and Mauritania. However, it is correct to argue that the Israeli issue is one of the outer skins of the onion, the core usually being disputes over perceived threats to national interests. So, for example, the Saudis are increasingly apprehensive about Iranian ambitions; North and South Yemen are locked in their interminable struggle; Algeria and Morocco continue to shadow box in the Sahara; and the war of rhetoric, punctuated by threatening military gestures, rages on between Egypt and Libya. The Arab-Israeli conflict finds its way into all of these disputes one way or another, but it is not as central to any of them as it was, for example, to the manoeuvring between Nasser and the Syrian Baathists in 1966-7. The Lebanese civil war, in which the Israelis have intervened directly, is the major exception to this new rule of regional politics, but even in this instance, where the issue of Israel is close to the heart of the matter, that dubious honour must in the final analysis be bestowed on the hostility between Lebanese Maronites and Muslims. So the Arab preoccupation with Israel, which after 1948-9 reached its height in the latter half of the Nasser era, is now being replaced by a sort of Hobbesian war of all against all in the region, with no single regional power able to consistently orchestrate events beyond its borders, and with all states on the lookout for advantageous alliances with others, irrespective of ideological leanings. Thus the Iraqis, having made the biggest show of rejectionism following Sadat's *Mubaadarat* (peace initiative), were so desparately afraid that the Syrians might steal their Baathist thunder that they quietly and unofficially restored economic relations and political contacts with Egypt and simultaneously fostered political and military ties with the Saudis. In this era of Middle East multipolarity, which finds such bizarre coalitions as the temporary unification of Tunisia and Libya, virtually anything goes, and when so much is indeed going, the Israeli issue is consciously or unconsciously moved to the back burner.

Alone among the Arab states, Egypt cannot afford the luxury of ignoring the Israeli question. Syria has its preoccupations in Lebanon and with the Iraqis, and while Israel does remain a threat and an occupier, financial success helps the Syrians swallow this bitter pill. The other front-line state, Jordan, withdrew into the wings at the 1974 Rabat Conference when the PLO was recognised as the legitimate representative of all Palestinians, including the inhabitants of the West Bank, and until Sadat is joined by other Arab heads of state in urging Hussein to come on stage once again, the King is wisely sitting it out. Therefore, it is the Egyptians, with their economy collapsing about their ears, who are left to deal with the Israelis. For Cairo, then, a negotiated settlement with Israel is absolutely essential, and it is to the domestic situation in Egypt, and its ramifications for negotiations, that we now turn.

VI

According to Sadat, the Egyptian economy was 'below zero' in 1973, so he had no choice but to launch the October war. While the same has not been reflected by him regarding his motives in going to Jerusalem in 1977 and signing the Camp David agreement in 1978, there can be little doubt that paramount among them was the desire to save Egypt from the twentieth-century equivalent of the *Caisse de la Dette* forced upon Khedive Ismail in 1876. The stark realisation of the country's desperate economic plight is lost on no one and even those Egyptians fortunate enough to reside in Cairo's most luxurious flats and drive Mercedes cars must nevertheless cope with the collapse of that city's entire infrastructure and with galloping inflation. While there are well-founded suspicions that the high living of some fellow countrymen is not helping matters, and that the *infatah* (economic opening) has simply opened the door to a flood of imported luxury items, there is also the knowledge that economic problems are essentially unsolvable until, and maybe not even after, the heretofore interminable conflict with Israel is brought to an end. This then is the great reserve of support that Sadat can and does fall back on, for almost no one sees a simple solution to Egypt's problems and leftists and rightists alike agree that the number one item on the agenda is the resolution of the Israeli issue. There are of course those, as Mohamed Hassanein Heikal and Khaled Muhyi al Din, who believe that they could better deal with the problem, but they lack the support necessary to gain the position which would enable them to try out their theories. Others, including presumably most top-ranking officers, are rather less sure of their diplomatic skills and strategies and would prefer to see Sadat continue to carry the ball as long as there remains a chance of success.

As a result, debate in Egypt on Israel is becoming focused increasingly narrowly on the various sticking points of diplomatic negotiations, while broader questions which formerly served as the main talking points—such as should we or should we not negotiate—have been eclipsed. Now those on the left, right and in the centre, argue over various solutions to such problems as the status of Jerusalem and the West Bank, the possibility of an Israeli presence in Sharm al Sheikh, and/or what should happen in the Golan Heights. While debates on these issues can be extremely heated, they are nevertheless disagreements over bargaining strategies and not over fundamentals and are therefore susceptible to reconciliation and compromise within an overall package. In summary, Egypt is propelled down the road towards peace by her domestic economic problems and by the realisation that she is no longer the home of a modern Salah al Din, capable of uniting Arabs for the great effort of ousting the Jewish crusader from his stronghold. Having been cut down to size in the region and forced inevitably to the conclusion that it too is a Third World country that lacks the resources to conduct an adventurous regional policy, Egypt is ready for a peace settlement, if, and this is still a big if, the right formula is found.

VII

There are historic turnings in nations' histories and presumably, therefore, potential turnings that are missed or simply postponed. The Israeli elections of May 1977 may well be an example of the latter. The elections that brought Begin to power for what probably will be the 'last hurrah' of the products of the *aliya* from Eastern Europe could easily have produced a very different result. More importantly, the splintering of the Israeli Labour Party, largely as a result of the generation gap which divides most of the Israeli elite, suggests that in the not too distant future younger, native-born Israelis will come to power. How different that group will be from the present European-born Zionists remains to be seen, but there are good grounds to suspect that the rigidity of those committed to Zionism from the distance of Poland and out of ideological considerations will not be nearly so characteristic of those simply born into Zionism and Israeli statehood. While those *sabras* who have matured politically as clients of Eastern European immigrants, such as Moshe Dayan, continue to espouse the ideology of their now deceased patrons, they are not representative of the younger generation, as the well-attended peace rallies held recently in Israel suggest. Therefore, while the future is bright for Arab-Israeli co-operation, as ageing takes its inevitable toll of the incumbent elite, that may not be a terribly encouraging thought for those Egyptians presently trying to negotiate with a man whose political perceptions seem to have been formed irrevocably and unalterably in the Europe of his youth.

A corollary of the passing of the torch to a new generation of native-born Israelis is that American influence in Israel will decline, for just as in the Arab world where the phase of radical Arab nationalism was necessarily coterminous with heavy dependence on the Soviet Union, so in Israel radical Jewish nationalism has required outside support to fulfill its ambitions. Paradoxically, the regional political stance of hardline European-born Zionists necessitates considerable dependence on the US for the wherewithall to conduct such a foreign policy and, just as paradoxically, it renders the architects of this strategy more vulnerable to US pressure than more accommodating Israelis would be. If America is to play the Big Brother role in negotiations between Israelis and Arabs, then it is probably necessary that it does so while Begin, or a similar individual, remains in power, for when the torch finally does pass to the younger native-born generation, it will be much more likely to come to some agreement with Israel's neighbours on its own. What remains to be seen is whether or not the US administration will play its winning cards against the Begin Government and force it to give up land for peace, or whether it will continue to abstain until the region explodes in yet another war; or the Israelis, under new leadership, take the bull by the horns themselves. So far, despite increasing verbal demonstration of the Carter administration's displeasure at Israel's intransigence following the Camp David summit, there does not seem to be any sign that the type of concrete pressure required to end such intransigence is being contemplated by Washington.

While the preceding observations on American involvement in the Middle East may suggest that sustained US pressure on the Begin Government is unlikely, there are a constellation of factors working in the opposite direction and which appear to orbit around the political personality of President Carter. Unlike several of his predecessors, he gives few signs of having a gut emotional commitment to Zionism and seems rather to have tailored his policy towards Israel, thus far at least, on the basis of domestic political pressures, perceptions of national interests, and bureaucratic infighting. In each of these areas there have been developments which give Carter greater room to manoeuvre and an incentive to do so. In the first instance, the monolithic Zionist lobby has shown signs of weakening as influential politicians like Senator Ribicoff begin to desert the fold on at least some issues, as the various American Jewish organisations begin to argue openly about Israeli policies, as Arab-Americans become better organised, and as American public opinion swings away from automatic support of Israel and its leaders.

With regard to perceived national interests, US dependence on imported Arab oil—and this is bound to become more intense as post-Shah Iran moves out of the American orbit—and America's pre-eminent position in the Gulf have become so salient that any threat to oil supply has to be very carefully evaluated. The lynchpin of American strategy in the Arab world is the Saudi connection, and having brought this relationship under pressure already by choosing to rely on Iran as the Gulf's policeman, the US might be playing with fire if it does not at least appear to twist Israeli arms, and appearances in the absence of reality are becoming harder and harder to maintain. Furthermore, in the wake of the turmoil in

Iran, Saudi Arabia's importance to US strategy in the Gulf and the Middle East is bound to increase manifold. There are the unmistakeable signs that the Saudis are becoming rather impatient with American bumbling, not only in the Middle East but also in Africa, and King Khaled, Crown Prince Fahd, Foreign Minister Saud al Faisal and Minister for Petroleum Sheikh Yamani are four Arabs who can gain access to the Oval Office at a moment's notice.

Finally, the very fact that bureaucratic politics within the Carter administration are so polycentric, with no one individual or institution having as yet attained a commanding position, leaves open the possibility for the President to take bold steps. With a veritable babble of advice coming from the State and Defense Departments, the CIA, the National Security Council and even the UN delegation, Carter may finally decide that the buck actually does stop at his desk. In that case developments pointed to above in domestic politics and in perceptions of national security should lead the President to exert much greater pressure on Israel than he has done to date. While Israel has lots of room for manoeuvre as long as America procrastinates, there is no doubt that the approximate peace package Sadat has offered (including his post-Camp David utterances on the West Bank) would be much more pleasant for Tel Aviv than the alternatives, were America to threaten to cut the umbilical cord. In conclusion, the short-term Israeli response depends on America's stance, while over the long haul the changing composition of the Israeli political elite will significantly affect that state's regional policy.

VIII

King Hussein learned his politics in the school of hard knocks, and he seems to have mastered his lessons. Having been cast overboard in the wake of the October war and the following Rabat Conference, Hussein has clung on waiting for events to rescue him. While Sadat has extended a helping hand, Hussein is clever enough to realise that the Egyptian President is himself standing on a slippery patch and more Arab heads of state must demonstrate their willingness to pull the Jordanian king aboard before it would be wise for him to abandon his uncomfortable but tenable position. If the final outcome of the peace negotiations leaves him with control over the West Bank, presumably in some sort of condominium status with Israel for a specified period of time, he will have to weather a storm of abuse from many Palestinians and their radical supporters. In this situation he would have very little to worry about if the Egyptians, Saudis and Syrians were behind him, but if, for example, the latter ended up on the other side of the fence, they could unleash the Palestinians to do their dirty work. Therefore, Hussein simply is forced to sit tight until he is certain that the front-line Arab governments and their key supporters can agree upon a peace package. Once this happens, even in the face of Palestinian opposition, he can move—for he is fully aware that without the backing of an effective regional patron the Palestinians cannot pose a formidable threat to his regime. Even in the longer term, Hussein's position looks brighter than one could possibly have foreseen some four years ago, for if the West Bank is returned in whole or in part to Jordan, the King will have a claim to the title of 'Liberator of Palestine'. While that may ring hollow to most Palestinians in the *diaspora* and to politicised Palestinians in Israel and on the West Bank, it might have some credibility within the West Bank Arab community. Moreover, as the man with control of the purse strings for the new entity, he will be in a strong position to use patronage to develop a clientele, so that, if after five years a plebiscite on the future of the West Bank were to be held, Hussein might carry the day. He would of course face opposition from a variety of Palestinian sources, but these forces may well lack the resources to pry the West Bank away from some sort of confederal status with Jordan.

The Saudi stance on Sadat's peace initiative, subsequent negotiations and the Camp David summit, illustrates the strengths and weaknesses of Riyadh's petro-dollar diplomacy. Like the Pope, the Saudi's lack divisions so they cannot hope to forge ahead of their Arab brothers. Instead they have to resort to quiet diplomacy, relying on cash inducements to swing things their way. For this approach to work they have to play the role of mediator (a role they played brilliantly at the Baghdad Rejectionists' meeting following the Camp David accord), avoiding overly close alliances with other parties so that the words to the wise they whisper in Arab ears will not be thought of as simply messages from Cairo or elsewhere. As 'fixers' of this sort the Saudis are absolutely essential to the success of a peace package, but they cannot afford to take bold, and indeed desperate, initiatives in the manner of Sadat. It can be expected, therefore, that when and if Sadat nears his goal the Saudis will begin to whisper more urgently and incessantly to Assad, Hussein, Arafat and probably even Saddam Hussein. In the final analysis it may be the webs established through behind-the-scenes Saudi activities that knit together a sufficiently broad Arab front to make an agreement work, that is if such a front can be formed at all.

Syria is sitting on the fence, despite appearances to the contrary, simply because it has nowhere else to go. Despite apparent evidence to the contrary, including the recently concluded Iraqi-Syrian agreement to set up a federated state of Syria and Iraq, Assad can hardly move his country into tandem with Iraq; neither can Syria go it alone. Relations with Amman have cooled considerably since the Sadat initiative, the Saudis are underwriting the so-called deterrent force in Lebanon and therefore their wishes have to be accommodated, and even relations with Moscow are not at all what they once were. In addition to the problems of regional and international isolation, President Assad continues to court disaster in Lebanon, while his rather narrowly-based Alawite regime must contend increasingly with war weariness of the Egyptian variety. That the lack of popular enthusiasm for another round of war with Israel seems to be concentrated in the Sunni-dominated cities of Damascus, Homs, Hama and Aleppo, can hardly be reassuring for a schismatic Muslim from Latakia. A way out of these various impasses could be provided by a reasonable peace agreement with the Israelis, which would presumably take the heat off in South Lebanon and elsewhere in the country, provide some balm for the national pride in the form of at least the partial return of a demilitarised Golan Heights, and finally, would realign the country with the Egyptians, Jordanians and Saudis, thereby providing Assad with several friends to help fend off the inevitable abuse from Baghdad. If, however, this option does not appear to be realistic as a result of continuing Israeli intransigence, Assad must have a counter-strategy prepared to protect his flanks. It is in this context that the recent Syrian-Iraqi federation agreement becomes important. President Assad's hardline statements should, therefore, be viewed as symptomatic of his awkward position and as diplomatic posturing, rather than as an irrevocable commitment to rejection.

IX

For several reasons the outlook in the region is not bright for radical Palestinian nationalists. Never truly capable of operating independently of the Arab states, the lifeblood of Palestinian organisations is the disunity of Arab countries. As the shock troops in inter-Arab combat, both verbal and military, they lend their support to one side or another in Arab squabbles in exchange for assistance or simply promises of assistance for the liberation of the homeland. If all the front-line states were therefore to agree to a peace package, none would have use for the Palestinians and all would want them contained. States further removed from the sources of action, such as Libya, Iraq and Algeria, would presumably embrace the Palestinian cause even more closely, but in the face of a Damascus-Amman-Cairo-Riyadh axis, there is little any or all Palestinian organisations could do to upset the apple cart, even if they were to have the wholehearted support of the hardline rejectionist states. Moreover, as the war of attrition between Iraq and the PLO, recently fought out in the streets of London, Paris, Karachi, Kuwait and elsewhere suggests, the possibilities of fraternal co-operation between mainstream PLO elements and the Saddam Hussein regime in Baghdad are rather remote.

It should also not be considered a foregone conclusion that Arafat and the mainstream of the PLO would reject out of hand a settlement that provided for some sort of Jordanian-Israeli or just Jordanian control over the West Bank for a stipulated period, with the promise of the possibility of self-determination at the end of the probation period. The possible cost to Arafat of refusing to go along with such an agreement could easily be that he and his organisation would be frozen out of the Palestinian future by Hussein, a scenario Arafat would wish to avoid at all costs. He would have to weigh this against the possibility of upsetting the whole affair, a strategy which would necessitate a close working alliance with Palestinian Rejectionists and their supporters, not a very palatable thought while the latter are shooting at Fatah guerrillas in Lebanon and the organisation's spokesmen around the world. So Arafat could well decide to beat his swords into ploughshares and try to best Hussein in the race for final sovereignty over a mini-Palestinian state on the West Bank. After all, Arafat is a consummate politician but a mediocre general, and he may well feel up to outmanoeuvring Hussein in Arab capitals and in the towns and villages of the West Bank, but rather less inclined to chase around from hideout to hideout in areas as far flung as Iraq and Libya.

If Arafat's proclivity would be to go along with a peace package that promised him the possibility of becoming head of a Palestinian state at some time in the future, it must be asked whether his 'indians' would follow their chief. The PLO and even Fatah are showing the strains brought on by the Lebanese disaster and

Arafat's control is clearly not what it once was. But two factors suggest that he could pull the fat out of the fire. The first is that Fatah is still much the strongest of the Palestinian organisations, as its military successes in combat with more radical organisations in South Lebanon have demonstrated.[15] If Fatah were to hang up its guns, the resistance would be emasculated, and if they were to turn them on their competitors, there is little doubt about the outcome. Secondly, Arafat is not only the most successful Palestinian politician, he is virtually the only one who could convincingly wear the label of 'Father' of his country. While his lieutenants may be envious of his political stature and might nurture ambitions of their own, they have remained so much in the background that they lack the necessary broad-based following to translate their aspirations into reality. More flamboyant competitors, such as George Habash or Nayef Hawatmeh, are debilitated either for health reasons, or because they are overly identified with a particular political ideology and its related practical alliances, or because they are thought of as little more than the hired guns of one Arab regime or another. Almost by default Arafat remains very much the preeminent Palestinian chieftain and where he goes, so by necessity goes a large segment of his wandering tribe.

While the carrot of possible future sovereignty over the West Bank and the stick of harassment by the front-line Arab states may be enough in themselves to propel the PLO in the direction of accepting a peace settlement, there are contributing factors that may also nudge this grouping of Palestinian nationalists along. First, the prognosis for continued relative freedom of operations in the last remaining base in the area, namely South Lebanon, is not good, particularly if a peace agreement were to be signed. Talk of a Palestinian state emerging in that particular region is not convincing and what is more likely is that the Syrians, acting either directly or indirectly through a surrogate Lebanese government, or possibly even some other party, will in the not too distant future put the 1969 Cairo agreement to rest once and for all. Such an outcome would be a heavy blow for the Palestinian national liberation movement, for removed to the periphery of the area, say in Iraq, they could make few convincing claims to being liberationists.

A second consideration is that the Palestinian *diaspora* is like a relentless tide carrying Palestinians out of the immediate region of their homeland and to the Arabian Peninsula, Europe, North America and even as far afield as Australia. As they begin to build their personal futures in these distant lands they are in many cases lost forever to the cause in the sense that they would not return to a liberated Palestine, whatever its size. Since the struggle with Zionism is essentially a demographic one, this trend bodes ill for future victory, even of a limited sort. It could presumably be arrested and possibly slightly reversed by the creation of a mini-Palestinian state and that realisation must also be part of the PLO's calculus.

Finally, and to return to our earlier preoccupation with the superpowers, it must be observed that the Palestinians have never enjoyed uninterrupted and generous patronage from the Soviet Union. Arafat is suspect in Moscow on ideological grounds and because of his ties to the Saudis, while more radical Palestinians who call for the destruction of the State of Israel, are, it should be remembered, out of tune with Soviet thinking on this issue. As is the case with many other aspects of their Middle East policy, the Soviets have not really developed an adequate response to the presence of the Palestinian liberation movement, a failure which may suggest an underlying fear that the Palestinians could get out of hand and wreck Moscow's position in the area. If this is indeed the case, then American decision-makers ought to proceed with great caution in the current negotiations, for if the Soviets are given no stake in a final agreement and if at the same time their positions in Baghdad and Damascus are seen to be crumbling, they could become more adventurist since they would have little to lose by throwing more of their weight behind radical Palestinians. While this eventuality can easily be headed off by carefully considered American moves, the climate of relations between Washington and Moscow is becoming so chilly that there is a danger that the Carter administration might damn the consequences, and go on full steam ahead, ignoring Soviet sensitivities. Despite the limited success of Camp David diplomacy, this would be an unnecessary error, and possibly one which could undermine otherwise carefully laid plans.

X

To label that collection of Arab states and Palestinians who are opposed to a settlement with Israel the 'Rejection Front' is to overstate the cohesion that exists in this fragile alliance. Even in the wake of Sadat's 'sell-out', Iraq could not see its way clear to sit through a conference in Libya, while Sadat's telling observation that it is those furthest removed from the battle who are most willing to spill blood has not gone unnoticed, even outside Egypt. As a group then, the Rejectionists suffer from the fact that they are not united and also because none of them, with the exception of Syria, which should more correctly be described as a fence-sitter, shares a border with Israel. Taken individually their capabilities are equally unimpressive. Iraq, the most bellicose of the Arab states, has never matched words with deeds for the very good reason that it is not in a position to do so. While the 1975 agreement with the Shah brought the war with the Kurds to an end, that running sore can be re-opened at will by Iraq's enemies. Possibly even more important is the realisation by Iraq's Sunni Baathist leaders that both their religion and their party affiliation places them in groups conspicuous in their status as minorities. Keeping the lid on at home in such a situation is a full-time job and an adventurist-interventionist foreign policy could very quickly cause the whole political system to come unstuck. Realising this, uncomfortably aware of their isolated position in the Arab world, and afraid of communist machinations in the country as well as Syrian intrigues across the border, the Iraqis have been trying hard to mend their fences with Egypt and Saudi Arabia. In short, they need not be taken seriously as a threat to a negotiated settlement.

What is true of Iraq is also true of Libya and Algeria, although for different reasons. While Saudi Arabia has developed a foreign policy strategy that maximises its petro-dollar influence, the Libyans, by trying to be among a self-defined vanguard instead of playing a mediatory role behind the scenes, have simply outrun their resources. With a population base somewhere around two million and with oil wealth no doubt taking its toll in terms of the masses' enthusiasm for selfless sacrifice for someone else's cause, the Libyan elite cannot muster the troops for the battle against the 'traitors to the Palestinian cause'. The Algerians, beset with innumerable development problems at home and located in the culturally distinct and very distant Maghreb, are simply too far away and too much involved in their own affairs, particularly now with the passing away of Boumedienne, to spare much time or energy for the Palestinian cause.

The slender resources of the Palestinian Rejectionists cannot make up for the short-fall elsewhere in the ranks: therefore, while poorly co-ordinated activities of all sorts could be expected to originate from the Rejectionist quarter following a negotiated settlement, not too much strength of will would be required on the part of the concerned parties, Palestinian and non-Palestinian, for them to successfully ride out the storm of radical Palestinian opposition.

XI

Those actors in the region who have little more than applause to add to whatever agreement might be reached should nevertheless be mentioned, for their reactions are not entirely inconsequential. For example, King Hassan of Morocco, riding the crest of a wave of popularity following the 'Green March' in the Sahara, has supported Egypt in both war and peace and such assistance must be gratifying to Sadat. Jaafar Numeiry in the Sudan has likewise thrown his weight behind Egypt's efforts to negotiate a settlement. Although this may be of relatively little account, were the opposite to be the case and were the Sudanese to be virulently opposed to Sadat's methods, Egypt could find itself in an uncomfortablely exposed position in North East Africa. Tunisia has virtually opted out of regional Arab politics until Bourguiba passes from the scene and the succession struggle plays itself out, but, for what it is worth, Tunis is also backing a negotiated settlement. The states of the Peninsula from Kuwait to Oman, more concerned with their own affairs than with what goes on along the shores of the Mediterranean, would nevertheless be relieved to see a mini-Palestinian state emerge and take some of the political pressure off them and some of the Palestinian guest workers away from their countries. On the other side of the Gulf, despite the Shah's departure, no matter who rules Iran will not find Tehran's interests inconsistent with supporting a negotiated settlement of the Arab-Israeli conflict. So from the very periphery of the Middle East—the North African region—to its centre, with the exception of some relatively weak centres of rejectionism, there is a general drift towards a negotiated settlement, a trend of opinion which the astute President of Egypt no doubt detected before gambling his future on a plane trip to Jerusalem.

XII

The strategic importance of the Middle East and its vast deposits of oil made the area one of vital concern to the superpowers in the post-World War II era, while the lack of competition from Europe, Japan or elsewhere, the Arab-Israeli conflict, the radical nationalisms of both sides in that conflict, and the relatively poorly-developed economic and political systems of the states of the area provided opportunities for both the US and the USSR to play important, indeed dominant, roles in the region. That era is, however, passing, not because the Middle East is of less strategic or economic importance now than it was a decade or more ago but because the superpowers are being challenged economically, politically and militarily by global and regional polycentrism. In the more complex world of the mid and late-1970s, the superpowers are seeing the sun set on their neo-colonial empires in the Middle East and both of them lack the resources to reverse that process.

The consequence of declining superpower influence for peace in the Middle East can at this relatively early stage only provide grounds for speculation, for in this volatile region anything can still happen. However, a not altogether unlikely scenario can be constructed. As long as the 'radical' Arab regimes were backed exclusively or mainly by the Soviet Union, and Israel by the United States, there was little chance for peace. In that circumstance not only did the regional combatants have to come to a meeting of the minds, but their major supporters had to do so as well, and inducing that many parties to agree at any one time to a specific proposal proved to be impossible. With Egypt having swung entirely out of the Soviet orbit, with the other most important 'radical' Arab states, including Syria and Iraq, having loosened their ties to Moscow, and with Jordan and all the states of the Peninsula with the exception of South Yemen firmly in the Western camp, the Arab-Israeli conflict has become somewhat analogous to the conflict between Greece and Turkey in that the main protagonists on both sides are at least nominally on the same side of the Cold War fence. This in itself lessens the likelihood of a shooting war, as the analogous case suggests, and also increases the probability of a settlement, for as Sadat and his backers know, if negotiations break down, the Soviets, having had their noses rubbed in the Nile mud, are very unlikely to bail the Egyptian President out of his predicament. Therefore, it is one of history's curiosities that the US, having some years earlier reached and passed its zenith of influence in the Middle East and the world generally, finds itself cast in the role of arbiter of the Arab-Israeli conflict. Understandably, American decision-makers, having been caught flat-footed, have as yet to demonstrate mastery of the situation, which they indeed may never do. But assuming that the US is able to meet the demands of a situation which could well be its last 'big hurrah' in the area, a more or less final settlement of the Arab-Israeli conflict could be negotiated. While resolution of this protracted struggle would be a great accomplishment, it would not necessarily lead to overall peace and stability in the area, for with the presence of vast deposits of oil and with increasing regional polycentrism and therefore innumerable localised disputes, any one of which can attract superpower attention, there is always the possibility of renewed and moderately widescale conflict. But it is unlikely that any other bone of contention would be so divisive for so long. Therefore, while the superpowers may continue to dabble in the region, with the resolution of the Arab-Israeli conflict they are unlikely to find themselves so deeply involved in another regional conflict in the foreseeable future. This may in turn considerably reduce their capacity to manipulate regional actors for their own global and regional ends.

Notes

1. For a presentation of this particular theory, see 'Conspiracy of Silence: U.S.S *Liberty* Cover Up', *Palestine Forum*, no. 22 (September-October 1976). See also Anthony Pearson's articles on the same subject in *Penthouse*, June and July 1976.

2. There have been allegations that Cuban troops played an instrumental role in Abdul Fattah Ismail's ouster of Salem Rubaya Ali in South Yemen. See for example the pro-Iraqi Beirut newspaper, *Al Liwa*, 28 June 1978. See also the UPI dispatch for that date.

3. This is the conspiracy theory mentioned above.

4. That the Begin Government continued to sanction the establishment of Jewish settlements in the West Bank even after Sadat's peace initiative of 1977 and, what is more, continues to be recalcitrant on this issue even after the Camp David summit of 1978, is but one example of the Israelis thumbing their collective nose at the US.

5. The Egyptians, for example, eventually wearying of Ghaddafi's exuberance for union and desirous of cementing the Saudi connection, turned their back on Libyan aid.

6. For a discussion of Egyptian 'divide and not be ruled' strategies over the past century, see Robert Springborg, 'Khedivalism Along the Nile: The Strategies and Tactics of Egyptian Dependency', *World Review*, vol. 17 no. 3. (August 1978).

7. Evaluation by Egyptian engineers of Soviet electrical gear used in the electrification of the High Dam has, for example, been very negative. Such feelings were expressed openly and vehemently in discussions held by the Syndicate of Engineers in Cairo in 1971 and 1972. The January 1972 issue of the syndicate's magazine, which contained an article highly critical of Soviet electrical equipment, was removed from the news-stands by the government.

8. The largest agricultural project in the country, the Jebal al Akhdar Authority in Cyrenaica, is a joint undertaking with the South Australian Ministry of Agriculture.

9. A Franco-Iraqi arms deal, under negotiation since 1975, was finally signed in mid-1977. It calls for the purchase of military equipment worth $1.4 billion, including 72 Mirage F-1s, Puma helicopters, Matra Magic air-to-air missiles, etc.

See Roger F. Pajak, 'French and British Arms Sales in the Middle East: A Policy Perspective', *Middle East Review*, vol. 10, no. 3. (Spring 1978), pp. 45-54.

10. On managerial and revolutionary elites, see John Kautsky, 'Revolutionary and Managerial Elites in Modernizing Regimes', *Comparative Politics*, vol. 1, no. 3 (July 1969), pp. 441-54.

11. On Russian methods in Egypt, see Mohamed Hassanein Heikal, *The Road to Ramadan* (Collins, London, 1976).

12. Donald Bergus, head of the US Mission in Cairo, even went so far as to draft his own proposal for a partial accord, an act which led to confusion on all sides. See William Quandt, *Decade of Decisions 1967-1976: American Policy Toward the Arab-Israeli Conflict* (University of California Press, Berkeley, 1977), pp. 142-3. Sadat was so taken with the idea of a national security adviser that he created the same post in Egypt, filling it with Hafiz Ismail, who at that time was his closest adviser on foreign policy.

13. On the prospects for an Arab arms industry, see Wolfgang Mallmann, 'Arms Industry is Viable, but ...', *The Middle East*, no. 29 (March 1977), pp. 26-7.

14. On the growing hostility between these two countries see 'Iran and Saudi Arabia: Rivals for the Superpower Role', *The Middle East*, no. 43 (May 1978), pp. 16-32.

15. On that round of fighting, see the *Egyptian Gazette*, 15 July 1978. On the strength of Fatah as compared to other elements of the PLO, see Jean Gueyras, 'Abu Nidal Versus Arafat', *Le Monde*, 5 August 1978, reprinted in *Guardian Weekly*, 13 August 1978.

5 Cyprus

JOHN ZAROCOSTAS

I

Cyprus, situated in the north-eastern corner of the Mediterranean, is intrinsically an inconsequential micro-state,* but its geo-strategic location has made it disproportionately vital to international politics. Over the last few decades its special vulnerability to foreign manipulation and intervention has permanently disabled it.

It will be the objective of this chapter to present a critical analysis of the interlocking aspects of the Cyprus problem. Particular emphasis will be placed on extrapolating the linkage between the local, regional and global actors and determinants of the Cyprus issue.

The origins of the Cyprus problem date back to the period of British colonial rule.[1] In 1878 the island was ceded to Britain by the Sublime Porte in return for a British undertaking to extend military assistance to Turkey[2] in defence of the Ottoman Empire's Asiatic possessions against Russia.[3] The island, however, did not come under *de jure* British control until the Treaty of Lausanne in 1923. The sovereignty of Cyprus, left by Disraeli—at least nominally—in Turkish hands, formally passed to Britain under Article 20 of the 1923 treaty[4] by which Turkey recognised the annexation of the island proclaimed by the British government on 5 November 1914. In 1925 Cyprus became a British Crown colony.

The British, who took over Cyprus in order to strengthen their imperial lifeline through the Mediterranean and the Suez Canal to India, in fact found little strategic interest in it until the 1950s. British control of Palestine, Egypt, and South Arabia, proved sufficient for strategic purposes until after the Second World War.

However, with the gradual demise of British influence in the Middle East, Cyprus once again emerged as a key strategic post. The British withdrawal from Palestine in 1948 and from Suez in

* The population of Cyprus is 78 per cent Greek and 18 per cent Turkish with the remainder being Maronites and Armenians.

1954 resulted in the British establishing their new Middle East headquarters in Cyprus. This stiffened British resistance to the revival of Greek Cypriot demands for 'enosis' (union with Greece).[5] The British refusal to accede to the Greek demand for Greco-British talks over Cyprus[6] forced Greece to bring the question before the United Nations in 1954.[7] Moreover, the key position that Cyprus was given in the Baghdad pact reinforced Greek Cypriot fears that Britain was reluctant to change the status quo. In retaliation they launched a campaign of guerrilla warfare and terrorism in April 1955 which was led by Colonel Grivas and EOKA (National Organisation of Cypriot Fighters).[8] In order to counter the EOKA threat, Britain embarked on a policy aimed at fomenting trouble between Greece and Turkey.[9] The British encouraged the Turkish version of self-determination, 'taksim' or partition.[10] In 1956 first 'Volkan' and then TMT (Turkish Resistance Organisation) emerged on the Cyprus scene.

A distinct change in British strategic requirements in 1957 resulted in the British abandoning their formerly intransigent line.[11] The shift in British policy,[12] along with the mounting pressure by NATO[13] for a rapprochement between the three camps, in the light of the looming Berlin and Middle East crises, interacted to bring about an imposed solution of the Cyprus question. In February 1959 the Greek and Turkish governments reached an agreement at Zurich, which was endorsed by the British government, to establish a Republic of Cyprus.[14] The republic came into being with the granting of independence on 16 August 1960. The legacy of communal discord on the island, a by-product of colonial rule, was, however, institutionalised in the 1960 constitution. Drafted by the Greek and Turkish governments, and not by the Cypriots themselves, it contained in it provisions for segregation at all levels between the Greek and Turkish communities, thus making the constitution virtually unworkable.[15] The incorporation of British, Greek and Turkish interests in the structure of the constitution,[16] as subsequent events demonstrated, made it a perfect instrument for the obliteration of the republic. With the British base facilities endorsed by the Treaty of Guarantee and the treaty itself entrenched in the constitution, British influence in Cyprus was made secure. The rigid constitution facilitated the process of bicommunal constitutional deadlock.

In November 1963 the deadlock induced Makarios to prepare thirteen constitutional amendments.[17] After Ankara and the

Turkish Cypriots rejected this unilateral revision an outbreak of intercommunal violence erupted. Although the crisis was essentially domestic in character, the existence of the Treaty of Guarantee and the fact that each community was supported by one of the guarantor powers, Greece or Turkey, provided international overtones to the crisis. Whereas in the 1950s Cyprus was basically a colonial problem kept within the jurisdiction of the imperial power, in 1963 Cyprus was a full-fledged member of the world community. It was also no longer an exclusive Western preserve. Its pursuit of an active policy of non-alignment implied that any major conflict that threatened its sovereignty would most probably invite some sort of Soviet involvement.

As clashes spread over Cyprus a limited peacekeeping effort undertaken by British troops at the request of the Cyprus government failed to restore peace on the island.[18] One of the salient features which emerged as the crisis entered a more critical phase was the diminution of British influence despite its nominal presence on the island. On 25 January 1964 the British made clear their intention of seeking a broader peacekeeping force through NATO, adding that if there was no solution forthcoming they were ready to drop the Cyprus issue in the lap of the United Nations.

The United States proved receptive to British proposals, and from February 1964 it assumed the initiative. President Lyndon Johnson stressed that it was the task of statesmanship to prevent the danger in Cyprus from exploding into disaster.[19] In the hope of a peaceful solution, on 28 January 1964, Johnson sent General Lemnitzer, the NATO commander in Europe, as his personal envoy to Athens and Ankara. This opened a new stage in the Cyprus crisis with American diplomacy introduced formally for the first time. As a result of Lemnitzer's trip a NATO peace plan was drawn up for Cyprus.[20] The American undertaking, however, also opened the way for Soviet involvement in the Cyprus crisis. On 7 February 1964 Khrushchev warned that 'The Soviet Union, although it does not border directly on the Republic of Cyprus, cannot remain indifferent to that situation which is developing in the area ...', and that any move against the island would be 'the source of international complications fraught with grave consequences'.[21]

Following the rejection of a Western peacekeeping force by Makarios, the Cyprus problem was placed before the United Nations. The Anglo-American plan failed because Washington proved incapable of viewing the problem in other than NATO terms. On the other hand, Makarios held the view that the UN would serve as the most reliable mechanism for the realisation of his internal political goals.[22] Besides the adverse effects that the crisis threatened to have upon NATO solidarity, United States interests over Cyprus had also been activated in part because of the possibility that the crisis might be removed from the hands of the guarantor powers once it was inscribed on the UN agenda. Such a move raised the possibility that the Soviet Union might enter an area which had so far remained a Western preserve.

On 4 March the Security Council adopted a unanimous resolution recommending the creation of UNFICYP—the UN force in Cyprus—and the appointment of a mediator.[23] In 1964, as in later crises over the island, both Greece and Turkey viewed the Cyprus dispute almost exclusively in the light of their respective national interests. With both these powers designating a greater priority to the Cyprus issue than to NATO cohesion, the United States was presented with a serious policy dilemma in trying to avert a Greek-Turkish clash over Cyprus which would have weakened the entire eastern flank of NATO defences. Washington now came to the conclusion that the continued independent existence of Cyprus was a threat to US interests.[24] As it became clear that the pre-established arrangements were not working, President Johnson personally intervened. On 5 June 1964 Johnson warned Ismet Inonu, the then Turkish Prime Minister, that Turkey might not receive NATO help in the event of a Soviet attack if a Turkish invasion of Cyprus were carried out.[25] Turkey acceded to Washington's demands for restraint. However, Johnson's ultimatum was taken as a serious intervention in Turkey's affairs and precipitated a deterioration of relations between Ankara and Washington. Nevertheless, this ultimatum succeeded in preventing a Turkish military intervention which, it was reported, was being planned.

In a bid to rapidly break the stalemate the United States also launched a diplomatic offensive. Washington openly put pressure upon the Secretary-General of the UN to sponsor an American mediation effort under Dean Acheson. In a compromise agenda the Secretary-General agreed to accept a secondary role for the US in discussions at Geneva.[26] The American proposed solution was the 'Acheson plan'.[27] Both Greece and the Makarios regime however rejected it as unacceptable asserting that it was another form of partition. Makarios was apprehensive that Greece might accept an Acheson proposal which would fall short of total enosis.[28] Soviet-

Makarios co-operation was also facilitated by the latter's distrust of NATO plans. However, in August 1964, Moscow abandoned its previous truculence.[29] Henceforth Soviet tactics appeared somewhat contradictory and cautious. Khrushchev told Makarios that although he sympathised with the latter he believed a ceasefire would be an important contribution to peace. The sudden reassessment of the issue by the Kremlin was in line with its new policy to use the Cyprus issue to detach Turkey from NATO. The timing was ideal with Turkish-American relations adversely affected by Johnson's ultimatum and Washington's refusal to espouse the Turkish cause. However, despite these calculated shifts in policy, the Soviet Union followed a cautious policy.[30] Especially after the fall of Khrushchev it restricted its policy in such a way as to exclude overt interference in the island's affairs.

The unstable political situation in Greece during the years 1965-7 had an adverse effect on diplomatic initiatives over the Cyprus issue.[31] By consolidating themselves in their barricaded enclaves the Turkish Cypriots sustained the *de facto* segregation of the island. Relations between Athens and Nicosia deteriorated during this period as the minority governments in Greece tried to persuade Nicosia to agree to the implementation of modified versions of the Acheson plan.[32] The intra-Greek rift widened with the seizure of power in Athens by the military on 21 April 1967. The new regime, isolated at home and abroad, desperately sought a resolution[33] of the Cyprus problem in order to raise its own prestige.[34]

Extreme tension between Greece and Turkey built up in mid-November 1967 as a result of a fresh outbreak of communal fighting in Cyprus.[35] Realising the weak international position of the Greek military junta, Turkey sought to shift the balance of power in Cyprus. Ankara, perceiving the communal clashes as Greek inspired,[36] first of all demanded the removal of the Greek soldiers on the island who were there in violation of the Treaty of Alliance.[37] This was a reference to the 10,000 to 15,000 troops which Greece had clandestinely placed on the island in 1964. The Turkish demands were seen in Athens as aimed less at protecting the Turkish Cypriots than at humiliating Greece and scoring a diplomatic victory. The Greek reluctance to meet all of Ankara's terms for ending the new crisis heightened the tension between them.[38]

In a co-ordinated effort to avert war between Greece and Turkey, the United States on 22 November 1967 chose to join with Britain and Canada in proposing a settlement formula. The package proposal presented by Canadian Prime Minister Lester Pearson, however, failed to achieve a consensus which could resolve the dispute.

On 22 November 1967 President Johnson appointed former Deputy Secretary of Defense, Cyrus Vance, as special envoy to prevent the outbreak of war between Greece and Turkey. On the same day U-Thant appointed Rolz-Benett as his special representative to handle the crisis. Two days later Athens and Ankara accepted a third mediator, Manlio Brosio, the Secretary-General of NATO. Johnson authorised the Vance mission with considerable reluctance. The Turkish reaction to his letter in 1964 and the problems of Vietnam made the American President extremely wary of involving America in the Cyprus conflict for a second time. It was argued, however, that the prospect of war between two allies was worth the risk.[39]

Once again the US was forced to play the 'honest broker' in the running dispute between its allies and once more it was forced into an uneasy position between them. The American mediator, by patiently extracting agreement on one point after another, managed to salvage the situation.[40] In his diplomatic efforts Vance was strongly supported by the active participation of Brosio and Rolz-Benett. The international consensus in this instance also included the Soviet Union. The low-key role of the Soviet Union helped the American mediator. Had the Soviet Union intervened in a forceful way, as it had done in 1964, Vance's ability to manoeuvre in the dispute would certainly have been drastically curtailed. In retrospect, the crisis witnessed a modicum of effective co-operation between Washington, NATO and the UN. The 1967 episode also illustrated a number of lessons in crisis control. The most important of these, undoubtedly, was that a superpower which does not abdicate its responsibility for crisis control, and which possesses significant influence over both parties to a conflict, could indeed play a constructive role.[41]

During the years 1968-74 various factors, both local and international, intermeshed to produce a pattern of politics in which force and the threat of force became the dominant features. The formation of the 'National Front' in 1969 and EOKA B[42] in 1971 (both pro-enosis extremist organisations) resulted in intra-Greek-Cypriot hostilities. Suspicions by the Nicosia regime that the Athens military junta was behind these organisations caused a bitter rift between Nicosia and Athens.[43] The Colonels' regime used the clandestine importation into Cyprus of 10,000 light arms from Czechoslovakia on 21 January 1972 as a pretext for intervention in Cypriot issues. Rumours spread of a possible coup by Grivas or the Athens government. In the view of the Nixon administration Athens acted too precipitately over the Czech arms issue.[44] Washington immediately launched an intensive diplomatic offensive to limit the impact of this stroke. Nixon instructed Ambassador Tasca to seek an immediate meeting with the Greek dictator, Papadopoulos, and to warn him against any violence in Cyprus.[45] The Nixon White House had no great admiration for Makarios[46] because of his flirtation with the Eastern bloc and his non-aligned policy which often clashed with American objectives.[47] However, in 1972 Washington decided that more harm than good would be done if the Greek government forced a confrontation on Makarios.

Moreover, the Nixon administration did not want to attract any additional international criticism to itself at a moment when it was negotiating for new naval bases in Greece.[48] Contrary to this line of thought it could be argued that the home-porting negotiations inspired the Papadopoulos regime to seek the overthrow of Makarios. Assuming a non-partisan American reaction, the coup might have succeeded. The timing, however, was not ideal and the coup attempt backfired. With Nixon's historic Peking trip scheduled for 20 February, the State Department did not want to have to face another Cyprus crisis. It was afraid that the Soviet Union would exploit any international incident to minimise the impact of Nixon's trip. On the other hand, after Peking Nixon was preparing for the Moscow summit and SALT I in May 1972. Hence it was imperative to forestall a crisis which could have drawn in the Soviet Union and threatened the prospects of the forthcoming summit. Finally, the strong objection to an Athens-supported coup in Cyprus that was demonstrated by a large cross-section of the international community probably helped to convince American policy-makers of the high risk of the proposed Greek venture.[49] Meanwhile, the Heath Government in Britain categorically stated during the crisis that 'the latest developments in Cyprus were the concern of Greece and Cyprus and did not directly concern Britain'.[50] By abdicating its responsibilities under the treaty the United Kingdom was clearly undermining its residual position in Cyprus, but this action formed a part of the major trend in British policy over Cyprus which had originated in the early 1960s.

II

The 1972 scenario was, however, replayed by the Greek junta in July 1974. On 15 July 1974, a bloody *coup d'état*, staged by the Greek National Guard and EOKA B, ousted the incumbent President Makarios and installed Nicos Sampson, a figurehead President selected by Athens.[51] A wide range of motives could be discerned behind the Greek junta's Cyprus *putsch*. The crisis may have been stoked up originally by the Athens regime largely for internal reasons in order to restore their deteriorating position in the armed forces and in the country as a whole. This explanation appears plausible in the light of the fact that since the fall of Papadopoulos in November 1973 the military had been divided into five factions: the 'royalists' demanded the return of the King, the 'conservatives' were lobbying for a transfer to civilian rule, the 'Quaddafist' faction wanted the junta to shift to a radical nationalist line. The group of the new military strongman, Brigadier Ioannides, firmly believed that for 'purification' reasons Greece still needed a couple of years of dictatorship. Finally, a less defined group called for the restoration to power of the deposed dictator Papadopoulos. It is also probable that the Greek military junta believed that the time was appropriate to pull off the annexation of Cyprus without having to fight a real war. With Turkey convalescing from thirty months of semi-military rule, with the new Ecevit-Erbarkan Coalition Government insecure, and its decision to lift the ban on Opium-poppy cultivation having deeply angered Washington,[52] which at the time was also distracted by the Watergate crisis, the junta must have believed it was a proper moment to take action.

It was symptomatic of the Greek junta's incompetence that it should have assumed that Turkey would not react vigorously to a provocation in Cyprus. The abrupt developments of July 1974 undermined the island's fragile status quo and caused the revival of the dormant Cyprus conflict. The new crisis set off a chain reaction which plunged the island into civil war and threatened the stability of the whole region. The coup gave the pretext for Turkish forces to invade and occupy 40 per cent of the island in two separate offensives which began on 20 July and 14 August 1974 respectively. The move led Greece and Turkey to the brink of war, and induced a renewed arms race between them thus giving rise to a new intramural crisis within NATO. Moreover, in protest over the failure of Washington to halt the Turkish invasion, Greece withdrew from the military structure of NATO. The American Congress later reprimanded Turkey by imposing a controversial arms embargo against it. As a result, Turkey closed American bases on its territory and threatened to pull its forces out of NATO also. The intramural crisis was probably seminal in the collapse of America's Mediterranean policy, after nearly thirty years of undisputed supremacy.

The complex policy dilemmas that have confronted American foreign policy since 1974 in the eastern Mediterranean region are to a large degree a by-product of Washington's disastrous intervention in the Cyprus crisis of that year. In order to achieve a clear perspective of the reasons why American policy in the aftermath of 1974 has been faced with unprecedented problems in the region, an analysis of Kissinger's 'tilt' diplomacy is necessary.

Once again, as was the case in January 1972, the Intelligence community in Washington received information in March 1974 of a forthcoming Athens-inspired coup in Cyprus. At that stage, however, Kissinger instructed the US Ambassador in Athens, Tasca, to avoid admonishing the military regime—a radical departure from the 1972 policy. The increasing instability in Italy, plus the Portuguese crisis and the open Soviet support for Cunhal, now meant that anything that reduced American strength in the Mediterranean was interpreted by Washington simply as an adverse shift in the global balance of power. Kissinger's decision was consistent with US policy to defend the Greek junta and to take timely steps to prop it up whenever it seemed to be in trouble. The rationale for this was the American need for the use of air and naval bases in Greece for the defence of the eastern Mediterranean.

The Nixon administration stressed that 'political differences aside, the United States and Greece had mutual security interests that could not be lightly dismissed'.[53] Despite rising criticism of the Colonels' regime by a large group of Congressmen in the spring of 1974, the White House continued to accord pre-eminence to military and strategic considerations over political and moral values. However, this time the Arab-Israeli conflict in the wake of the October war, rather than NATO security, influenced the State Department to continue to show preference for the Greek Colonels in 1974. Although the Greek government had remained officially neutral during the October war in the Middle East, it fully co-operated with the US insofar as allowing the latter access to American communications facilities in Greece and to other facilities such as Athenai airbase and Souda Bay airfield. There were no restrictions placed on the movement of the vessels of the Sixth Fleet home-ported in the Athens area or on the use of logistic facilities for the re-supply of the Sixth Fleet.[54] American policy-makers had, as a result of the 1973 episode, concluded that this security relationship was an important ingredient in the strength of the political-military posture of the United States in the eastern Mediterranean particularly as it related to the Middle East situation.[55]

In late June 1974 Washington received a flood of a new warnings about the planned coup.[56] This time Kissinger instructed Tasca to warn the junta against such action. Tasca, it has been asserted, failed to pass on the warning to the Greek rulers.[57] On 5 July a blueprint of the proposed coup appeared in the Cypriot paper *Apogeumatini*. The next day the same paper published President Makarios's prophetic letter to General Ghizikis, the Greek President.[58] On 8 July Mr Tetenes (Greek Foreign Minister), Mr Tjounis (Director-General for Political Affairs in the Greek Foreign Ministry) and Mr Vlahos (Secretary General of the Greek Foreign Ministry) resigned in protest over the proposed coup.

Despite all these ominous warnings the White House remained firm in its support for the Greek junta and avoided making an executive decision which could have averted the coup. The State Department failed to warn the Athens government formally, for example, either by calling in the Greek Ambassador in Washington or by despatching a special emissary to Athens or releasing a White House statement which could have had the same effect on the Greek junta.

At the height of the crisis State Department area specialists contended that unless Kissinger denounced the appointment of Sampson his silence might be interpreted by the Turks to signify a virtual takeover of Cyprus by the Greek junta and could prompt Turkey to invade the island. Kissinger rebuffed their counsel partly because he assumed that Makarios had lost power physically and was unlikely to be restored by the UN (which is what the Soviet Union was advocating).[59] Kissinger, in the first few days of the crisis, did nothing to minimise the effect of the coup. On 17 July the State Department rejected the possibility that the coup was of Athens' making. Instead the Department alluded to the coup as an internal situation. It stated: 'In our view, there has not been outside intervention.'[60] Contrary to the American position, the Soviet Union moved speedily to denounce the coup; so did the British.

On 16 and 17 July the American representative in the Security

Council threatened to block any resolution that stated the obvious fact: that Athens had planned and executed the Cyprus *putsch*. The US delegation wasted precious time by indulging in delaying tactics by using the pretext that more facts were needed before it could approve UN action.[61]

British Foreign Office officials emphasized to their American counterparts that it was difficult to put pressure on the Greeks unless the US took a position supporting the restoration of Makarios. In the US however, when the Washington Special Action Group met on 16 and 17 July it opposed the withdrawal of Greek troops since according to it their removal would create a power vacuum. The UK went on record with a demand to the Greek government that it replace 600 or so officers assigned to the Greek National Guard, most of whom had evidently participated in the coup.[62] In addition, the British Foreign Secretary, James Callaghan, tried to persuade Kissinger to exercise America's more powerful influence in Athens and to recognise the dangers in countenancing a regime in Cyprus as unstable and unsavoury as the puppet government of Sampson.

Kissinger's early indifference deprived Washington of credibility or leverage in both Athens and Ankara as the crisis escalated. In the meantime, without American support the British strategy for the resolution of the crisis by diplomatic means was doomed to failure. After Washington had created the impression that it was tilting towards a *de facto* recognition of the Sampson regime, Kissinger sent Joseph Sisco, Under-Secretary for Political Affairs, to Athens and Ankara but apparently without a mandate to put pressure on either government. Washington's 'low profile' diplomacy however failed to come up with positive results. When Sisco reached Athens the junta had virtually disintegrated. While Sisco was trying to persuade Ecevit that Turkey should postpone its invasion for 48 hours the Turkish Prime Minister ordered the invasion.[63] Ankara had no intention of becoming entangled in protracted negotiations that would permit the Sampson regime on Cyprus to consolidate its hold on the island and present the world with a *fait accompli*. Ecevit reasoned that further delay would only create the impression of Turkish weakness in Greek eyes.

On 20 July the Security Council in its resolution 353(1974) demanded an immediate end to foreign military intervention and called upon the three guarantors to enter into negotiations without delay.[64] Ignoring the dictates of resolution 353, Turkey continued its onslaught until a ceasefire was reached on 23 July. In the meantime the military regime in Athens collapsed when the chiefs of staff rejected Ioannides's orders to mobilise Greek forces into action against the Turks.[65] On 24 July Greece returned to civilian rule with ex-Premier Karamanlis heading the new government. An important factor in the armed forces chiefs' decision to turn over power was the reluctance on the part of the United States after 20 July to support their disintegrating military government as well as US pressure that a Greek-Turkish conflict must be avoided at all costs. This lends support to the critics' case that if US pressure had been applied on Athens from the very beginning of the crisis it might have been successful in removing Sampson and defusing the crisis before the Turkish invasion took place.

American shortcomings in policy-making and execution continued in the next phase even after the signing on 30 July of the interim ceasefire agreement by the guarantor powers.[66] While State Department officials insisted that US policy had not tilted towards Turkey, the US did remain publicly silent when the Turkish invasion force expanded its Cyprus bridgehead, violating the ceasefire agreement. On 30 July Makarios warned that unless the US attitude to the invasion was made more clear and more decisive there would be a possibility of serious disturbances in that sensitive area and also within NATO. Just after the first stage of the Geneva talks Assistant Secretary of State for European Affairs Hartman told the Karamanlis Government that the US opposed an early complete withdrawal of the Turkish invasion forces from Cyprus because such action would lead to anarchy.[67] Hartman disregarded the possibility that a temporary increase of UNFICYP could have prevented this from happening. The State Department continued to tilt its policy towards Turkey after 8 August when the Geneva talks resumed. However, on 13 August the talks collapsed and on the 14th Turkish forces resumed full fighting, finally occupying 40 per cent of the island.[68]

The United States reacted to the series of Turkish ceasefire violations by emphasising only restraint rather than condemning the continuation by the invasion forces of 'the peace operation', as Ankara liked to call it. The US also failed to apply pressure on Turkey to revert to the status quo *ante*. Instead, Washington recommended that Makarios not return to Cyprus since it might exacerbate the situation on the island.[69]

During the first half of the August talks, when Kissinger intervened with the Turkish Prime Minister to postpone the deadline for

Turkish demands, he was successful. Again, on 13 August Kissinger asked Ecevit for a further 36-hour extension of the second Turkish ultimatum.[70] This time the Turks refused to budge and walked out of the Geneva talks. The British Foreign Minister declared that the negotiations had broken down because of Turkey's arbitrary and unreasonable refusal to allow a delay so that all parties could consider the plan for a federated government. In calling for a Security Council meeting, Callaghan warned the Turks that there could be no military solution that would stick.[71]

In an incredible display of bad timing, if not bad policy, at the crucial juncture of the talks, the US issued a statement on 13 August which stressed that Washington supported a greater degree of autonomy and protection 'for the Turkish Cypriot community'. It appeared from the timing of the statement and the stress laid on Turkish grievances that Washington was supporting Ankara's position in Geneva.[72] The Turks seized on the statement as American acquiescence in the second Turkish military drive into Cyprus. Makarios believed that the US was fooled by the Turks, or perhaps fell into the trap when Turkey said it would be a limited operation—a police action to restore constitutional order in two days. Perhaps it understood only later what Turkey's actual plans were.[73]

Turkey claimed that the real reason for the second offensive was diplomatic. In the first place the Turks wanted to improve their bargaining posture. When the Greeks finally refused to negotiate at gunpoint, Ankara implemented phase two, arguing that they were simply adhering to the thesis that they could not win at the conference table what they had not won on the battlefield. More likely, it is possible that the Turkish military commanders, afraid that their forces would be in an exposed position if they remained in the Kyrenia-Nicosia wedge, decided to advance. As George points out, military leaders have a strong advocate's role in determining policies and once a diplomatic crisis erupts into warfare their bargaining position within the policy-making arena becomes even stronger.[74] With the absence of any bold initiative on the part of the US to avert the Athens-inspired coup or the Turkish landing, Ankara correctly estimated that Washington would not intervene to stop their second advance.

Only after Greece's withdrawal from the military wing of NATO on 14 August did the US condemn Turkey's renewed assault. Kissinger recognised that there was no easy and permanent way of reconciling the competing interests of Greece and Turkey, and once he had lost the pliable Greek military junta he decided to side with the stronger party, namely Turkey. American thinking was apparently dictated by the conviction that the US could no longer sit on the fence over Cyprus and hope to keep both Greece and Turkey in NATO. Turkey was more important to the US and NATO than the unpredictable government that had just been installed in Greece.

In Western geo-strategic thinking, Greece does not have the same importance as Turkey. It is Turkey which directly borders on the Soviet Union and is an important link in the chain of direct encirclement of the Soviet Union and was geo-strategically and organisationally the link between the NATO and CENTO powers. What is more, Turkey controls the Dardanelles and holds a grip on the Kurdish ethnic group which lies astride the most direct route between the Soviet Union and the Middle East. Moreover, Turkey's neighbours, Iraq and Syria, were already too firmly pro-Soviet for Washington to want to risk angering Ankara into adopting a similar attitude. This resolve was all the more important in the context of Kissinger's post-1973 diplomacy in the Middle East where US prestige was visibly committed to the solution of the Arab-Israeli problem unilaterally with the long-term objective of drastically reducing, if not completely expelling, Soviet influence from this strategic region.

Kissinger rejected accusations by Athens that the US had tilted in favour of Turkey because it regarded its military bases there as more important then those in Greece. He said the situation on Cyprus 'tilted not because of American policy but because of the actions of the previous Greek government which destroyed the balance of forces as it had existed on the island'.[75] Kissinger further argued that during the 1974 crisis the US decided that under the circumstances quiet diplomacy would be the most effective course. Kissinger refused to accept that America was partly responsible for the outcome of events. The Secretary of State, in response to criticism, argued that a threat to cut off military aid to Turkey would have been ineffective as far as stopping the Turkish advance in Cyprus was concerned. Secondly, alluding obliquely to the American interest in Turkey's strategic position bordering the Soviet Union, Kissinger declared that cutting off aid to Turkey would have had the most drastic consequences for the Western alliance.

III

A number of crisis scholars, such as Coral Bell, have asserted that the 1974 Cyprus crisis illustrated the fact that superpower detente reduced the sense of threat for the local adversaries thus reducing the diplomatic leverage of the great powers over their middle or small-power allies.[76] Bell's thesis is certainly valid as far as the 1964 crisis was concerned. In the 1967 and 1974 crises, however, although neither of the local adversaries felt vulnerable to the Soviet Union, the US, nevertheless, still had sufficient influence with both its allies to give it adequate room for manoeuvre. In relation to the Cyprus crisis the institutions that detente neutralised were NATO and the United Nations. In earlier crises both institutions had played constructive mediatory roles. In the case of NATO, detente had limited its ability to act. Kissinger's failure to give his European allies advance information of his China breakthrough or the SALT I negotiations alarmed West European leaders. Moreover, Kissinger failed to give his European allies advance notice of the 1973 nuclear alert over the Middle East. Most of the Western leaders resented Kissinger's secrecy and his summit diplomacy which had the stabilisation of relations between the superpowers as its primary objective. The end result was a deterioration in NATO solidarity and cohesiveness. The neglect of the consultative process had weakened the crisis-management machinery in the Western alliance which had had its roots in the Cold War. In 1974 it utterly failed to work in the case of Cyprus. At the height of the crisis NATO was thus powerless to act. The alliance failed to make any authoritative decisions, and without US support the prospect of NATO members intervening effectively as mediators appeared bleak. The spirit of detente had managed to corrode the political mediatory and consultative machinery which in the days of the Cold War had operated effectively.

On its part, the UN, meeting 15 times and passing eight resolutions, was still unable to effectively intervene in 1974. Although the UN had successfully intervened in the 1960s, the process of detente had relegated this institution also to observer status in the 1970s. During the heyday of the Cold War, the UN, as an influential forum, had attracted the active participation of the great powers. As detente gradually emerged and summitry became the *modus operandi,* the superpowers increasingly by-passed the UN. In the period of detente the UN crisis-management mechanism operated effectively only when the superpowers agreed to lend their support, for example in the authorisation of the UN to implement resolution 242 in the Middle East after the October war. When the superpowers did not see their own interests strongly involved the UN, as the 1974 Cyprus developments demonstrated, was not able to coerce even a minor power such as Greece or a middle power like Turkey.

IV

The 1974 developments radically changed the political environment of Cyprus making the American and UN-sponsored intermediaries' search for a viable and lasting peace extremely difficult. Agreement between the two ethnic communities in Cyprus was a necessary prerequisite for even a minor breakthrough to be achieved. The events of 1974, however, widened the traditional gulf between the Greek and Turkish views on what should be the final status of the island. In November 1974 Makarios declared, 'I can't recognise a fait accompli, I can't legalize with my signature a situation created by the use of force.'[77] However, with 35,000 Turkish troops occupying 40 per cent of the island (but representing in economic terms 70 per cent of the island's production from all sources), plus the fact of 200,000 Greek Cypriot refugees, the local balance of power shifted for the first time in favour of the Turkish Cypriot minority. This change in the status quo, however, blocked the road to any form of effective reconciliation. From their newly acquired position of strength the Turkish Cypriot leadership in 1975 proclaimed the Turkish-occupied area as the 'Turkish Federated State of Cyprus', headed by Rauf Denktash who assumed the position of President. On the other hand, since November 1967 the Greek Cypriot government had followed a policy which stated that 'though enosis was a cherished dream of the Greek Cypriots, its achievement was under the circumstances not feasible'. From then on the Makarios Government had striven to establish a firm basis for an independent state.[78]

The Turkish Cypriot initiative further exacerbated the level of intransigence between the two camps. The Greek Cypriots opposed federation on a geographical basis. Makarios believed it would lead to partition of the island and to 'double enosis', which would mean the end of Cyprus as an independent state. The Greek Cypriots favoured federation but on an administrative basis not a geographical one.

The obstinate negotiating tactics of the Greek and Turkish Cypriot sides resulted in an impasse in the UN-sponsored intercommunal talks despite the fact that in February 1977 Makarios and Denktash had reached an agreement in principle regarding the intercommunal talks. The first point of the agreed guidelines had stated that the two sides were seeking an independent non-aligned, bicommunal Federal Republic.[79] The two sides, however, failed to reach a consensus on the agreed attributes of the Federal Republic.

Shortly after this Makarios renewed his 'long struggle' campaign. This was directed at internationalising the Cyprus problem by recourse to international forums like the UN and the Non-Aligned Conference. Although the diplomatic campaign helped the Greek Cypriot cause, Makarios was aware that in reality the US was the only country which could exert pressure on Turkey and force it to undertake a moderate policy and persuade Ankara to direct Denktash to make concessions. Makarios also believed that if the two superpowers were in agreement they could help solve the issue, but at the same time he realised that since there was no such agreement over the future of Cyprus they would not co-operate towards the solution of the problem.[80]

The death of Makarios in August 1977 led a number of observers to assume that the new Greek Cypriot administration might shift to a moderate position *vis-à-vis* the Turkish Cypriots. However Kyprianou, Makarios's successor, opted to continue the policy he had inherited from the Archbishop, except for a few minor changes. Despite the setback received by them as a result of the US decision to lift the arms embargo against Turkey, the Greek Cypriots continued to demand a return to the status quo *ante* agreements as a basis for new arrangements. On the other hand, the Turkish Cypriots pointed out that the former agreements had failed to work.

Thus, without any prospect of a breakthrough in sight, the problem remains dangerously unresolved. Besides local intransigence, Greek and Turkish policies over Cyprus are also largely responsible for this state of affairs.

V

In one form or another Greece and Turkey have always played a key role in the island's affairs. The latter has always directed major Turkish Cypriot initiatives. Traditionally, Greece has also supported the Greek Cypriots. However, the liaison between Athens and Nicosia has been far from perfect. Since independence the Makarios administration had demonstrated a high degree of independence from Athens. As already shown above, attempts by various Greek governments (especially by the military regime from 1967 to 1974) to impose their particular policies on Nicosia had usually produced intra-Greek rifts.

The Karamanlis administration, conscious of the previous schisms between Athens and Nicosia, has been apprehensive of being involved directly in the issue. Since 1974 it has pursued a policy which assumes that the solution of the Cyprus problem lies not in Athens and Ankara but in Nicosia. In the meantime, Athens has fully supported the Greek Cypriots in their diplomatic campaign to gain support for their position in international forums. Policy priorities, national security and diplomatic tactics also underlie Greece's unprecedented low profile on the Cyprus question. Greek entry into the Common Market, reconciliation between Greece and Turkey and Greek re-entry into NATO ranked above Cyprus in the priority list of the Athens government. In the meantime, by rejecting the Turkish demand to elevate the Cyprus issue to the level of Greco-Turkish relations, the new Greek government improved Greece's diplomatic and strategic position over Turkey. By rejecting the offer Greece enhanced the chances of the US arms embargo against Turkey being prolonged. If it had agreed to the Turkish demand the arms embargo would have probably been lifted earlier. The Treaty of Paris of 10 February 1947 prohibited Greece from fortifying the Dodecanese and other islands close to Turkey.[81] Athens, however, used the Turkish invasion of Cyprus as a pretext to militarise the islands, improving further its diplomatic leverage on the 'Aegean issue'.

The deteriorating economic position of Turkey, plus the 'political vacuum' that continued to prevail in Ankara, ruled out the possibility of any Turkish government directing Denktash to make concessions, despite the fact that the arms embargo was undermining Turkey's strategic position in the Aegean.[82] The National Salvation Party that held the balance of power in the last few years included Cyprus in its irredentist policy and was stridently opposed to any concession over the island.

At the Greco-Turkish summit at Montreux on 10 and 11 March 1978 the Cyprus problem was officially separated from bilateral Greco-Turkish relations.[83] The shift in the Carter administration's position over Cyprus was instrumental in Ankara's policy shift. The lifting of the arms embargo in August 1978 put an end to the regional strategic imbalance.

With Karamanlis under political pressure from the ascending opposition leader, Papandreou, who would like to pull Greece entirely out of NATO and who holds a hawkish position on the Aegean issue, Athens has been forced to harden its stance on the Aegean dispute and over the protracted deliberations in NATO about the special status requested by Greece some three years ago. Turkey, however, has made its consent to this arrangement conditional on a redistribution of NATO's operational jurisdiction in the Aegean sea and air space which had been left under Greek control.[84] Turkey has also made political capital out of Greece's breakthrough with the EEC, symbolised by the agreement in December 1978 by which Athens would become a full member of the community in 1981.[85] Ankara has accused Athens of lobbying in an effort to persuade the EEC states to economically sabotage Turkey. At present, bilateral disputes between Athens and Ankara rank ahead of the Cyprus issue in the priorities of both governments. As of now it seems improbable that Greece and Turkey will focus their attention on reaching a compromise settlement on Cyprus until their differences over the Aegean are solved.

VI

From the very outset of the Cyprus crisis Moscow has held 'NATO circles' responsible for the problem.[86] The Soviet Union opposed all attempts to settle the conflict within NATO as a quasi-internal affair. The primary goal of Soviet policy over Cyprus still continues to be the removal of the British sovereign-base areas and the prevention of a possible division of Cyprus between Turkey and Greece, both NATO members. Despite the presence of AKEL, the strongly pro-Moscow Cypriot Communist Party which commands about 40 per cent of the Greek Cypriot votes, the Soviet Union has charted a cautious course over Cyprus. Moscow, while supporting the Nicosia regime, has restrained itself from overtly interfering in Cypriot affairs. The Soviet policy of 'good neighbourliness' towards Turkey requires Moscow to follow a policy that does not offend Ankara. Hence its twofold approach limits its manoeuvrability over the issue.

Although Britain had a legal right and a moral obligation to find a solution to the dispute, in 1974 it lacked the influence needed to restrain the Turkish invasion. Whitehall argued that circumstances had so changed that the importance of Cyprus to Britain was no longer the same as it was in 1960. Considerations of policy played their part in Britain's non-intervention.[87] The British Foreign Secretary suggested that it was politically inexpedient to seek to uphold the 1960 Treaty of Guarantee because it had become a dead letter. As the former colonial power, Britain was also sensitive to charges of intervention.

Because the British sovereign bases are entrenched in the Cyprus constitution, a decision by Britain to withdraw from them will probably set off another crisis on the island. As *de facto* NATO and American bases, the sovereign areas are important as maritime air bases from which surveillance and other air operations can be conducted for the control of the eastern Mediterranean. The October war in the Middle East added a new dimension to the Mediterranean power-play with the elevation of 'ocean strategy' as a mutual lever of deterrence in the region. High-ambient noise levels in the Mediterranean make sonar conditions extremely difficult creating a problem for anti-submarine operations. Under such conditions effective air surveillance is vital.[88] A strong correlation has always existed between the nature and magnitude of the Soviet naval presence in the Mediterranean and the Soviet Union's ability to meet its requirements for sea and land-based air support.[89] American naval strategists argue that for effective deterrence the US must secure air support for the Sixth Fleet and that, at the same time, it should seek to curtail Soviet access to sea and land-based support.

The Pentagon's policy over Cyprus is a preventive one. Its foremost aim is to prevent the Soviet Union from gaining a foothold in Cyprus. It is also equally interested in maintaining the sovereign British airbases and its own surveillance stations at Yerolakos, Karavas and Nea Milia, plus its vital OTH radar at Mount Olympus.[90]

For the United States, salvaging its relations with Greece and Turkey and putting an end to NATO's intramural crisis related to Greek-Turkish rivalry in the eastern Mediterranean, dwarfed the importance of the Cyprus issue *per se* for its policy-makers. Contrary to Congressional opinion,[91] President Ford argued that the US embargo on arms supply to Turkey had called into question the ability of an ally to continue to fulfil its essential NATO responsibilities and had jeopardised vital defence installations which Turkey and the US jointly maintained.[92] Ford and Kissinger tried to separate the question of the lifting of the embargo from the question of a Cyprus settlement. They emphasised that the embargo would not make for an improvement in relations between Greece and

Turkey without which a Cyprus settlement could not be reached. Security interests prompted the Ford regime to state that no linkage should be made between the Cyprus question and US-Turkish military relations.[93] The embargo, argued Kissinger, had harmful effects on the triangular relations between Turkey, Greece and NATO. Moreover, the embargo delayed the passage of multi-million dollar defence co-operation agreements the administration had negotiated with Greece and Turkey as part of its policy aimed at strengthening NATO's weakened southern flank.[94] With the support of the 'Greek lobby', Congress, however, continued to insist on the formula: 'no Cyprus concessions—no arms agreement.'

The new Carter administration, in a policy review of the eastern Mediterranean, temporarily linked aid to Turkey to concessions from Turkey on Cyprus. The shift undermined further the US-Turkish alliance which was already under stress. The adoption of a more independent and flexible yet tougher foreign policy approach by Ecevit[95] in 1978 however prompted the Carter administration to accept the Kissinger line that preserving the strength of a NATO ally outweighed the moral considerations that Turkey had breached agreements with the US and committed human-rights abuses in Cyprus.[96] On the Carter administration's urging,[97] on 2 August 1978 Congress lifted the controversial embargo by a hairline majority of 208 to 205. The American government, in a move to vindicate by deeds the expectations it had invoked in asking for the lifting of the embargo, proposed in November 1978 a twelve-point plan for a negotiated solution of the Cyprus dispute.[98] Britain and Canada assisted in the drafting of the plan which was designed to break the deadlock. The Greek Cypriots had argued in the past that the issue of the withdrawal of the Turkish army of occupation was non-negotiable. Ankara and the Turkish Cypriots, on the other hand, had stressed that its presence was a deterrent against the Greek Cypriots and that if it were suddenly removed the Turkish Cypriot leverage would be eroded. The precarious internal political balance in Turkey seems to rule out the possibility of Ecevit urging Denktash to seek a compromise solution. Such a move could be used by extremist minority leaders such as Erbarkan and Turkes to topple the government.

It has often been stated in the past that whether the impasse is broken hinges on Western influence, in the sense that NATO powers and particularly the US are in a better position than anyone else to help find a solution to the Cyprus issue.[99] Historical precedents have shown that Washington, after intervening to de-escalate a crisis in Cyprus, has, due to policy shifts, particularly in the context of other new crises drawing its attention elsewhere, shelved the Cyprus issue.

In retrospect it appears that had it not been for the 1974 crisis temporarily institutionalising American involvement, the US would most probably have only shown a temporary interest in the problem. With the lifting of the arms embargo American foreign policy has returned to its traditional position of placing its security interests, as well as its interest in improving relations between Greece and Turkey in the name of NATO cohesion, ahead of a search for a solution to the Cyprus problem.

VII

The political upheaval in neighbouring Iran in late 1978 and early 1979 and the subsequent climate of political uncertainty that has prevailed in that region has augmented Turkey's strategic importance in the area. The fear that Turkey might go the way of Iran has caused Washington to focus special attention on Ankara. With a severe economic recession and mounting political violence and governmental instability confronting the 'sick man of the Bosphorous', the possibility that Turkey might drift towards a non-aligned posture[100] unless it received sufficient Western support has evoked Washington's special interest in Turkey, despite assurances by Ecevit that his country will remain in NATO. In February 1979 the Carter administration proposed $300 million in military and economic aid for Turkey during the next fiscal year, while at the same time negotiating a new five-year defence co-operation agreement with Ankara.

With American leverage diminished in Ankara as a result of regional instability, it seems most unlikely that Washington will push Ankara at this juncture to make concessions over Cyprus.[101] Moreover, given the continuous tension in Greco-Turkish relations, there seems to be little chance of a Cyprus solution emerging from a joint Greco-Turkish initiative.

The prospect of a solution to the Cyprus problem in the near future, therefore, appears bleak. A large portion of the responsibility for this continuing deadlock must be shared by the two regional mentors of the Cypriot communities—Greece and Turkey—who have put other issues, vital to their national security and regime survival, ahead of the search for an equitable solution of the island's problems. It must also be shared in substantial measure by the NATO powers, particularly the US. The latter, as the major source of external support for both Athens and Ankara, has put its global strategic considerations in the eastern Mediterranean and the Middle East far ahead, in terms of its priorities, the resolution of the Cyprus conflict. But then that is the nature of international politics where larger problems—strategic and political—tend to take precedence over smaller local issues; and great powers, whether in the regional or the global sense, are more concerned with improving their own strategic and political positions in their respective operational arenas and have little time to spare to contribute to a solution of primarily local issues—that is until another crisis is triggered off in the region as a result of the non-solution of what might have appeared a minor problem. Cyprus provides no exception to the rule.

Notes

1. For the pre-independence history of Cyprus see the following works: Sir George Hill, *History of Cyprus* (4 vols., Cambridge University Press, Cambridge, 1940, 1948 and 1952); Sir Harry Luke, *Cyprus Under the Turks 1571-1878* (Oxford University Press, London, 1921); Doros Alastos, *Cyprus in History: A Survey of 5,000 years* (Zeno, London, 1955).
2. Excellent accounts of this arrangement appear in D.E. Lee, *Great Britain and the Cyprus Convention Policy of 1878* (Harvard University Press, Cambridge, Mass., 1934), especially pp. 77-86; Capt. C.W.J. Orr, *Cyprus Under British Rule* (Scott, London, 1918). For full text of the convention see pp. 35-9.
3. Besides the strategic factors, Cyprus was also offered as a security to Britain for the Ottoman debt. See D.C. Blaisdell, *European Financial Control of the Ottoman Empire* (Columbia University Press, New York, 1929), pp. 114-17.
4. See no. 701—Treaty of Peace, signed at Lausanne, 24 July 1923. *League of Nations—Treaty Series*, vol. 28, no. 1 (1924), p. 12299.
5. The 'enosis' movement started in the middle of the nineteenth century, its leaders being the high dignitaries of the Cypriot Orthodox Church. When Britain took over the island, the movement was already flourishing. Although the Greek Cypriots soon became discontented with British rule, the Greek government advised them to be patient, for in view of Greco-Turkish negotiations over Epirus and Thessaly, Greece could ill afford to offend the British. In October 1915 the British Foreign Secretary, Sir Edward Grey, offered to cede Cyprus to Greece if Greece joined the Allies. This offer was refused and Cyprus remained in British hands. With the exception of the 1931 riots for enosis the issue lay dormant until a church-held plebiscite on 15 January 1950 registered a 95.7 per cent Greek Cypriot vote in favour of Union with Greece and revived the enosis movement. See *Cyprus: Background to Enosis* (Royal Institute of International Affairs (RIIA), London, February 1958), pp. 2-10 and E. Kofos, *Greece and the Eastern Crisis 1875-1878* (Institute for Balkan Studies, Thessaloniki, 1975).
6. On the dispute over bipartite negotiations see A.A. Kyrou, *Hellenike Exoterike Politike* (Zombolas, Athens, 1955), pp. 272-6; Nancy Crawshaw, *The Cyprus*

Revolt (Allen and Unwin, London, 1978), pp. 71-89; S.G. Xydis, *Cyprus Reluctant Republic* (Mouton, The Hague, 1973), pp. 40-1, 63-4 and, 'Toward "Toil and Moil" in Cyprus', *The Middle East Journal*, vol. 20, no. 1 (Winter 1966), pp. 6-9.

7. For an analysis of the Cyprus problem as a UN issue, see the following works: S.G. Xydis, *Cyprus, Conflict and Conciliation 1954-1958* (The Ohio State University Press, Columbus, 1967) and 'The UN General Assembly as an Instrument of Greek Policy: Cyprus 1954-1958', *The Journal of Conflict Resolution*, vol. 12, no. 2 (1968), pp. 141-58; N. Rosenbaum, 'Cyprus and the United Nations: An Appreciation of Parliamentary Diplomacy', *Canadian Journal of Political Science*, vol. 33, no. 2 (May 1967); and U.H. Bayulken, 'The Cyprus Question and the United Nations', *Dis Politica* (Ankara), vol. 4, nos. 2-3 (1974), pp. 71-142.

8. About the EOKA campaign see G. Grivas-Dighenis, *Apomnimonevmata* (Athens, 1961); D. Alastos, *Cyprus Guerrilla* (Heinemann, London, 1960); R. Stephens, *Cyprus A Place of Arms: Power Politics and Ethnic Conflict in the Eastern Mediterranean* (Pall Mall, London, 1966).

9. See Sir Anthony Eden, *Full Circle* (Cassell, London, 1960), p. 400; Harold Macmillan, *Tides of Fortune 1945-55* (Macmillan, London, 1969), pp. 664-5.

10. On 19 December 1956, the Secretary of State for the Colonies, Mr Lennox-Boyd, remarked that 'the exercise of self-determination should be considered on a communal basis and therefore partition must be included as one future possibility'. See *Cyprus: The Dispute and the Settlement* (RIIA, London, June 1959), p. 32; Xydis, *Cyprus Reluctant Republic*, p. 153.

11. During the period 1955-8 the British government offered a succession of proposals for the future. However, it should be stressed that the British plans, including the Winster constitution of 1948, the Radcliffe plan, and the Macmillan-Foot plan were drafted in a way that assured the British, and secondarily the Turkish and Greek governments, a maximum of manoeuvre in Cypriot foreign affairs, defence and finance. See Sir Hugh Foot, *A Start in Freedom* (Hodder and Stoughton, London, 1964), p. 158; Linda Miller, *Cyprus: The Law and Politics of Civil Strife* (Occasional Papers in International Affairs, Harvard University Press, no. 19, June 1968).

12. Duncan Sandys, Minister of Defence is supposed to have made a strategic re-evaluation of Cyprus in the summer of 1957. Command paper 124, issued in April 1957, presented a new approach to Britain's defence needs that already had implicit in it a shift in this role expected for Cyprus. British military policy was changed to centre on integration of British with NATO forces, dependence on a nuclear deterrent, and reduction of the armed services to small and mobile professional contingents. See J. Frankel, *British Foreign Policy 1945-1973* (Oxford University Press, London, 1975), pp. 290-306. Field Marshal Lord Harding, 'The Cyprus Problem in Relation to the Middle East', *International Affairs*, vol. 34, no. 3 (July 1958), p. 293; P. Darby, *British Defence Policy East of Suez 1947-1968* (Oxford University Press, London, 1973), p. 121; N. Rosenbaum, 'Success in Foreign Policy: The British in Cyprus 1878-1960', *Canadian Journal of Political Science* (December 1970), p. 623.

13. See *Discussion on Cyprus in the North Atlantic Treaty Organisation, Sept.-Oct. 1958, Command Paper 566* (HMSO, London, 1959).

14. See Xydis, *Cyprus Reluctant Republic*, pp. 477-519.

15. For example, according to Article 62 a ratio of 70 per cent Greeks and 30 per cent Turks was provided for communal representation in the House. Article 46 provided for the same ratio in the Council of Ministers, and Article 123 provided similar communal participation in the Public Service. For an in-depth legal analysis, see S. Kyriakides, *Cyprus: Constitutionalism and Crisis Government* (University of Pennsylvania Press, Philadelphia, 1968), especially pp. 53-103.

16. The Treaty of Guarantee, a pact between the United Kingdom, Greece and Turkey gave the guarantor powers the constitutional right to act as 'philosopher

kings' in the constitutional development of the republic. Any developments in Cyprus interpreted as detrimental to the interests of any of the three guarantors could lead to collective or unilateral action directed towards re-establishing the state of affairs created by the treaty. Similarly, the Treaty of Alliance, a defence treaty between Cyprus, Greece and Turkey, made provision for permanent stationing of Greek and Turkish troops in Cyprus. For texts of the treaties see *Cyprus Command Paper 1093* (HMSO, London, 1960), pp. 86-7 (Treaty of Guarantee), pp. 88-90 (Treaty of Alliance).

17. See Makarios, 'Proposals to Amend the Cyprus Constitution', *Cyprus Today*, vol. 1, no. 6 (November-December, 1963).

18. On British initiative a conference was called for 15 January 1964 to be held at London. The conference, attended by the three guarantor powers and the two Cypriot communities, however, failed to achieve a permanent peace settlement. For a detailed account see E. Weintal and C. Bartlett, *Facing the Brink: An Intimate Study of Crisis Diplomacy* (Scribners, New York, 1967), pp. 18-19.

19. See *Department of State Bulletin* (16 March 1964), p. 399.

20. Under the proposed plan a NATO recruited peacekeeping force of 10,000 men under British command with political guidance from a North Atlantic non-NATO country. See P. Windsor, 'NATO and the Cyprus Crisis', *Adelphi Papers*, no. 14 (November 1964), pp. 13-14.

21. 'Chairman Khrushchev's letter to President Johnson', *Department of State Bulletin* (23 March 1964), pp. 446-8; 'N.S. Khrushchev's message on Cyprus', *U.S.S.R. Mission to the U.N.* (press release, no. 4, 7 February 1964).

22. Linda Miller, *World Order and Local Disorder* (Princeton University Press, New Jersey, 1967), especially pp. 122-6.

23. U.N. Doc. S/5575 (March 4, 1964), especially para. 5.

24. George Ball, 'The Responsibilities of a Great Power', *Department of State Bulletin* (5 September 1964), pp. 476-7; 'Undersecretary Ball comments on Cyprus situation', *Department of State Bulletin* (31 August 1964), p. 301.

25. For Johnson's ultimatum see 'Correspondence between President Johnson and Prime Minister Inonu', *The Middle East Journal*, vol. 20, no. 3 (Summer 1966), pp. 386-93.

26. V. Coufoudakis, 'United States Foreign Policy and the Cyprus Question: A Case Study in Cold War Diplomacy' in M.A. Attalides (ed.), *Cyprus Reviewed* (Zavallis, Nicosia, 1977), especially p. 113.

27. This plan proposed to safeguard American interests in the dispute. It contained the following points: first, enosis of Cyprus with Greece in return for a thirty to fifty-year lease of a military base to the Turks. The Turks would have sovereignty over the base whose size was to be approximately equal to one-fifth of the island; second, the cantonisation of the island creating two parallel governmental structures, one for each of the two ethnic groups; third, a joint military command for Greece and Turkey. A. Papandreou, *Democracy at Gunpoint: The Greek Front* (Penguin, Harmondsworth, 1973), p. 139.

28. A. Xydis *et. al.*, *Ho Makarios Kai Hoi Symmachoi Tou* (Gutenberg, Athens, 1973), especially pp. 91-7.

29. 'Aggressive Schemes Against Cyprus', *Current Soviet Documents*, vol. 2, no. 6 (10 February 1964), p. 12.

30. For an analysis of Soviet policy towards Cyprus see T.W. Adams and A.J. Cottrell, *Cyprus Between East and West* (Johns Hopkins Press, Baltimore, 1968).

31. Cyprus was partly implicated in the Greek political upheaval during 1965-7 through the ASPIDA affair. ASPIDA (shield) was the name of an alleged left-wing military conspiratorial group that supposedly drew its membership principally among the Greek forces in Cyprus. See Papandreau, *Democracy at Gunpoint*, p. 151.

32. The minority governments tried to negotiate a bilateral solution of the Cyprus problem with Ankara. Cyprus was not a party to these secret negotiations

which had been instigated by the US. The most significant of the negotiations was the one held in Paris on 16 December 1966 between the Greek and Turkish foreign ministers. The meeting resulted in the signing of a protocol which provided *inter alia* for enosis. A major Greek concession involved the granting to Turkey of the Dhekelia military base (one of the two British sovereign-base areas). As a further provision, Greece offered the 'Karagatch triangle', a strategic area on the Evros river that greatly interested the Turks. This protocol was never implemented as the Stephanopoulos Minority Government fell some 48 hours later for reasons unrelated to the Cyprus issue. See C. Christides (psd) (Damonides), *Akros Aporreton: To Protocollo Tes 17 Dekembriou 1966* (Athens, 1973); S. Gregoriades, *Istoria Tes Synhhronou Ellados 1941-1974* (Kapopoulos, Athens, 1975), vol. 5, especially pp. 158-9; *Akropolis* (Athens daily), 2 March 1975.

33. Mr Muley, the British Minister of State for Foreign Affairs, confirmed the report that shortly after the military seized power, the new leaders offered the Turks a settlement on lines which corresponded to the NATO solution proposed by Dean Acheson in 1964. *The Times*, 28 July 1967.

34. The Military regime's overtures to Turkey led to a Greco-Turkish summit over the Cyprus question at Kesan and Alexandroupolis on 9-10 September. However, with the Greeks proposing enosis and the Turks invoking the Zurich-London agreements the talks eventually collapsed. A. Xydis provides a useful analysis of the talks in his article, 'The Military Regime's Foreign Policy' in R. Clogg and G. Yannopoulos (eds.), *Greece Under Military Rule* (Secker and Warburg, London, 1972), especially p. 195. See also *Cyprus Mail*, 11 September 1967.

35. For an authoritative account of the communal crisis of 1967 see M. Harbottle, *The Impartial Soldier* (Oxford University Press, London, 1970), pp. 145-61. Also 'Special Report of the Secretary-General on Recent Developments in Cyprus', Security Council Official Records, 22nd year, supplement for Oct-Nov-Dec. 1967, UN Doc. S/8248.

36. On 16 and 17 November the Turkish National Assembly and Senate met in joint session and voted the government authority to use the Turkish armed forces abroad if circumstances required their use. *Middle East Record*, vol. 3 (1967), citing the Turkish daily *Cumhuriyet*, 16-17 November 1967.

37. T. Ehrlich, *Cyprus 1958-1967: International Crises and the Role of Law* (Oxford University Press, New York, 1974), p. 105.

38. Cemal Tural, who was chief of the Turkish General Staff during the 1967 crisis, wrote later that the cabinet took the decision to intervene in Cyprus but then decided to postpone the action. F. Ahmad, citing Yeni Ortam, in his book *The Turkish Experiment in Democracy 1950-1975* (Hurst, London, 1977), p. 415.

39. L.D. Battle and D.P. Williams, *Cyprus: A Decade of Crises* (The Middle East Institute, Washington DC, 1974), p. 8. Battle, former Assistant Secretary of State for Near Eastern and South Asian Affairs, was also the man in charge of Washington's 'crisis center', or operations room, during the November crisis.

40. In his nine-day stint Mr Vance travelled three times to Turkey, four times to Greece and twice to Cyprus. *The Economist*, 9 December 1967, pp. 1031-2.

41. *Strategic Survey 1967* (Institute for Strategic Studies, London, 1967).

42. The EOKA B was modelled on the pattern of EOKA. S. Papageorgiou, *Makarios: Poreia Dia Piros Kai Siderou* (Ladias, Athens, 1976), especially pp. 33-40.

43. For EOKA B-Greek government liaison see N. Kakaounaki, *2650 Meronykhta Synomosias* (Papazisi, Athens, 1976), vol. 2, pp. 136-40.

44. The following articles and documents are quite informative on the 1972 crisis: K. Mackenzie, 'Cyprus: The Ideological Crucible', *Conflict Studies*, no. 26 (September 1972); N. Brown, 'Cyprus: Victory in the first round for His Beatitude', *New Middle East* (May 1972); UN Doc. S/10564, UN Doc. S/10564/Add. 1, UN Doc. S/10564/Add. 2.

45. 'Testimony of Ambassador Henry Tasca', *Pike Select Committee on Intelligence, U.S. House of Representatives*, 94 Congress, 1st Session, p. 1537.

46. Quite possibly the CIA would have liked Makarios to be toppled in favour of somebody more NATO-oriented.

47. For example, Cyprus was one of the seven countries that had reneged on their commitments on 25 October 1971 which led to the US losing the fight to keep Taiwan in the UN, *Washington Post*, 27 October 1971. In 1969 Nixon ordered that all US foreign aid to Cyprus be cut off after Makarios refused to co-operate in restricting Cypriot shipping to North Vietnam. Richard Nixon, *RN: The Memoirs of Richard Nixon* (Macmillan, Melbourne, 1978), p. 1047.

48. Throughout February 1972 US officials negotiated with the Hellenic navy. Greek government authorisation was granted in March 1972. Declassified text of HNC letter, 4th Staff Office, K 575/2/72 of 25 March 1972. See *Implementation of Homeporting in Greece, H of R Committee on Foreign Affairs, Subcommittee on Europe*, 93 Congress, 1st Session, especially pp. 151-67.

49. The Soviet Union reiterated that the Greek government's interference in Cyprus was part of US policy aimed at converting Cyprus into a Western military base. Similarly, President Sadat of Egypt accused the US of weaving a plot against the Government of President Makarios. For Soviet commentary see *BBC SWB SU/3923/A4/1-5*, 18 February 1972. For Sadat's remarks see 'Anwar Sadat's speech to the Arab Socialist Union', *BBC SWB SU/3918/A4/3*, 18 February 1972.

50. *BBC SWB ME/3918/C/2*, 18 February 1972; *BBC SWB ME/3921/C/2*, 22 February 1972.

51. The following works give good accounts of the 1974 Cyprus crisis from various perspectives: N. Sarris, *I Alli Plevra: Politiki Kronografia Tis Eisvolis Stin Kypro* (Grammi, Athens, 1977), vol. 1; S. Pseharis. *Ta Paraskinia Tis Allagis* (Papazisi, Athens, 1975); S. Anastatakou, *Thyella Stin Athina* (Pleias, Athens, 1974); *Cyprus 1974* (special issue of *Dis Politika*), vol. 4, nos. 2-3 (1974); L. Stern, *The Wrong Horse: Intervention and the Failure of American Diplomacy* (Quadrangle, New York, 1977).

52. W.J. Spain, 'The United States, Turkey and the Poppy', *The Middle East Journal* (Summer 1975), pp. 295-309.

53. R.P. Davies, 'United States Policy Toward Greece', *Department of State Bulletin* (9 August 1971), p. 161.

54. A.A. Hartman and R.P. Davies, 'The Impact of the Middle East Crisis on the Atlantic Alliance', *Department of State Bulletin* (18 March 1974), pp. 279-82.

55. In bolstering the Colonels' regime the United States ventured on a policy which was far from secure. If the Colonels lost power, the US, because of its close association with them, risked suffering a serious political setback and even ran the risk of being deprived of Greek naval facilities. For a critique of Washington's foreign policy towards Greece and Cyprus see J.C. Campbell, 'The United States and the Cyprus Question, 1974-1975' in V. Coufoudakis (ed.), *Essays on the Cyprus Conflict* (Pella, New York, 1976), pp. 13-26 and 'The Mediterranean Crisis', *Foreign Affairs*, vol. 53 no. 4 (July 1975), pp. 605-23.

56. During the period May-June 1974 former US Ambassador to Cyprus Belcher was told in very strong terms that there was documentary evidence available to the government of Cyprus that the CIA was financing EOKA B through money passed through Ioannides in Athens. 'Testimony of Ambassador Belcher', *Pike Select Committee on Intelligence*, p. 760; L. Pain, *The CIA at work* (Hale, London, 1977), pp. 135-42.

57. 'Tasca Testimony', *Pike Select Committee on Intelligence*, pp. 1563-5.

58. *Apogeumatini* (Nicosia daily), 5 and 6 July 1974.

59. *Washington Post*, 18 July 1974.

60. *New York Times*, 19 July 1974; 'Tasca Testimony', *Pike Select Committee on Intelligence*, p. 1568.

61. See statements by Ambassador Scali, *UN Monthly Chronicle*, vol. 2, no. 8 (August-September 1974), p. 8; *USUN* press release 88, dated 16 July 1974.

62. *The Times*, 18 July 1974.

63. See 'Cyprus Operation received full Cabinet support', *Translations Western Europe*, no. 563 (1974), citing *Milliyet*, 4 September 1974.

64. UN Doc. S/RES 353.

65 At the same time in Cyprus Sampson abdicated. Glafcos Clerides, president of the House of Representatives during the Makarios period, assumed temporarily the leadership of the government according to the 1960 constitution. Makarios returned to Cyprus in December 1974.

66. For full text of Geneva declaration see *The Times*, 31 July 1974.

67. *Pike Select Committee on Intelligence*, pp. 1294, 1558, 1559, and 1568.

68. For a critique of US diplomacy during phase two, see the series of well-informed articles by S. Karnow, 'Premier Ecevit's Perspective on Cyprus: Tough Turkey', *The New Republic* (5 October 1974), pp. 12-15; 'America's Mediterranean Bungle', *Atlantic Monthly* (February 1975), pp. 6-14; 'Foul-up in the Mediterranean', *The New Republic* (7 September 1974), pp. 6-7.

69. *Pike Select Committee on Intelligence*, p. 1558.

70. *New York Times*, 14 August 1974.

71. *The Times*, 15 August 1974.

72. 'Cyprus 1974', *Hearings before the House Foreign Affairs Committee, Subcommittee on Europe*, 93 Congress, 2nd Session, 1974; 'Crisis on Cyprus: 1974', *Study Mission Report of the Subcommittee on Refugees of the Senate Committee on the Judiciary*, 93 Congress, 2nd Session, 1974.

73. Makarios interview with Oriana Fallaci, November 1974, in *Interview with History* translated by John Shepley (Liveright, New York, 1976), pp. 315-6.

74. A.L. George *et al.*, *The Limits of Coercive Diplomacy: Laos-Cuba-Vietnam* (Little Brown, Boston, 1971), pp. 4-5.

75. Text of Secretary of State Kissinger's news conference of 19 August 1974.

76. Coral Bell, *The Diplomacy of Detente: The Kissinger Era* (Martin Robertson, London, 1977), p. 155.

77. Fallaci, *Interview with History*, p. 315.

78. *The Times*, 5 October 1971.

79. *Cyprus Intercommunal Talks: New Series, First Round Vienna, 31 March-7 April 1977* (Nicosia, April 1977). See also Makarios's interview in *The Middle East* (February 1977).

80. Text of President Makarios's last press conference, 21 July 1977.

81. *United Nations Treaty Series*, vol. 49 (1950), p. 134.

82. Since the discovery of oil deposits in the Aegean in 1973 Greece and Turkey have periodically threatened to go to war over the demarcation of the Continental Shelf in the Aegean. The letter of the relevant international law was mostly on Greece's side. See L. Gross, 'The Dispute between Greece and Turkey in the Aegean', *The American Journal of International Law*, vol. 71, no. 1 (January 1977), pp. 31-59; G. Timagenous, *To Dikaion Tis Thalassis Kai Tò Aigaion* (Athens, 1975).

83. On Greco-Turkish relations see G. Maurou, *Ethnikoi Kindynoi* (Atlantis, Athens, 1978); M. Ploumidi, *I Ellinotourkiki Krisi* (Estias, Athens, 1975).

84. *The Times*, 7 October 1978.

85. *International Herald Tribune*, 22 December 1978.

86. *The Current Digest of the Soviet Press*, vol. 26, no. 32 (1974), pp. 16-17.

87. For an outline of the official government position during the crisis see *Report from the Select Committee on Cyprus Session 1975-1976* (HMSO, London, April 1976).

88. For strategic assessments of the Mediterranean see the following works: Vice-Admiral C. Margaritis, 'A Strategic Analysis of the Eastern Mediterranean and

the Black Sea', *United States Naval Institute Proceedings* (March 1973), especially pp. 122-4; Admiral I.C. Kidd, 'View from the Bridge of the Sixth Fleet Flagship', *United States Naval Institute Proceedings* (February 1972), p. 25; Admiral H. Rivero, 'Why a U.S. Fleet in the Mediterranean?', *United States Naval Institute Proceedings* (May 1977), p. 69; J.W. Lewis Jr, *The Strategic Balance in the Mediterranean* (American Enterprise Institute for Public Policy Research, Washington DC, 1976).

89. R.G. Weinland, 'Land Support for Naval Forces: Egypt and the Soviet Escadra 1962-1976', *Survival*, vol. XX, no. 2 (March-April 1978), especially pp. 73-6.

90. The OTH is a useful tool both for military and for oceanographic and ionospheric studies. As well as detecting aircraft and missiles, OTH also reveals nuclear bursts. P. Laurie, 'An Eye on the Enemy Over the Horizon', *New Scientist* (7 November 1974), pp. 420-4.

91. For the pros and cons of the arms embargo debate see 'Controversy Over US Military Aid to Turkey', *Congressional Digest*, vol. 54, no. 4 (April 1975), pp. 97-128.

92. 'US Military Aid to Turkey', *Weekly Compilation of Presidential Documents*, vol. 11, no. 28 (1975), pp. 722-3.

93. Defense Department strategists assumed that US military influence in the Middle East would suffer substantially if Turkey were to turn her back on the US. Taken in their entirety, US intelligence facilities in Turkey were extremely valuable. America used these facilities to monitor Soviet compliance with the ABM agreement and needed their renewed availability in maintaining Soviet compliance with the pending SALT II agreement. R.F. Ellsworth (Assistant Secretary for International Security Affairs), 'Strategic Importance of Turkey', *Outlook* (Ankara), no. 518 (17 November 1976); *Greece and Turkey: Some military implications related to NATO and the Middle East*, House Committee on International Relations, a study prepared by John M. Collins for the Special Subcommittee on Investigations, Washington DC. 28 February 1975.

94. P.C. Habib, 'Department Urges Congressional Approval of Agreement with Turkey on Defense Cooperation', *Department of State Bulletin* (4 October 1976), pp. 424-7.

95. B. Ecevit, 'Turkey's Security Policies', *Survival* (September-October 1978) pp. 203-5.

96. On the shift in the Carter administration's policy, see M. Kondracke, 'The Greek Lobby', *The New Republic* (19 April 1978), pp. 14-16.

97. 'The Situation in Cyprus', *Weekly Compilation of Presidential Documents* (21 July 1978), p. 1331; 'The President's News Conference of 14 June', *Weekly Compilation of Presidential Documents* (14 June 1978), p. 1091.

98. The US initiative was the outcome of shuttle diplomacy by Deputy Secretary of State Warren Christopher. *International Herald Tribune*, 30 November 1978.

99. Speech by the President of the Cyprus Republic, Mr Spyros Kyprianou, 28 February 1978.

100. B. Lewis, 'Turkey Turns Away', *The New Republic* (18 February 1978), pp. 18-20.

101. In March 1979 Turkey followed the example of Pakistan and Iran and withdrew from CENTO. Thus, with Turkey in an anti-Western mood, Washington cannot risk agitating an unstable government, which could retaliate by deciding to withdraw from NATO either temporarily or permanently.

6 The Horn of Africa*

MOHAMMED AYOOB

I

The major contradiction in the regional politics of the Horn of Africa has been the conflict between Ethiopia and Somalia which has assumed various manifestations at various times. It has sometimes manifested itself in the local Somali resistance in the Ogaden to Amharic overlordship and at other times in the clash of nationalist Somali irredentism with Ethiopian imperial ambitions. The involvement of global powers in support of their client states has given this conflict yet another dimension and made it an integral part of East-West rivalry for the political allegiance of the grey areas of the globe, i.e. the Third World. While other sources of conflict, the Eritrean one foremost among them, have affected the course of political developments in the Horn, it is the Somali-Ethiopian rivalry which has left the most lasting impression on the politics of this region and has proved to be the most important regional conflict as far as its implications for the international system are concerned. This chapter, therefore, will be concerned almost exclusively with the Somali-Ethiopian conflict. References to other conflicts in the region will be made only when they are considered essential to the central theme of the chapter.

II

The Somali offensive of 1977-8 in the Ogaden, the Ethiopian retreat and then the Ethiopian-Cuban-Soviet counter-offensive which restored the status quo *ante*, together form an important turning point in the recent political history of the Horn, symbolising as they do the deep-rooted nature of regional rivalries as well as the ephemeral character of international alignments in the Third World. These events have also provided us with the incentive to

*In preparation for this chapter, the author has drawn heavily on his earlier work, *The Horn of Africa: Regional Conflict and Super Power Involvement* (Canberra Papers on Strategy and Defence, no. 18, Strategic and Defence Studies Centre, Australian National University, 1978).

take a closer look at the domestic, regional and international aspects of the crisis (or series of crises) that has overtaken that part of the world. These events have also demonstrated the validity of the thesis that the problems of post-colonial nation-building in vast areas of the Third World have been compounded by the vagaries of colonially-drawn borders which cut across ethnic, linguistic, tribal and sometimes (as in the case of Somalia) national boundaries. However, these borders are considered sacrosanct not only by the European metropolitan powers involved in their establishment but also by Third World ruling elites. Since most, if not all, of these countries are faced by potential threats of secessionism in one form or another, the elites who have fallen heir to the colonial powers tend to impose a degree of sanctity on these boundaries which is often difficult to sustain either in terms of actual control of peripheral areas or of real, as opposed to assumed, interaction within the 'political community' encompassed by a particular boundary.

Africa, more than any other continent, is replete with instances of such problems which derive their origins from the vagaries of colonial boundaries. The conflict on the Horn dramatically symbolises these problems. The roots of the conflict go back both to the European colonial experience which this part of Africa underwent in the last half of the nineteenth and the first half of the twentieth centuries as well as to the ambitions of a 'native' empire—Abyssinia, later to be known as Ethiopia—to forestall its European competitors by acquiring a large portion of Somali-inhabited territory between the Abyssinian highlands and the Red Sea, forming almost one-third of present-day Ethiopia.[1]

In the closing years of the nineteenth century the Shoan Emperor Menelik persuaded his major European competitors to acquiesce in accepting Abyssinia's 'historical' claims to the region in return for his acceptance of the legitimacy of their rule over the Somalilands. Menelik's strategic importance, particularly to the British, was greatly increased by the Mahdist uprising in the Sudan. This led to the British acceptance of a large part of Menelik's claims and the surrender in 1897 of large expanses of the British Somali Protectorate to the Abyssinian monarch. But, as Lewis points out, as of 1897 no Ethiopian claims could be supported 'by a firm Ethiopian occupation on Somali soil beyond Jigjiga'.[2] He goes on to point out that

> It was not until 1934, when an Anglo-Ethiopian boundary commission attempted to demarcate the boundary, that British

> protected Somalis became aware of what had happened and expressed their sense of outrage in disturbances which cost one of the commissioners his life.[3]

On the basis of these and other facts, W. Michael Reisman of the Yale Law School has gone to the extent of arguing that Ethiopia's claims to the Ogaden have no legal foundation since they are based on the Anglo-Ethiopian Treaty of 1897 which itself was null and void. Reisman argues that the 1897 treaty

> was void because it presumed an authority which the Somalis had never accorded Great Britain. The Somalis gave no authority to the British to transfer Somali territory to another state. Ironically, the British had committed themselves to protect the Somali territory and this was the manifest reason for the Protectorate. In attempting to transfer the land to Ethiopia, the British were acting without competence, exceeding their jurisdiction and concluding an agreement without the participation of the Central party. Moreover, the treaty violated the fundamental trust which was expressed in the protectorate Agreements on which the British rested their authority with regard to the Somali Territory.[4]

The dispute over the Ogaden, however, did not hit world headlines until after 1960 when the Somali Republic was established as an independent state by the union of Italian and British Somalilands.

The formation of the Somali state was the culminating point of the development of national consciousness among the people of the Somali coast which can be traced back at least to the emergence in the 1890s of Sheikh Mohammed Abdille Hassan who combined the roles of religious messiah and national leader in his charismatic personality—a Somali Mahdi in short. It is no matter for surprise that Sheikh Abdille Hassan's phenomenal rise coincided with the extension, at least formally, of Menelik's imperial authority to the Ogaden and the consolidation of European colonial possessions on the Somali coast. The first conscious rumblings of Somali nationalism were, in fact, provoked by these very events. This embryonic consciousness was nurtured, on the one hand, by growing opposition to European colonial power on the coast, which became more and more evident as the three occupying powers—Britain, Italy and France—found themselves involved in the Second World War, and on the other by the harsh treatment meted out to the Somali inhabitants of the Ogaden by the Christian Amharic rulers of Addis Ababa—a treatment which was often a mixture of feudal condescension and military plunder.

The national aspirations of the Somali people received a boost both during and immediately after the Second World War, when all areas inhabited by the Somalis, with the exception of French-ruled Djibouti, came under the control of a single power, viz. Great Britain. Britain occupied Italian Somaliland and also took over administrative control of Ethiopia from the retreating Italians, pending the return of Emperor Haile Selassie. To Italian and British Somalilands and the Ogaden were added the Northern Frontier District (NFD) of Kenya, which itself was a British colony. The return of the Ethiopian Emperor to Addis Ababa in 1941, after the expulsion of Italy from the Horn, created a difficult situation for Britain, particularly regarding the Somali-inhabited Ogaden. Britain got around the problem by concluding an agreement with the Emperor in 1942 which restored full sovereignty to Ethiopia and confirmed its pre-war boundaries. This was, however, qualified by a military convention granting Britain temporary administrative control over the Ogaden and the reserved area which included the Haud and the grain-producing areas west of British Somaliland.

The unification of almost all Somalis under the British 'raj' had two far-reaching results. First, it accelerated the growth of Somali national-consciousness and, as a corollary, of nationalist activity, particularly among the urban population. This culminated in the efforts of a group of young activists who succeeded in establishing the first modern Somali political movement, the Somali Youth Club (SYC). The SYC became by 1947 the 25,000-strong Somali Youth League (SYL).

A second result of the unified administration was an increasing appreciation among the local British officials of the need to continue this experiment in order to alleviate the economic conditions of the Somali tribes, a large number of whom were denied access by artificial boundaries to traditional sources of pasture and water. The needs of the British Empire and humanitarian considerations coincided to prompt the then British Foreign Secretary, Ernest Bevin, to propose in 1946 that 'British Somaliland, Italian Somaliland, and the adjacent part of Ethiopia, *if Ethiopia agreed*, should be lumped together as a trust territory'.[5] But the proposal, as Tom Farer has pointed out,

> however well intentioned, was intrinsically flawed by the provisions requiring Ethiopian agreement and proposing a British trustee. The former could not be satisfied. The latter, although it was not put forward as an essential condition, nevertheless encouraged perception of the plan as a strategem for British imperial expansion.[6]

Eventually, in 1950 Italian Somaliland became a UN Trust Territory under Italian administration on the condition that it should become independent in ten years. However, with the failure of what was essentially a feeble British effort to establish a unified Somali entity, the grounds for conflict between a truncated and, therefore, irredentist Somali state and the Ethiopian Empire were firmly laid. Compared to the polyglot nature of Ethiopia, the Somali people have been one of the few in Africa who, despite tribal and clan cleavages, have had a well-developed sense of national identity even before they attained formal statehood. As Farer has pointed out,

> The Somalis are as culturally uniform as the Ethiopians are mixed. From Djibouti in the north to Kenya's Tana River in the south, they speak a common language, enjoy a rich oral literature centred on poetic forms, organise communal life around similar, egalitarian social institutions, distinguish themselves from their Bantu and Nilotic neighbours by emphasising a genealogy stretching back to an original Arab ancestor, and manifest a powerful devotion to Islam. These cultural factors as well as the millennial occupation of contiguous territory and at least 500 years of intermittent conflict with the Christian occupants of the Ethiopian plateau make for an undisputable shared sense of nationhood. Surviving as well the political divisions imposed initially during the colonial scramble and partially sustained—in some ways aggravated—through the era of decolonisation, that sense now constitutes the root of the Somali problem.[7]

The 'political divisions' imposed during this colonial period were partially obliterated when on 1 July 1960 the former Italian and

British Somalilands united to form the Somali Republic and to constitute themselves into the core of a Somali state which aspired to unite French-controlled Djibouti (about half Somali), the NFD of Kenya (overwhelmingly Somali) and the Ogaden region of Ethiopia (almost exclusively Somali) to the new republic. Somali irredentist ambitions regarding Djibouti and the NFD, while relevant to the main theme of this paper, are marginal and cannot be analysed in any detail. Suffice it to say that Djibouti emerged in 1977 as an independent republic, though with a sizable French military presence in the tiny state, and that Somali efforts at annexing the NFD failed to bear fruit when the British decided, despite initial vacillation, against its detachment from Kenya when the latter received its formal independence in December 1963.[8] At the moment both of these issues are relatively dormant, partially because of Somali preoccupation with the Ogaden and partially because the Issa (Somali) and Affar populations of Djibouti are so evenly matched that any attempt by Somalia to acquire the former French territory is bound to lead to civil war. The NFD has been relatively quiet after an initial outburst of anti-Kenyan activity from 1964 to 1967. However, if Nairobi suffers from political instability in the post-Kenyatta period, the issue may once again become live. The Somali claim on the NFD is the major reason why Kenya has supported Ethiopian claims to the Ogaden despite the vastly different characters of the two regimes at present.

III

While the basic contradiction between the Ethiopian Empire and the Somali Republic emerges out of the fact that 'perhaps as many as one million Somalis occupy, more or less exclusively, nearly one fifth of Ehtiopia',[9] tension in the Horn has been exacerbated by the involvement of great and, particularly, superpowers for reasons which are often not directly related or relevant to the Somali-Ethiopian rivalry. For example, the conflict potential of the region has been enhanced by its proximity to the major theatres of Arab-Israeli conflict and because of the strategic importance to Israel of the Straits of Bal-el-Mandeb, the narrow waterway between the Horn of Africa and the Arabian Penisula.[10] Because of the West's, and particularly America's, commitment to Israel's conception of 'absolute security' for the Jewish state—often to the extent that Israeli conceptions are allowed to determine US policies towards the Middle East at the expense of America's own interests in the region[11]—regional conflicts in the Horn have in the West come to be viewed to some extent as extensions of the Arab-Israeli conflict. The accession to power of radical regimes, particularly in Somalia and South Yemen (PDRY) which received political and military support from the Soviet Union, further convinced policy-makers and strategists in the United States that the area had become an important target for the expansion of Soviet political influence. On its side, Soviet involvement in the Horn has evolved partially from its involvement in the Middle East conflict and partially from its desire to find counterweights to US-supported regimes in Ethiopia and Saudi Arabia on the Red sea littoral. Soviet interest in the Horn has also been partially determined by its newly acquired active role in the Indian Ocean from the late 1960s and its desire to find facilities on the Indian Ocean littoral for its increased naval deployment.

The Soviets have, however, been late arrivers in the Horn. They began to establish their links with Mogadishu at least a decade after the United States had established itself firmly as Addis Ababa's major external supporter and arms supplier in the early 1950s. Moreover, it was not until after the military takeover in Somalia in 1969 that the Soviet-Somali relationship began to acquire the warmth which made the latter the most firm ally of the USSR in the African continent until its decision in November 1977 to cut all ties with Moscow.

The United States, the first superpower to arrive on the scene, looked upon its Ethiopian connection to a large extent in the Cold War context. It not only gave Washington a foothold in a continent poised for decolonisation, but also conferred certain concrete dividends, the most important of them being the (formerly Italian) Kagnew communications base near Asmara in Eritrea. For two decades this base remained an important link in the worldwide network of US military communications stretching from the Philippines through Ethiopia and Morocco to Arlington, Virginia. The US acquired the Kagnew facility as part of a deal with Ethiopia under which Washington extended support at the UN to the Ethiopian annexation of Eritrea and also provided military aid to Addis Ababa.[12] The Kagnew base, named after the Ethiopian contingent that fought in Korea,[13] was leased to the US in 1953 for 25 years. While the lease technically was to run out in 1978, in the mid-1970s the US began to transfer the functions of the Kagnew base to its newly established facility in Diego Garcia. This transfer had far-reaching implications for the level of US support to Addis Ababa to which we will return later.

John Spencer, the former (American) Chief Adviser to the Ethiopian Ministry of Foreign Affairs, has pointed out in his testimony to a US Senate subcommittee that Ethiopia was able to persuade the US to extend arms assistance to Addis Ababa by exploiting the 'Northern Tier' concept being developed at that time by Secretary of State Dulles, culminating in the Baghdad Pact. The negotiators for Ethiopia (apparently John Spencer included) presented the argument that Addis Ababa should form part of a 'Southern Tier' or secondary line of defence against communism in the Middle East. This type of argument made it possible for the Secretaries of State and Defense to 'find' that the defence of Ethiopia was essential to the defence of the 'Free World'. Again, as in the case of the base agreement, the arms assistance agreement was related not to Africa as such but to the Middle East and 'defence' against communism.[14]

On the basis of the above-mentioned considerations, to which were added new ones, particularly those of close Soviet-Somali relations from the mid-1960s onward, the US supplied Ethiopia with \$350 million in economic aid and \$278.6 million in military assistance until 1976. An additional \$6 million worth of military aid to Ethiopia had been programmed for 1977.[15] According to US Arms Control and Disarmament Agency (ACDA) estimates, from 1966 to 1975 Ethiopia received \$151 million of arms of which \$120 million came from the United States.[16] According to International Institute for Strategic Studies (IISS) estimates, this equipment has included 24 M-60 medium and 54 M-41 light tanks, about 90 M-113 armoured personnel carriers (APC), four Canberra B-2 bombers, eleven F-86F fighter bombers and 16 F-5/AE fighter bombers.[17] According to Stockholm International Peace Research Institute (SIPRI) estimates, Ethiopia was the largest importer of major weapons in sub-Saharan Africa through the 1950s and the 1960s, accounting for over twelve per cent of the total throughout the period. It also became the first black African country to acquire supersonic aircraft when it received the F-5 Freedom Fighters from the US in 1965. Moreover, up to 1962 nearly the entire US military aid to sub-Saharan Africa went to Ethiopia and from 1962 to 1969 Ethiopia's share of this aid averaged 70 per cent.[18]

Until 1960, when the Somali Republic gained independence, and in fact for a further three years, US influence in the Horn was practically unchallenged. Throughout the 1950s two of its NATO allies—Italy and Britain—were in effective control of the major Somali territories, and France was firmly ensconced in Djibouti. Moreover, during the initial years of Somali independence, Mogadishu was primarily dependent upon its erstwhile colonial masters, Italy and Britain, for external political support and for the supply of the limited quantity of military hardware it was able to obtain. However, in 1963 Somali relations with the Western powers deteriorated considerably mainly because of the British refusal to separate the Somali-populated northern district from Kenya before granting that country independence, and because of continued US support to Ethiopia which kept the regional balance of power tilted very much against Somalia. It was in this context that Mogadishu turned to the only other major source that could help redress the regional imbalance and, if possible, tilt it in Somalia's favour, viz. the Soviet Union.

On its part, Moscow, having attained both a degree of strategic parity with Washington and, for the first time, a global reach in terms of its military and political capabilities, was not averse to extending aid to the Somali Republic if it helped diminish the military superiority of the American ally, Ethiopia. Such an opportunity was all the more welcome from the Kremlin's point of view since it provided the Soviet Union with a foothold in the Horn of Africa, strategically placed next to the volatile Middle East and at the junction of the Red Sea and the Indian Ocean. In October 1963 Somalia accepted a Soviet offer of military assistance in the form of a long-term rouble credit worth $30 million. The main objective of this aid was to expand the Somali army from 4,000 men to 10,000—this target was revised to 20,000 after the military came to power in 1969—and to build, by African standards, a significant air force. Somalia received its first supply of MIG aircraft (six MIG-15 UTI trainers) in November 1963 and additional MIG-15 and MIG-17 aircraft in 1965-6. It also received T-34 tanks from the USSR in 1965. The Somali-Soviet relationship, although it had its ups and downs, remained very close, particularly from 1969 when the military came to power until 1977 when dramatic events in the Horn led to equally dramatic shifts in international alignments, thus making obsolete all the traditional assessments of regional conflict and superpower involvement in that part of Africa.

According to the IISS estimates, Somalia had an army of 22,000, before the outbreak of the Ogaden war, as compared to Ethiopia's

47,000. The Somali army had at its disposal 200 T-34 and 50 T-54/55 tanks. It had an airforce of 2,700 men with 66 combat aircraft (as compared to Ethiopia's 2,300 and 36 respectively) which included ten IL-28s, forty-four MIG-15s and MIG-17s and twelve MIG-21s. However, the IISS publication also pointed out that 'spares are short and not all equipment is serviceable'.[19] With the outbreak of the Ogaden war not only had both armed forces lost a great deal of equipment and trained manpower,[20] but the shift in international alignments had affected the composition of their arsenals as well. This has been particularly true of Ethiopia which has received a good deal of modern weaponry from the Soviet Union and its East European and Cuban allies. But to this we will return later.

As a *quid pro quo* for Soviet military and economic assistance to the Somali Republic, the latter had extended certain base facilities to Moscow at the port of Berbera. These included a military airport and two Soviet communication facilities that opened in December 1972. Despite Soviet and Somali denials, the first and unrevised report of the three experts appointed by the UN Secretary-General in 1974 to report on great-power naval rivalry in the Indian Ocean had identified Berbera as a Soviet base.[21] There is enough evidence on record now—including US aerial photographic reconnaissance and the visits of US Congressional teams—to conclude that it was a naval facility used by the Soviet Union and had storage and handling facilities for naval missiles and although 'nothing has actually been seen here that is bigger than the Styx (missile) which has a range of about 20 miles ... the handling gear and the buildings could obviously handle something much larger'.[22] In 1974 the Somali Republic and the Soviet Union signed a Treaty of Friendship and Co-operation which made provisions for 'training of the Somalian military personnel and the mastering of weapons and equipment delivered to the Somali Democratic Republic for the purposes of enhancing its defence potential'.[23]

Recent political and military changes in the Horn have, of course, radically transformed the character of the Soviet-Somali relationship resulting in the abrogation of the treaty, the termination of Soviet base facilities at Berbera, the repatriation of Soviet military and civilian advisers in Somalia who at the height of the relationship had numbered between 5,000 and 6,000 and all-out Soviet-Cuban support to the Ethiopian counter-offensive which forced Somalia to withdraw from the Ogaden. But in order to understand this drastic alteration of international alignments one must first look at recent changes in the domestic environments of Ethiopia and Somalia—particularly of the former—and evaluate their effects on the balance of power within the region and consequently on intra-regional relationships.

IV

The event that acted as the major catalyst for change in the Horn of Africa was the overthrow of Haile Selassie's *ancien régime* in Addis Ababa in early 1974 and its eventual replacement—after a period of uncertainty and confusion—by a military government controlled by the Provisional Military Administrative Committee, better known as the Dergue.[24] This body, which had begun as a democratic movement within the armed and police forces initially with the objective of forcing reforms on the unwilling Emperor, soon found itself desperately trying to fill the power vacuum which was created by the unexpectedly swift disintegration of the *ancien régime* under the impact of a widespread upheaval of protest against the old feudal system. The Dergue found itself divided on the basis of policies and personalities and its leadership locked in a power struggle which resulted in a series of purges until in early 1977 Colonel Mengistu Haile Mariam emerged as the victor.[25]

Under Mengistu the Dergue moved increasingly in a Marxist direction, at least in its rhetoric, partially because of domestic requirements and partially because of the leftist predilections of a section of its leadership. Such a leftward orientation on the part of Ethiopia's new rulers was also the result of their urgent need to enlist external support in order to shore up the Dergue's shaky position *vis-à-vis* local dissidents and secessionist forces, particularly those operating in Eritrea and the Somali-inhabited Ogaden.[26] After an initial bout of enthusiasm for close relations with China,[27] Mengistu apparently came to the conclusion that 'although the Chinese maintain a low-profile presence in the Horn of Africa, they are not in a mood to play super-power politics in the area—unlike the Soviet Union'.[28]

The Ethiopian lurch towards the left, and particularly towards the Soviet Union, was to a considerable extent dictated by a deterioration of relations between Washington and Addis Ababa which in turn was based to some extent on the accession to power in Ethiopia of a regime apparently wedded to 'scientific socialism' (although in a peculiarly Ethiopian fashion). Considerable criticism of the Dergue's Marxist predilections was voiced in US Congressional circles. Simultaneously, as has been mentioned earlier, American interest in propping up the Ethiopian Empire declined with the transfer of the most important functions of the Kagnew communications base to Diego Garcia, thereby reducing Ethiopia's strategic significance to the United States. Growing US links with Saudi Arabia also prevented Washington from giving open support to Mengistu's genocidal plans for Eritrea, where the nationalist insurgency was being supported, among others, by Riyadh.

With American support to Ethiopia remarkably reduced, the Dergue decided that it was time to switch sides. In April 1977 Mengistu decided to cut off all ties with the United States, thus formally ending Ethiopia's near-total dependence on Washington for military aid and political support. He turned instead to the Soviet Union to replace the US as the major source of arms supply and military training. Among the reasons which seem to have prompted Mengistu to take this course, other than his Marxist predilections, was the way the war was going in Eritrea and the expectations of a showdown with Somalia over Djibouti when the French withdrew from their coastal enclave in mid-1977. Despite American military assistance (and Israeli help in training counter-insurgency units) the war in Eritrea was moving slowly but surely towards a total Ethiopian rout and the two Ethiopian ports on the Red Sea, Assab and Massawa, both in Eritrea, had become virtually unusable because of Eritrean nationalist control of territory between the ports and the Abyssinian highlands. No government in Addis Ababa could have survived the fall of Eritrea. Combined with Somali success in the Ogaden, where the West Somali Liberation Front (WSLF) had been increasing its physical control of Somali-inhabited territory, and with half a dozen other secessionist groups waiting in the wings, Eritrean independence would have heralded the total break up of the Ethiopian Empire. Mengistu was apparently impressed by the degree of Soviet involvement in Angola where Moscow had done its best, including the introduction of Cuban troops, to help its allies win control of that country. The Soviets, in contrast with the Americans, therefore, appeared more reliable allies to him on the Eritrean front. Moreover, given the Soviet Union's leverage with the Somali Republic, Mengistu must have reasoned that a Soviet Union friendly to Addis Ababa would be willing to restrain Somali intrusions into the Ogaden as well as into Djibouti since such intrusions could force Ethiopia into another major war at a time when Eritrea was unmanageable.

The Soviet Union responded with surprising alacrity to Ethiopian overtures. As Colin Legum has pointed out, 'Already in 1974, Moscow began to show a tentative interest in backing the Dergue but without upsetting the Somalis.'[29] Moscow's calculations seem to have been based, among other things, on the need to get a firmer foothold in the Horn than was provided by Somalia. Ethiopia, with a population almost nine times that of Somalia and with two outlets to the Red Sea, seemed, at least on paper, a good horse to bet on. At the same time, given the Horn's proximity to the Middle East, Moscow must have reasoned that the losses it had suffered in terms of reduction of influence in Egypt and Sudan could be at least partially made up by the acquisition of a friendly Ethiopia. This was an inviting prospect, particularly since it was to be, at least technically, at the expense of the United States. Moreover, with Egypt and Sudan, along with arch-conservative Saudi Arabia, as the main supporters of the Eritrean nationalists, Moscow must have calculated that an Ethiopian victory in Eritrea, particularly with some sort of a Marxist government in Addis Ababa, would be in the Soviet interest.

Moscow also could have been secretly worried that Saudi overtures to Mogadishu in the shape of offers of massive economic and military aid plus political support to woo Somalia away from the Soviet orbit might prove too tempting for the latter to decline. The development of intimate relations between stridently anti-communist Saudi Arabia and Somalia was bound to endanger Soviet influence in Somalia as a whole and its presence in Berbera in particular. All through 1976 there had been reports of Saudi offers of assistance to Mogadishu—including funds for the purchase of arms in the West—if Somalia broke with the Soviet Union. According to one report,

> the figure of proffered Saudi aid mentioned most often in Arab circles here (in Mogadishu) is $300 million to $350 million, although Saudi diplomats in the region say that this is a vastly exaggerated estimate of Somali needs. Last year (1976) Saudi Arabia gave Somalia $28 million, so far this year (1977) it has furnished $16-18 million.[30]

At one stage in 1976, James E. Akins, former US Ambassador to Saudi Arabia, charged the Ford administration with having ignored a Saudi proposal, made while Akins was ambassador in Riyadh, to reduce Soviet influence in Somalia because the removal of the Soviet base at Berbera would have weakened the administration's case on Diego Garcia at a time when the US Congress was considering appropriations for the base.[31]

Compared to all this activity on the Somali front, Ethiopia's isolation in the region, since it had successfully alienated almost all its neighbours as well as the United States for different reasons, made Addis Ababa appear a much more dependable client to Moscow. Ethiopian 'dependence' and, therefore, its 'dependability' stood out in sharp contrast to an increasingly self-confident regime in Somalia which had become a member of the Arab League and was on friendly terms with rich conservative as well as radical governments in the Arab world. Furthermore, the Soviet Union may have been confident enough of its leverage—political, military and economic—with Somalia to take the risk of wooing its major rival while yet hoping to retain Mogadishu's loyalty.

There is some reason to believe that Moscow felt relatively optimistic about its capacity to impose a sort of *Pax Sovietica* on the Horn by acting as the Godfather for both the Somali and Ethiopian regimes. Any optimism on this score, however, must have suffered a drastic setback when Somalia rejected out of hand Fidel Castro's proposal in March 1977 to join the two neighbours plus the PDRY in a sort of Marxist confederation around the Red Sea. As far as the Somali perception of Soviet activities in Ethiopia was concerned, it was summed up by Somali President Siad Barre's remark to the Kuwaiti newspaper, *Al-Yaqash,* on 27 June 1977, that:

> If it should transpire that the arms sent by the Soviet Union to Ethiopia constituted a threat to Somalia, then Somalia would take a *historic decision* against this armament. We would not be able to remain idle in the face of the danger of the Soviet Union's arming of Ethiopia. Despite our good relations with the Soviet Union, its outlook on Ethiopia is different from ours.[32]

However, at the same time, one Somali leader pointed out to a Western correspondent the pitfalls of breaking relations with the Soviet Union and becoming exclusively dependent on the United States:

> Look at what happened to Sadat. Washington promised him the moon and left him defenceless against Israel.[33]

Despite its misgivings regarding the West, Somalia finally decided to cut all its ties with the Soviet Union in November 1977. What was it that prompted Mogadishu to take this 'historic decision'? What happened between June and November that made such a break inevitable? In one sentence, what intervened was the Ogaden war. This conflict made the Somali-Soviet relationship completely untenable in the light of all-out Soviet support for Ethiopia in the latter's desperate action to preserve a semblance of Ethiopian authority in the Somali-inhabited south-eastern region of the crumbling Empire.

V

The last major clash between the two countries over boundary claims in the Ogaden had taken place in 1964 when the American-equipped Ethiopian army had had much the better of the infant Somali army. Throughout the 1960s and the 1970s a Somali nationalist movement, which came to be known as the West Somali Liberation Front (WSLF), had operated in the Ogaden and had frequently harassed the Ethiopian rulers. With increasingly chaotic conditions prevailing in Ethiopia following the fall of the Emperor and the intensification of the Eritrean insurgency, the WSLF had also extended its activities and had been able to wrest substantial portions of the Ogaden from Ethiopian control. The Somali Republic had never tried to hide its sympathy and support for the WSLF although it had denied charges of direct involvement in anti-Ethiopian activities in the Ogaden. As far as Ethiopia's new rulers were concerned, one of the major reasons for their decision to develop intimate links with the Soviet Union was their calculation that Moscow would be able to keep Somali ambitions in check while the Dergue was neck-deep in its troubles in Eritrea and elsewhere in the country. But, paradoxically, the Soviet decision to support the new Ethiopian regime, militarily and politically, was responsible, more than anything else, in triggering off the Somali offensive in the Ogaden in mid-1977.

According to relatively reliable Western intelligence estimates in June-July 1977, the Soviet Union started to supply Ethiopia not only T-34, T-54 and T-55 tanks (some of which were brought in from Aden) and armoured personnel-carriers (APC) but also Sam-7 anti-aircraft missiles, MI-8 helicopters, 140 mm rocket-launchers and self-propelled guns.*[34] According to the same sources, this augmentation of Ethiopian military strength was very worrisome for Mogadishu. But what was even more disturbing to the Somali leadership and to the West was Mengistu's reported promise to the USSR, when he visited Moscow in May 1977, 'that he would allow the Russians to turn (the Eritrean Red Sea port of) Massawa into a large naval base able to serve warships and submarines with its own shipyard'.* This would drastically reduce Soviet dependence on Somali facilities in the Red Sea-Indian Ocean area as well as present the Soviet Union with a base facing pro-West Saudi Arabia, 'behind the backs of Egypt and Sudan'.*

The Somali decision to escalate the fighting in the Ogaden seems to have resulted directly from this shift in Soviet strategy in the Horn since it worked to the detriment of Somali interests. First, with Ethiopia available to the Soviet Union as an ally-client and with Massawa a possible (although, given the situation in Eritrea, not very likely) replacement for Berbera, Somali leverage with Moscow would be drastically reduced. This switch would be reflected in Soviet policies in the Horn which would then tend to completely subordinate Somali interests to those of its larger and more important ally, Ethiopia. Second, an accretion in Ethiopian armed strength, particularly when such an augmentation might be at the expense of Soviet arms deliveries to Somalia, might tempt the Ethiopian junta, especially given the unstable conditions at home, to take military action against Somalia in order both to bolster its domestic image and to force Somalia to reduce, if not completely stop, its support to the WSLF. Both these outcomes of the shift in Soviet strategy, but particularly the latter, were unacceptable to the Somali leadership which was specially worried about the adverse effects of a tilt in the military balance in the Horn in favour of Addis Ababa. The intensification of the WSLF activities in the Ogaden and the Somali decision to join the WSLF in an all-out offensive against Ethiopia was, therefore, to a large extent prompted by the desire to take advantage of Somali military superiority *vis-à-vis* Ethiopia while it lasted and before it was altered by the infusion of large-scale Soviet weaponry into Ethiopia and the adaptation of the Ethiopian armed forces to Soviet weapon-systems. A secondary objective of the Somali offensive seems to have been the attempted discrediting of the Mengistu regime as a result of military defeat and its replacement by either a right-wing (therefore, anti-Soviet) or an extreme left-wing (therefore, again anti-Soviet) government in Addis Ababa which would force Moscow once again to mend its fences with Mogadishu, this time on the latter's terms.

It was this calculation of speedy military success coupled with the possibility of a reassessment of Soviet policies in the Horn that prevented the Somali government from totally rupturing its ties with the Soviet Union, particularly since in ideological terms the West was still anathema to the socialist rulers of Somalia. The Somali leadership was, however, not averse to shopping for arms in the West to make up for losses in the Ogaden and to augment its military strength generally, particularly through the good offices of Saudi Arabia. It was with this aim in view that President Barre of Somalia paid a visit to Saudi Arabia on 13 July 1977. However, the Saudis, although very interested in helping the Somalis, apparently made the total expulsion of the Soviet Union a precondition for any large-scale Saudi help.[35] The Somalis responded with a substantial cutback of Soviet advisers in the country—a process which was confirmed by Western sources[36]—but, once again, stopped short of complete rupture with Moscow.

While later reports from Western intelligence sources disclosed that President Barre had made a promise to King Khalid of Saudi Arabia and President Sadat of Egypt on the eve of the Ogaden offensive that he would throw the Soviets out of Somalia completely,* the thesis that Barre was signalling Moscow and giving it time to reassess its policy in the Horn appears a more plausible explanation of the often contradictory moves and statements emanating from Mogadishu between June and November 1977. The responses from both the Soviet Union and the West (and the latter's friends in the Arab world) were equally mixed and often confusing. Initially, following the Soviet decision to make major political and military investments in Ethiopia and the consequent cool that descended upon Somali-Soviet relations, the US seemed prepared to step in to fill the political and military gap left in Somalia as a result of the shift in Soviet policy. President Carter's statement that the United States was prepared to 'aggressively challenge, in a peaceful way, the Soviet Union ... for influence in areas of the world we feel are crucial to us now or potentially crucial'[37] appeared to be directed primarily towards parties in conflict in the Horn. This was borne out by the reported American decision 'in principle' to supply arms to Somalia to defend 'its present territory', and the report that Washington was consulting with 'friends and allies'—Saudi Arabia, Egypt, Iran, Pakistan, France, Italy and Germany—on how best to supply arms to Somalia.[38] The report that the US had decided to supply arms simultaneously to Sudan (which had thrown out Soviet advisers) strengthened the possibility of an imminent American decision to send major weaponry to Somalia, most probably through third parties.

However, indications that Washington was having second thoughts about a major military and political commitment to Mogadishu were available almost immediately after the decision 'in principle' was taken. US vacillation was the result of a number of factors: first, the socialist character of the Somali regime (even though it was supported by such conservative Arab states as Saudi Arabia); second, its refusal to break totally its ties with Moscow unless a firm offer of military assistance from the West was forthcoming; third, fear of Congressional disapproval of another African involvement after the Angolan misadventure; fourth, pressure from the Jewish lobby, both inside and outside Congress, which considered a Somali victory in the Horn anathema both since Muslim Somalia was a member of the Arab League and since it was bound to hasten Eritrean control of the Red Sea ports of Assab and Massawa which Israel was helping to oppose by supplying military advisers to Ethiopia. But more important than all these was the outbreak of the Ogaden conflict in July and its intensification in August which contributed greatly to the American decision not to supply Somalia with arms which might be used to dismember the Christian Amharic Ethiopian Empire which, despite its current aberrations, had been America's traditional ally in a part of the world where distrust of the West had become almost a matter of political instinct. Apparently, the French were also not too happy with any accretion in Somali strength because of the latter's aspirations regarding Djibouti which, although it had gained independence from France in June 1977, was virtually under French military protection. Pro-West Kenya, afraid that the Ogaden example might embolden its Somali population in the erstwhile NFD to rise again in revolt and provide Mogadishu with an excuse to intervene, also reportedly pleaded with Washington not to do anything which might increase Somali capabilities.

These factors, which were working against US material support to Somalia, were considerably reinforced when regular Somali troops brazenly crossed the international frontier to attack Ethiopian forces in the Ogaden. It should be noted at this stage that the Somali argument that Ethiopia had participated in the nineteenth-century partition of Somali territories and that the WSLF, therefore, was a legitimate liberation movement failed to impress the eight-nation mediation committee which had been set up by the OAU to mediate the Somali-Ethiopian dispute. The committee, meeting in Libreville between 5 and 9 August 1977, passed a resolution 'reconfirming the inviolability of African frontiers and condemnation of all forms of political subversion'.[39] As Mayall has argued, this 'issue of principle stood in the way of any unambiguous American commitment' to Somalia, and that 'in the end, it was the orthodox OAU view of the conflict which prevailed in Western capitals as in Africa itself'.[40] Given the strong commitment on the part of African ruling elites to the inviolability of colonial boundaries, and the initiatives that had been undertaken by the Carter administration in 1977 to woo African elites through the medium of the Andrew Young style of diplomacy and pressure on Ian Smith for a solution of the Rhodesian problem acceptable at least to 'moderate blacks', it was understandable why, at that juncture, Washington was not willing to launch itself upon a course that might prove detrimental to its larger policy objectives in Africa.

This African commitment to the inviolability of state boundaries also helped to legitimise the escalating Soviet-Cuban involvement in Ethiopia on behalf of a 'legitimate' government and in defence of 'recognised' boundaries. Therefore, even the most die-hard anti-Soviet elements in the African leadership found themselves incapable of openly taking an anti-Ethiopian and pro-Somali stand on the Ogaden issue because of the potential risk that the Somali example might be followed in other cases to their own disadvantage and to the detriment of the legitimacy of the regimes over which they presided.

It was almost inevitable in such a situation that there would be differences of opinion within the policy-making apparatus in Washington over US policies towards the Horn. It was reported that the National Security Council under Brzezinski was taking a 'hard' line *vis-à-vis* the Soviets and the Ethiopians and the Africa Bureau of the State Department was advocating a 'soft' line and a low profile for the US in the conflict in the Horn.[41]

The various pressures upon the Carter administration and its own assessment of what a projected Somali victory would do to the regional political dynamics of the Horn, to Israel's presumed security requirements and to great power positions in the Red Sea and the Indian Ocean, led to the State Department spokesman's statement on 1 September 1977 that in view of the current clash in 'Ethiopia's Ogaden region' the US had decided that providing arms (to Somalia) 'would add fuel to the fire we are more interested in putting out'. US State Department officials also pointed out that no transfer of US military equipment to Somalia from third countries would be approved.[42]

Somalia's chagrin at the US decision was understandable, especially since Mogadishu had been led to believe through private communications from Washington that the US was not only ready to replace the USSR as its major arms supplier if the tab could be picked up by its wealthy Arab supporters, but also that Washington was not averse to the extension of Somali control over the Ogaden in order to teach Ethiopia a lesson for having deserted the Western camp. This seems to have been the gist of the message communicated to President Barre through Dr Kevin Cahill, Barre's longtime American physician, when he flew to Mogadishu in mid-June 1977 after meeting high-level State Department advisers. Cahill reportedly told Barre he had a message from the 'very top' that Washington 'was not averse to further guerrilla pressure in the Ogaden and that the US was prepared to consider Somalia's legitimate defence needs'.[43] Later denials by US officials were confined to the contention that the message might have been misinterpreted either by Cahill or by Barre and did not dispute the fact that a message was sent through Barre's physician. While the confusion in American policy might have resulted from the tussle within the administration between the 'White House (backed by the Pentagon) aims of challenging the Soviets and Africa-oriented [State Department] advisers who took Somali claims of non-alignment more seriously and feared a Cold War approach would eliminate possible leverage in Ethiopia',[44] it provoked one high-ranking State Department official to comment that American diplomacy in the Horn of Africa was 'a classic case of incompetence and mismanagement'.[45]

All this led Mayall to conclude that

> To the extent that in the confusion [of intra-administration debate] the Somalis were able to listen to that side of the argument which they wanted to hear, the Washington policy debate had dire consequences in the Ogaden. For by the end of the year it was becoming increasingly clear that, strong as the Somalis' position on the ground might be, it could only be held if they could call on external support equivalent to that provided by the Soviet Union and Cuba to the other side.[46]

On the other side, given the cover of apparent legitimacy to their Horn adventure, the Soviet Union and its allies were less than inhibited in their support, both in terms of sophisticated Soviet hardware and trained Cuban manpower, to Addis Ababa. While, initially, the Soviet support to Ethiopia which resulted in the alienation of Somalia from Moscow, appeared like changing horses in mid-stream and a particularly hamhanded demonstration of Soviet diplomacy, the Soviets have been able, at least temporarily, to save the day by the massive support, in men and materiel, that they have extended to the Mengistu regime. This the Soviet Union accomplished by throwing almost all ideological pretensions overboard, and, in fact, by violating all forms of normal diplomatic behaviour, particularly *vis-à-vis* Mogadishu.

After having made a major investment in Somalia the Soviet Union performed such an about-turn in its policy as to transform completely the nature of politics in the Horn and trigger off a major conflict in the region. The belief, which from all indications the Soviet Union seemed to harbour until the fall of 1977, that Moscow could impose a *Pax Sovietica* on the Horn and force Mogadishu to play along with its Ethiopian strategy was, to say the least, misconceived. In its enthusiasm for the Ethiopian 'revolution' and the consequent worsening of US-Ethiopian relations, the Soviet Union completely ignored the real nature of that revolution, the imperial character of the Ethiopian state and the Dergue's refusal to change this character into a genuine federation, and, above all, the strength of Somali nationalist sentiment and its unwillingness and inability to contemplate perpetual subjection of the Ogaden Somalis even to a Soviet-backed Marxist regime in Addis Ababa. The 'major contradiction', to use a Maoist phrase, in the Horn was not between 'socialism' (and that of a peculiarly Ethiopian variety) and 'reaction' (the US and its allies—Saudi Arabia, Egypt and Sudan), but between the requirements of Somali ethnic nationalism (buttressed by a socialism far more genuine than the Ethiopian experiment) and the need of the Mengistu regime in Addis Ababa to maintain the integrity of Ethiopia's multinational empire (since the fortunes of the regime were inextricably enmeshed with the future of the imperial boundaries). By opting for Ethiopia, the Soviet Union seemed to be putting itself definitely on the wrong side of history.

As has been mentioned earlier, despite Moscow's tilt towards Ethiopia, President Barre desperately tried to maintain Somali links with the Soviet Union as long as Mogadishu's vital interests were not sacrificed. He in fact travelled to the Soviet Union at the end of August 1977 and met Soviet Premier Kosygin, Foreign Minister Gromyko and Communist Party theoretician Suslov. President Brezhnev, holidaying in the Crimea, did not meet Barre and this was interpreted in Western circles as a snub for the Somali leader.[47] The US announcement regarding its ban on arms supply to Somalia, made when Barre was in Moscow, immeasurably weakened the Somali bargaining position *vis-à-vis* the Soviet Union and, therefore, it was no surprise that the mission failed in persuading Moscow to tone down its support for Addis Ababa. The importance of the mission also lay in the fact that it was undertaken two weeks after a *Tass* statement and an *Izvestia* article critical of Somalia's 'armed intervention in Ethiopian internal affairs'.[48]

Despite these diplomatic setbacks, the Somali government was in no hurry to terminate its formal links with the Soviet Union. However, President Barre more than once expressed his displeasure at the Soviet and Cuban involvement with the Ethiopian regime and warned that Soviet and Cuban backing of Ethiopia was pushing the Horn of Africa to a 'war conflagration'.[49] Even at this stage in October 1977, when the Somali thrust into the Ogaden had stalled before Harar and Dire Dawa and Mogadishu was desperately seeking military supplies to bolster its defences against an expected Ethiopian counter-offensive now that Ethiopian forces had had time to assimilate the Soviet weapons, the Somali leadership was hesitant to expel Soviet advisers and formally terminate the Soviet presence in Somalia. This cautious Somali stance was, at least partially, related to reports regarding the Ethiopian regime's efforts to patch up its differences with the United States. These efforts were aimed both at neutralising Western support to Somalia and at pressurising the Soviet Union and its proxy, Cuba, to escalate their support to the crumbling Ethiopian regime.

Western intelligence sources reported that in mid-October 1977 the Ethiopian Foreign Minister visited Havana and Moscow to persuade Castro to send Cuban troops to Ethiopia *à la* Angola. While on his trip the Ethiopian minister reportedly told his hosts that if adequate Soviet bloc aid was not forthcoming then Addis Ababa might be driven to resort to 'desperate options'. These options apparently included renewal of military and political ties with the United States.

These Ethiopian requests and warnings coincided with the initial Somali success in the Ogaden and President Barre's decision on 13 November 1977 to terminate all Somali ties with Moscow, to expel Soviet advisers and to deny the use of naval facilities in Berbera to the Soviet Union. These Somali actions were to a large extent predicated on the assumption that Saudi Arabia—Somalia's new found friend—would be successful in persuading the US to extend military and political support to Mogadishu in its adventure in the Ogaden once the latter had demonstrated its 'good faith' by the expulsion of Soviet influence. President Barre's decision was also based on a Somali assessment that Moscow's commitment to Ethiopia was total and irrevocable. This had resulted in the almost complete cessation of Soviet arms deliveries to Somalia following the outbreak of the fighting in the Ogaden, while Soviet tanks, missiles and MIG fighters, accompanied by Soviet advisers (some of them transferred from Somalia) were arriving in Ethiopia in larger numbers. Somali leaders could have drawn no comfort from the Western estimate that an 'infusion of $500 million worth of Soviet arms to Addis Ababa could turn the tide of battle in the Ogaden'.[50]

Once the Somali advance had been halted before Harar, following the costly assault on Jigjiga, the time for decision in Mogadishu had become imminent. Somalia, having come to the conclusion that it had used its Soviet card to the utmost extent possible, decided to discard it for a fresh, and hopefully better, hand. However, the Somali trust in Saudi promises and American support appeared to be misplaced. While, on the morrow of Somalia's 'historic decision' to expel the Soviets, there was 'a consensus in diplomatic circles [in Mogadishu] that Barre's government had received some kind of assurances from the West that it will cover Somalia's arms supply losses resulting from the expulsion' and that 'the United States gave some kind of indication that it would not object to a third party, armed with US weapons, giving assistance to the Somalis',[51] there was also considerable scepticism about American behaviour because of its erratic pattern in the past. This scepticism was strengthened by Barre's statement at a news conference on 23 November 1977 that the US had rejected his appeal to counter Soviet support for Ethiopia despite his expulsion of Soviet advisers.[52] Although the US administration decided in early December 1977 to resume development aid to Somalia which had been cut off since 1971, 'US officials stressed that the decision to resume development aid does not signal any change in the Administration's policy of refusing to provide arms to Somalia'.[53]

This US posture effectively wrote 'finis' to the Somali attempt to integrate the Ogaden into the Somali homeland, particularly since just at this time the Soviets decided to pour in massive military supplies and fly in thousands of Cuban troops to shore up Ethiopian defences. 'Between November [1977] and January [1978] the Russians mounted an airlift of heavy armour and men which involved some 225 planes, about 12 per cent of the entire Soviet transport fleet, the launching of a control satellite and, on US estimates, strengthened the Ethiopian forces by up to 1,500 Soviet advisers and 10,000 Cubans.'[54] It was estimated that 'in a matter of several months ... $1 billion worth of equipment, including tanks, artillery and tactical aircraft', plus Cuban troops, were airlifted to Ethiopia.[55] The Soviets had also

> demonstrated that they could airlift several divisions, with heavy equipment, into the Middle East and Eastern Africa and support them on a sustained basis, without access to seaports. Moreover, because of the diversity of the routes flown, some without permission, the Soviets indicated that there were enough friendly countries, e.g. Yugoslavia and Libya, and sufficient range of the heavy IL-76 transports that denial of overflight rights was no longer a barrier to regional access.[56]

This massive Soviet-Cuban effort finally made its effects felt on the Ogaden front and the tide was turned against the Somalis. Within a few short weeks the Somali army, after being completely outmanoeuvred, was decisively defeated at Jigjiga where the campaign was directed apparently by General Vasily Ivanovich Petrov, First Deputy Commander of the Soviet ground forces.[57]

The American response to the massive Soviet-Cuban build-up, hamstrung by the apparent legitimacy of Soviet actions particularly in the context of the OAU endorsement of Ethiopia's 'traditional' boundaries, did not go much beyond President Carter's statement accusing the USSR of sending 'excessive quantities of weapons' to Ethiopia and of 'unwarranted interference in the area'.[58]

The only concrete contribution that the US made was in the last days of the Ogaden war when it was able to negotiate a formula with the Soviet Union which could allow Somalia to withdraw its forces without losing face completely and which guaranteed

Somalia's territorial integrity. This formula consisted of a pledge given by the Soviet Union that it would prevent its allies from crossing the international frontier into Somalia if the Somalis withdrew their regular forces from the Ogaden immediately.[59] By 15 March 1978 Mogadishu announced that the withdrawal of Somali forces from the Ogaden had been completed.

The generally low level of reaction demonstrated by the US during the Soviet-Cuban-Ethiopian counter-offensive in the Ogaden demonstrated among other things the fact that the State Department's soft line, now symbolised by Andrew Young's pronouncement over the Cuban role in Africa, had eventually won out over the Brzezinski line which had advocated linking the Soviet Union's 'forward' policy on the Horn to East-West detente and negotiations on SALT II. The NSC adviser had called for US retaliation in these spheres as a response to the Soviet involvement in Ethiopia.[60]

VI

There is one other important aspect of the conflict on the Horn which needs some elaboration before we move on to draw general conclusions regarding the conflict and great power involvement therein. This relates to the roles played by certain neighbouring countries in the conflict. The importance of these roles is based upon the fact that they cut across ideological lines and political alignments/commitments. They had much more to do with regional rivalries in the contiguous region of the Middle East than to the conflict in the Horn *per se* or to alignments with one or other of the superpowers. The most outstanding example of this phenomenon was the role played by Israel in the Somali-Ethiopian conflict. Until the overthrow of Emperor Haile Selassie of Ethiopia and particularly until Mengistu's tilt towards Moscow, Israeli policy in the Horn was completely congruent with that of the United States. In fact, as has been stated earlier, US support for Israel and its almost total commitment to the Israeli concept of security for the Jewish state, had been one of the major reasons for US support for Ethiopia. Situated as it is, commanding the western coast of the Red Sea and contiguous to the Bab-el-Mandeb, Ethiopia was considered a major ally by Israel in its strategy to deny control of the Bab to the Arabs and to keep the Red Sea approach to its southern port of Eilat open.

It was no wonder, therefore, that throughout the 1960s the Israelis were involved in some form of military co-operation with Ethiopia. 'From 1962 onwards Israeli advisers trained the Emergency Police, an elite counter-insurgency group of 3,100 men established to operate in Eritrea.'[61] There were also reports of Israeli-Ethiopian co-operation in ventures off the Eritrean coast. These reports seemed credible because one of Israel's major objectives in the region was to prevent the Eritrean coastline from falling into 'Arab' (i.e. Eritrean) hands. Moreover, as one analyst has pointed out,

> It is not widely known that the historic Israeli victory in the six day war [1967] was in the first instance made possible owing to the use of Ethiopian airfields, from which Israeli jets took off that famous Monday morning thus approaching from an utterly unexpected direction.[62]

Despite the Ethiopian decision under Arab pressure to break diplomatic relations with Israel in October 1973, military co-operation and trading relations between Addis Ababa and Tel Aviv were maintained.

The Ethiopian tilt towards the Soviet Union complicated matters for Israel but Tel Aviv took a pragmatic stance and refused to cut its military and economic links with Ethiopia despite US withdrawal from Addis Ababa. It was reported that the US looked upon the Ethiopian-Israeli link favourably since it provided Washington with a reliable conduit into Ethiopia. Even as late as July 1977, at the time of the Somali offensive in the Ogaden, it was reported that 'a small contingent of Israelis are in Addis Ababa training elements of the Ethiopian armed forces'.[63] While this number was estimated in July at 20 to 30, mainly involved in training Ethiopians in counter-insurgency techniques for use in Eritrea, by October 1977 the Jewish presence had increased substantially. It was then reported that Tel Aviv was involved in training Ethiopian tank crews in Israel in the use of Soviet tanks supplied to Addis Ababa which were of the same type as those captured by Israel during the October war. It was also reported that Israeli mechanics were in Ethiopia servicing US-made F-5 jet fighters. These Israeli activities were reportedly undertaken with tacit US approval.[64] In February 1978 the Israeli Foreign Minister, Moshe Dayan, went to the extent of declaring officially that Israel had sold some spare parts for American equipment to the Ethiopian air force. He went on to say that 'the fact that we are on the same side as the Soviets in this matter, well, that's a different question'.[65] Colin Legum has pointed out that 'because of the incautious public boast by ... General Dayan ... Colonel Mengistu reluctantly decided in April 1978 to suspend all his military and other relations with Israel'.[66]

The Israeli-Ethiopian connection is, however, only one, though possibly the foremost, example of the peculiar alignment in the Horn where Israeli advisers helped to train an Ethiopian force armed with Soviet weapons, not infrequently paid for with funds from Libya. The latter's antipathy towards Saudi Arabia, Egypt and Sudan—the major Arab supporters of Somalia—not to mention Iran, and its newfound friendship with Moscow placed it in the uncomfortable position of aiding Ethiopia against fellow-Muslim and fellow-Arab League member, Somalia. South Yemen was placed in a similar position although the ideological commitment of its rulers and their traditionally close ties with Moscow made the decision much easier for Aden.

A further noteworthy contradiction was revealed by the Iraqi policy in the conflict. Despite its role as Moscow's most reliable friend in the Middle East, Iraq openly pledged support to Eritrean and Somali guerrillas fighting for independence from Addis Ababa. Iraq, at one stage, warned Moscow, in an article in the ruling Baath party newspaper, *Al-Thawrah*, against aligning itself too closely with Ethiopia because that policy would mean losing Somalia and thereby 'benefit imperialist strategy'.[67] *Al-Thawrah*, with obvious reference to the turnabout in Soviet policy towards Eritrea, further declared: 'We cannot change our position as long as the Eritrean people are fighting for their just and legitimate rights.'[68] There were also reports from Western sources of Iraq supplying Somalia with tanks, guns, planes and necessary spare parts from its arsenal of Soviet weapons. These reports only demonstrated the extent to which Middle Eastern rivalries, not only Israeli-Arab but also inter-Arab, did not necessarily harmonise with the affiliation of the individual regional actors with the superpowers.

VII

After careful scrutiny of the conflict on the Horn and the involvement of external powers, in both the politics of the region in general and this conflict in particular, one comes to the following conclusions:

1. Recent events in the Horn of Africa, especially the international realignments, demonstrate the validity of the thesis that regional conflicts in the Third World are more deep-seated than either ideological commitments or alignments with big powers. While the regional conflicts are based most often on competing nationalisms and tenuous local balances which can be easily upset, a number of them, and this is particularly true of the Somali-Ethiopian conflict, owe their origins to colonial boundaries drawn by European powers without regard for divided tribes, peoples and nations.

2. This case study also demonstrates that imperial domination of large parts of Asia and Africa in the eighteenth, nineteenth and early twentieth centuries, although primarily European in character, was not exclusively so. Abyssinian expansionism during the late nineteenth century was a manifestation of imperial aspirations. This expansion under Emperor Menelik was at least as responsible for the current tensions in the Horn as were the European colonial powers with their legacy of colonial boundaries drawn with scant concern for the sentiments of the local population. It is worth repetition that the partition of Somali-inhabited territories in the Horn was the result of arrangements worked out between the European colonial powers—Italy, Britain and France—on the one hand and Ethiopia on the other, as well as among the European powers themselves.

3. The role of World War II as a catalyst for change in the Third World by exposing the mythical nature of supposed European invincibility, although most forcibly demonstrated in South-east Asia, was also in evidence on the Horn, particularly in relation to the Somali population. The consecutive defeats experienced by all the imperial powers in the Horn—Ethiopia (at the hands of Italy in 1935), Britain (by Italy in 1939-40), Italy (by Britain in 1941-2), Vichy France (capitulation of Vichy-ruled Djibouti to the British and the Free French in 1942)—and the later consolidation, however temporary, of all Somali-inhabited territories, except Djibouti, under British control strengthened the foundations of Somali nationalism which had been laid by Sheikh Mohammed Abdille Hassan in the late nineteenth century. The formation of the Somali Youth League (SYL), initially with the blessings of the British, provided the focal point at least in the cities for Somali nationalist activity which increasingly escalated its demands. The UN decision, following World War II, to constitute Italian Somaliland into a UN

Trust Territory with a set programme for independence in 1960 accelerated the pace of nationalist activity not only in the Trust Territory but in British Somaliland and the NFD of Kenya as well. This evolution of Somali nationalism and its assumption of concrete shape in 1960 with the creation of the Somali Republic (by the merger of Italian and British Somaliland) were bound to have important fallout effects on the Somali populations of French-ruled Djibouti and Ethiopian-controlled Ogaden.

4. Superpower involvement in the Horn of Africa began within a few years of the end of World War II. However, throughout the 1950s and during the early 1960s the only credible superpower presence in the Horn was that of the United States. While the US was firmly ensconced as Ethiopia's major ally providing it with political support and military hardware, America's European allies were in firm control of most of the Somali territories in the Horn (Britain and Italy until 1960 and France until 1977). Its northern hinterland—Sudan—was under effective British control till the mid-1950s. American involvement in the Horn was, however, related not so much to its interest in Africa, as to its general Cold War policy of 'containment' or pre-emption of the Soviet Union and, more specifically, to its support for Israel in the Middle East. The utility of the Kagnew Communications Centre near Asmara, in Eritrea, in America's global network of military communications, Ethiopia's role as Israel's only dependable regional supporter and its control of the Red Sea coast considered to be vital to Israel's security, combined to make Addis Ababa the major recipient of US military and economic aid in black Africa. The scale of such assistance, not inconsiderable by African standards, demonstrates the importance attached to Addis Ababa in America's global strategy and in the calculation of its strategic interests in the Red Sea, particularly in the southern seaward approaches to Israel.

5. As has been demonstrated in other cases, particularly in South Asia and the Middle East, the American strategy of 'containing' or pre-empting the Soviet Union by denying it local influence in the Horn and the Red Sea, once again, provided the opportunity for Soviet political and military intrusion which this strategy was supposed to prevent.[69] Just as US military and political support to Pakistan led to the strengthening of Indo-Soviet ties and the total US commitment to Israel resulted in the increasing tilt of important Arab powers towards Moscow, so US economic and military assistance, particularly the latter, to Ethiopia provided the opportunity

for the intrusion of Soviet power and influence into the Horn of Africa. However, it was not until the mid-1960s that the Soviet Union could establish a credible and competitive presence in the Horn. This lag was the result, first, of the lack of Soviet global reach in the 1950s, when it was still undergoing the gradual process of transformation from a regionally dominant to a global power, and second, of the absence of a regional competitor capable of challenging Ethiopian dominance in the Horn. The emergence of the Somali Republic with its anti-Ethiopian bias and its irredentist ideology at a time when the Soviet Union was becoming increasingly confident that it could challenge the Western, and particularly American, presence in the grey areas of the globe (having demonstrated this capability successfully both in South Asia and the Middle East), provided Moscow with the opportunity to enter the influence-building game in the Horn of Africa. Somali disenchantment with Western powers in the context of firm US support to Ethiopia led to Mogadishu's receptiveness to Soviet offers of aid and assistance. Although the first major transfer of Soviet weaponry to Somalia took place in 1963 (a decade after major American arms had been first supplied to Ethiopia), it was not until after the military coup in 1969, which brought President Barre to power in Mogadishu, that Soviet-Somali relations attained the high level of political and military intimacy which they retained until the Somali decision in November 1977 to expel the Soviet Union from Somalia lock, stock and barrel.

6. This dramatic decision, and the equally dramatic regional realignments which preceded it, demonstrated both the autonomy of local powers from their superpower patrons and the fragility of the base of superpower influence in areas of the Third World where such influence rests primarily on the exploitation of local tensions and regional conflicts. Moscow had earlier suffered the same fate in Egypt and Sudan where its services were dispensed with despite no such dramatic shift in Soviet postures *vis-à-vis* Cairo's and Khartoum's regional rivals as was evidenced in the Horn. (The Soviet Union's support to Libya escalated only after its expulsion from Egypt.) While the US has so far not suffered any parallel dramatic setback in this region (its withdrawal from Ethiopia was more gradual, caused by growing mutual disenchantment), the fragility of its regional influence base in South-east Asia has already been demonstrated by the rout of all American-supported regimes in Indo-China where the Americans had invested much more

heavily than any corresponding Soviet investment either in the Middle East or in the Horn of Africa.

7. Events on the Horn have also demonstrated the close connection which exists between different intra-regional rivalries within contiguous regions in the Third World. The importance of Indo-Pakistani tensions in South Asia and the Iraq-Iran rivalry in the Gulf region for Indo-Iranian relations has been demonstrated and documented by this author elsewhere.[70] Similar connections between tensions and conflicts within two further contiguous regions, the Horn and the Middle East in this instance, have been demonstrated above. The support extended to Soviet-backed Ethiopia by Israel on the one hand, and by Libya and South Yemen, the two most radical and, *vis-à-vis* Israel, 'rejectionist' Arab states on the other, is a phenomenon that can be explained only in the context of Middle Eastern rivalries, not merely Israeli-Arab but inter-Arab as well. Similarly, the support extended to socialist, but currently anti-Soviet, Somalia by conservative and moderate Arab states like Saudi Arabia, Egypt and Sudan on the one hand and Moscow's most dependable Arab friend, Iraq, on the other can be understood only in the context of the web of Middle Eastern rivalries. Moreover, as has been stated earlier, superpower attitudes toward rivalries in the Horn are also considerably conditioned by their appreciation of their own interests in the Middle East and their involvement with Middle Eastern allies, friends and adversaries. American support for Somalia was limited partly by the US commitment to Israel. Similarly, Soviet antipathy towards oil-rich and fanatically anti-communist Saudi Arabia and its desire to teach Egypt and Sudan a lesson for the humiliation inflicted by them upon Moscow has considerably affected Soviet perceptions of the situation in the Horn and its decision to support Ethiopia even at the expense of sacrificing its long-nurtured relationship with Somalia.

8. Although the most recent round in the Somali-Ethiopian conflict has been apparently won by Ethiopia with massive Cuban and Soviet support (in fact, had it not been for the active participation of over 10,000 Cuban troops in the battle for the Ogaden, Somalia might have well attained its objective in that territory), the last has not been heard either of Somali irredentism or of the liberation movement in the Ogaden. In fact, by its massive investment in Ethiopia in support of an extremely unstable and unpopular regime, the Soviet Union might well have been launched on the

process of acquiring its own Vietnam, although by (Cuban) proxy. The current Soviet-Cuban-supported Ethiopian campaign against the national liberation movements in Eritrea, particularly the EPLF, is, by Marxist definition itself, an intervention on the wrong side of history. Unlike the Angolan case, where Soviet-Cuban support to the MPLA was generally interpreted, both within and outside the former Portuguese colony, as basically anti-colonial, anti-Western and, particularly, anti-South African, Moscow's continuing involvement with Ethiopia could be interpreted in the unfavourable light of rendering assistance to a crumbling empire bent upon crushing nationalist uprisings in its peripheral regions. If you add to this the character of the Mengistu regime, the long-term has been the OAU's endorsement of Ethiopia's 'traditional' boundaries which gives the Soviet effort a certain amount of legitimacy in the eyes of African and Third World leaders. However, if the conflicts in the Ogaden and in Eritrea continue (as they promise to do given the strength and long experience of the Eritrean forces and the recently renewed guerrilla activity on the part of the WSLF in the Ogaden), such claims to legitimacy are bound to erode over a period of time. When this happens, given the intensity of their commitment to Addis Ababa, Soviet policy-makers, like their American counterparts in Vietnam, would find it extremely difficult, if not impossible, to extricate themselves from a very embarrassing situation, particularly if the Mengistu regime collapses.[71] In that event, the Soviets would acquire complete parity with the US as well as true superpower status. For it seems that the acquisition of one's own Vietnam has become the hallmark of that status.

Notes

1. For a detailed discussion of imperial exploits on the Horn, see I.M. Lewis, *The Modern History of Somaliland: From Nation to State* (Frederick A. Praeger, New York, 1965); John Drysdale, *The Somali Dispute* (Pall Mall Press, London, 1964); Robert L. Hess, *Italian Colonialism in Somalia* (University of Chicago Press, Chicago, 1966); G.N. Trevaskis, *Eritrea: A Colony in Transition* (Oxford University Press, London, 1960); Virginia Thompson and Richard Adloff, *Djibouti and the Horn of Africa* (Stanford University Press, Stanford, 1968).
2. I.M. Lewis, *Modern History of Somaliland*, p. 59.
3. Ibid., p. 61.
4. W. Michael Reisman, 'The Case of Western Somaliland: An International Legal Perspective', *Horn of Africa*, vol. 1, no. 3 (July-September 1978), p. 16.
5. *House of Commons Debates*, 4 June 1946, cols. 1840-1. Emphasis added.
6. Tom J. Farer, *War Clouds on the Horn of Africa* (Carnegie Endowment for International Peace, New York, 1976), p. 67.

7. Ibid., p. 50.

8. For details of the Djibouti problem see Thompson and Adloff, *Djibouti* and 'Affar vs Issa: Looming Conflict', *Africa Institute Bulletin* (Pretoria), vol. 15, no. 5 (1977), pp. 100-10. For details of negotiations about the NFD and the British decision see Drysdale, *Somali Dispute*, pp. 103-66.

9. 'Ethiopia and the Horn of Africa', US Senate Committee on Foreign Affairs, hearings before the subcommittee on African Affairs, 4-6 August 1976 (Washington, 1976), p. 75.

10. A good example of the Israeli preoccupation with the strategic importance of the Bab and therefore of the Horn is found in Mordechai Abir, 'Red Sea Politics', *Conflicts in Africa, Adelphi Papers*, no. 93 (December 1972), pp. 25-37.

11. For an interesting discussion of how the Jewish lobby influences US policy-making towards the Middle East, see Jane Rosen, 'US Middle East Policy Courtesy of the Jewish Lobby', *Guardian Weekly*, 25 September 1977, p. 9.

12. For details of the origins of the US-Ethiopian agreement, see the testimony of John H. Spencer, former Chief Adviser to the Ethiopian Ministry of Foreign Affairs in 'Ethiopia and the Horn of Africa', pp. 26-8.

13. Ethiopia was the only black African country to have supplied a military contingent for UN operations in Korea.

14. 'Ethiopia and the Horn of Africa', p. 27.

15. Ibid., p. 2.

16. US ACDA, *World Military Expenditures and Arms Transfers, 1966-1975*, (Washington, 1976), p. 79.

17. IISS, *The Military Balance 1976-77* (London, 1977), p. 42.

18. SIPRI, *The Arms Trade with the Third World* (Stockholm 1971), pp. 650-1.

19. IISS, *The Military Balance*, p. 44.

20. According to one assessment the Somalis lost a quarter of their tanks and over half their combat aircraft in their initially successful offensive in the Ogaden. Gwynne Dyer, 'Half-Time in the Horn of Africa'. *Canberra Times*, 4 January 1978.

21. UN Doc. A/AC. 159/1 (3 May 1974), p. 14.

22. Testimony of Geoffrey Jukes before the Australian Senate Standing Committee on Foreign Affairs and Defence; reference: *Australia and Indian Ocean Region, 1976, Official Hansard, Transcript of Evidence* (Canberra, 1976), p. 669.

23. Quoted in *Australia and Indian Ocean*. Report from the Australian Senate Standing Committee on Foreign Affairs and Defence, Canberra, 1976, p. 21.

24. 'Dergue' is the Amharic term for 'committee'. For the origins and course of the movement that led to the overthrow of the Emperor, the near anarchic situation in the country following the change in regime and the struggle for power within the Dergue, see Colin Legum, *Ethiopia: The Fall of Haile Selassie's Empire* (Africana Publishing Co., New York, 1975), and Colin Legum, 'Realities of the Ethiopian Revolution', *The World Today*, vol. 33, no. 8 (August 1977), pp. 305-12.

25. Possibly the best account of this transformation in Ethiopia, the intra-Dergue struggle and the true character of the Mengistu regime, is John Markakis and Nega Ayele, *Class and Revolution in Ethiopia* (Spokesman, Nottingham, 1978).

26. Constraints of space prohibit the author dwelling upon the recent developments in Eritrea and their effects on the fortunes of the Dergue. For background on the rise of Eritrean separatism and the present situation in Eritrea, see John Franklin Campbell, 'Rumblings along the Red Sea: The Eritrean Question', *Foreign Affairs*, vol. 48, no. 3 (April 1970), pp. 537-48; J. Bowyer Bell, 'Endemic Insurgency and International Order: The Eritrean Experience', *Orbis*, vol. 18, no. 2 (Summer 1974), pp. 427-50; Farer, *War Clouds*, particularly pp. 5-48.

27. John H. Spencer, 'Haile Selassie: Triumph and Tragedy', *Orbis*, vol. 18, no. 4 (Winter 1975), p. 1146.

28. Legum, 'Ethiopian Revolution', p. 310.

29. Ibid., p. 311.
30. *International Herald Tribune,* 4-5 June 1977.
31. *New York Times,* 5 May 1976.
32. Quoted in Legum, 'Ethiopian Revolution', p. 312.
33. *Newsweek,* 27 June 1977, p. 11.
34. The information given in passages asterisked here and below is taken from a commercially available publication, which is made available only on condition that it is not cited directly.
35. *Australian,* 20 July 1977.
36. Ibid.
37. *International Herald Tribune,* 27 July 1977.
38. Ibid.
39. James Mayall, 'The Battle for the Horn: Somali Irredentism and International Diplomacy', *The World Today,* vol. 34, no. 9 (September 1978), p. 337.
40. Ibid., pp. 338-9.
41. For a discussion of this controversy see Elizabeth Drew, 'A Reporter at Large: Zbigniew Brzezinski', *New Yorker,* 1 May 1978, pp. 90-130.
42. *Canberra Times,* 3 September 1977.
43. *Newsweek,* 26 September 1977, pp. 15-16; *Guardian Weekly,* 30 October 1977.
44. *Guardian Weekly,* 30 October 1977.
45. *Newsweek,* 26 September 1977, p. 15.
46. Mayall, 'Battle for the Horn', p. 341.
47. *International Herald Tribune,* 3-4 September 1977.
48. *Australian,* 16 August 1977 and *International Herald Tribune,* 17 August 1977. The *Izvestia* article, published on 16 August, said that even 'the plausible excuse of implementing the principle of self-determination' does not justify Somalia's action. It went on to state that 'fighting is going on between regular units of the Somalian Army and Ethiopian troops ... It is a fact that hostilities are taking place in Ethiopian territory and that it is Ethiopia and no other country that is the victim of armed invasion ... Armed intervention is in crying contradiction with the principles of the UN Charter and the Charter of the OAU. To justify such a violation by a desire to implement the principle of self-determination is to mislead the broad African public.'
49. *International Herald Tribune,* 22-3 October 1977.
50. Ibid., 14 November 1977.
51. Ibid., 17 November 1977.
52. Ibid., 25 November 1977.
53. Ibid., 7 December 1977.
54. Mayall, 'Battle for the Horn', p. 341.
55. Lawrence Whetten, 'The Soviet – Cuban Presence in the Horn of Africa', *RUSI,* vol. 123, no. 3 (September 1978), p. 41.
56. Ibid. See also 'Airlift to Ethiopia', *Newsweek,* 23 January 1978.
57. For details of the campaign, see 'The Ogaden Debacle', *Newsweek,* 20 March 1978.
58. *New York Times,* 13 January 1978.
59. Fred Halliday, 'US Policy in the Horn of Africa: Aboulia or Proxy Intervention?', *Review of African Political Economy,* No. 10, September-December 1978, p. 21.
60. For a discussion of the two lines within the US administration and the clash between them, see *Guardian,* 15 February 1978.
61. Halliday, 'US Policy in the Horn of Africa', p. 25.
62. W. Scott Thompson, 'The American-African Nexus in Soviet Strategy', *Horn of Africa,* vol. 1, no. 1 (January-March 1978), p. 43.
63. *International Herald Tribune,* 25 July 1977.

64. *Newsweek,* 31 October 1977.
65. *Sydney Morning Herald,* 8 February 1978.
66. Colin Legum, 'The Horn of Africa', *Current Affairs Bulletin,* vol. 55, no. 8 (January 1979), p. 13.
67. Quoted in *International Herald Tribune,* 17 August 1977.
68. Quoted in Ian Clark, 'The Communist Powers in Africa', *Current Affairs Bulletin,* vol. 55, no. 3 (August 1978), p. 22.
69. For the South Asian case, see the section on South Asia in Mohammed Ayoob, 'The Indian Ocean Littoral: Intra-Regional Conflicts and Weapons Proliferation' in Robert O'Neill (ed.), *Insecurity! The Spread of Weapons in the Indian and Pacific Oceans* (ANU Press, Canberra 1978); for the Middle East, see Fuad Jabber, *The Politics of Arms Transfer and Control: The United States and Egypt's Quest for arms, 1950-55,* Southern California Arms Control and Foreign Policy Seminar, Los Angeles, 1972.
70. Mohammed Ayoob, 'Indo-Iranian Relations: Strategic, Political and Economic Dimensions', *India Quarterly,* vol. 33, no. 1 (January-March 1977), pp. 1-18.
71. For a perceptive and detailed account of internal challenges to the Mengistu regime and the true character of the regime, see Markakis and Ayele, *Class and Revolution in Ethiopia.*

7 Rhodesia*

I.R. HANCOCK

I

For many years Ian Smith claimed that if Rhodesians were left alone they would eventually solve the Rhodesian problem by themselves. He argued that because he was obliged to appease the conscience of the West, and because the nationalists were being prompted by the 'communist bloc', it was impossible to reach a negotiated solution satisfactory to the relevant parties inside the country. What Mr Smith really meant, and why he was so often bitter on the subject, was that external intervention had prevented white Rhodesians from obtaining their basic objective: international recognition and acceptance of continued white rule in Salisbury. Rarely did the Rhodesian Prime Minister state the objective so crudely, and when he did so he was usually addressing the party faithful in closed session. For the most part he assumed an air of injured innocence, either protesting that outsiders were deliberately sabotaging progress towards a peaceful and harmonious settlement, principally because they wanted to advance the 'communist cause' in southern Africa, or insisting that the overwhelming majority of African opinion, as represented by government-appointed chiefs and other 'responsible' Africans, wanted an internal settlement which would preserve 'civilised standards'. Mr Smith also argued that militant nationalism had only limited popular support, especially in the rural areas, and could not survive without intimidation and moral and material assistance from outside. In his view 'intervention' by communist countries and by Western liberals had partly provoked and largely exacerbated the Rhodesian conflict, and the conflict itself could only be resolved by Rhodesians meeting each other inside the country and around the negotiating table. Ironically, when they did so, the result was the internal settlement of 3 March 1978, an agreement which not only failed to solve the

**Author's note.* This was written before the Rhodesian elections of April 1979; however, that event does not change the conclusions reached in the chapter.

Rhodesian problem but ran counter to the whites' basic objective. The important point, however, is that Ian Smith both tacitly and explicitly acknowledged that the source of his frustration was international involvement in the Rhodesian conflict.[1]

Yet just as he deliberately under-estimated the strength of militant nationalism inside the country, the Rhodesian Prime Minister exaggerated the role of outside forces in Rhodesian politics. It was, after all, more convenient to blame 'left-wing influences' in the British Foreign Office[2] for his failure to deliver to the white electorate what he called the 'first prize'—a constitutional settlement and the preservation of European rule—than admit his own failure to convince Africans that he could be trusted to implement the letter and the spirit of the Anglo-Rhodesian agreement of 1971. But what was convenient was also misleading. In the first place, the Rhodesian problem was local and not international in origin. As Colin Legum pointed out,[3] the root of the conflict in southern Africa is 'entirely indigenous' and arises from 'the determination of black Africans to bring an end to the white supremacist regimes there'; although he might have added that another kind of determination—evident in the whites' refusal to forgo their privileges or even contemplate majority rule—was equally important in promoting confrontation. The second point is that while outside forces helped to prevent white Rhodesia from obtaining the 'first prize', and did, finally, tilt the balance of power towards the nationalists, they were unable and unwilling to impose solutions. For more than a decade after UDI (the Unilateral Declaration of Independence) in 1965 there was a vast difference between what Mr Smith, in the face of international repudiation, could not achieve, and what, in the absence of sufficient international pressure, he was able to maintain. It was this gap which explains why confident predictions about the early demise of white Rhodesia proved so wildly wrong. And part of the reason why Mr Smith survived for so long was that the Rhodesian conflict remained essentially a local one, and in the local context the Europeans were firmly in control.

Clearly, however, the great powers were involved in the progress of the Rhodesian conflict. The object here is to determine more precisely the nature, extent and relative importance of that involvement by examining three particular themes: the several attempts of the British, and later in conjunction with the Americans, to force and persuade the white Rhodesians to make substantial concessions towards African advancement and to negotiate meaningfully with the black nationalists; the role of the Soviet Union and of China in supplying arms, training assistance and ideological guidance to the guerrillas; the attempts, especially from the mid-1970s, to ensure that the eventual outcome in south-central Africa would not, at the very least, be unfavourable to the interests of the particular powers. Basically the argument will be developed along the following lines: for a long time great-power interest in Rhodesian affairs was either marginal or ambivalent and for this reason, together with the determination and local strength of white Rhodesia, the overall declared objective of a transfer of power was not seriously pressed and was certainly not far advanced; that from the mid-1970s great-power involvement increased quite dramatically without at the same time becoming proportionately more influential and direct; that apart from the easy though important victory of denying white Rhodesia a legalised and secure independence, the net result of great-power intervention by the end of 1978 was an escalating war, an uncertain future and a weakened but continuing European dominance in Salisbury.

II

The initial step in this analysis must be to see how and why the Rhodesian conflict began. The key period was from the late 1950s until UDI. During this time two clear sets of views were formed inside Rhodesia, the one represented by a succession of nationalist parties which came to demand immediate majority rule, and the other, ultimately, by the RF (Rhodesian Front) which opposed any modification of the existing system. The divisions between the standpoints were fundamental, long-standing and irreconcilable. The history of African resistance goes back to the arrival of the first settlers in 1890 and although sometimes muted, and always well contained following the rebellions of 1893 and 1896-7, protest continued unabated in the twentieth century. When in 1957 the African National Congress was re-formed, beginning a new phase both in the intensity and the objectives of resistance, the leaders tapped deep sources of discontent about the level of wages and the living and working conditions on European farms and in the mines and the urban areas, and about the multitude of indignities and abuses endured under white rule. Perhaps Joshua Nkomo or Robert Mugabe or Ndabaningi Sithole did find inspiration in the contemporary stirrings of black America, in Nkrumah's Ghana or in the emotions and ideas of a broader African nationalism. But for the large majority of those who joined the Congress and much later ZAPU (Zimbabwe African People's Union) and ZANU (Zimbabwe African National Union) these sounds from abroad were appealing but distant. Their motivation was at home, in the Land Apportionment Act of 1930 and the Land Husbandry Act of 1951, in the industrial colour bar and the poverty and filth of the overcrowded African townships, in the pass laws, the mining compounds and the attitudes of white authority. Meanwhile the Rhodesian government added to their discontent when, in 1959 and 1960, Sir Edgar Whitehead introduced several pieces of repressive legislation and when, after the RF came to power in 1962, it proceeded even more rigorously to ban the nationalist parties and their activities. Under these circumstances, where constitutional methods were denied to them, serious nationalists did not need advice from overseas to seek redress through violence.[4]

On the other side white reaction hardened from the late 1950s. Stories brought by refugees from the Congo and by former European farmers in Kenya confirmed assumptions about the consequences of giving power to the African. Decolonisation meant the destruction of white privilege and of political stability and must be resisted to the end. On several occasions from the mid-1950s a small minority of white Rhodesians tried to suggest that unless the European was prepared to share power with moderate Africans his privileges would be forcibly taken away. The majority had no time for such cleverness, or for multi-racial idealism. Any attempt to alter the basis of white power was anathema, any proposal to modify the most trivial of its manifestations was suspect. So in 1958 Garfield Todd was eliminated from European politics because he sounded like a liberal and in 1962 Sir Edgar Whitehead was rejected because he behaved like one. When in 1964 members of the RF caucus felt that Winston Field was not sufficiently tough and uncompromising in defending white supremacy they elected Ian Douglas Smith to do the job for them. The argument was always that the European standard of living in Rhodesia depended ultimately on the ability of the whites to control the political system and, after all, the 'Rhodesian way of life' was only fair compensation for bearing that heavy responsibility of representing Christianity and Western Civilisation in the lands between the Zambesi and the Limpopo. Land apportionment, security of employment, residential segregation, separate health and education facilities, this vast body of discriminatory legislation and practice would be swept away in a transfer of power and replaced by expropriation, chaos and enforced racial integration. Convinced, therefore, that black rule was dangerous and unacceptable, that the only guarantee for preserving the 'Rhodesian way of life' was perpetual European rule, and that the only guarantee of permanent white supremacy was independence from the decolonising power, the electorate and its government moved inexorably towards UDI. And once UDI was declared the breach within Rhodesian society was complete.[5]

In 1965 Rhodesia was still a British colony and UDI was an act of rebellion. Apart from any moral obligation, Britain had a legal right to intervene. A quick decisive strike in November-December 1965 ought to have ended the matter but, instead, the British response was hopelessly inadequate and, for a time, even self-defeating.

For more than forty years successive British governments steadily relaxed their hold over the colony of Southern Rhodesia, assisted in their departure from responsibility by the determination and astute tactics of Sir Godfrey Huggins, Rhodesia's longest serving Prime Minister. As a result, by the 1950s, the Rhodesian Parliament had encroached on areas which under the 1923 constitution were excluded from its legislative competence, while the powers of reservation and disallowance, particularly those covering 'native affairs', were of little practical consequence. When the Central African Federation was formed in 1953 the Southern Rhodesian legislature surrendered considerable powers to the new federal government although it retained authority over African affairs and both politically and personally the federal government was closely identified with the European community. For a number of reasons the Federation failed, and during the process of disintegration Sir Edgar Whitehead's government sought a constitution which would be the basis for Rhodesian independence. In return for a substantial transfer of power to the Rhodesian executive and legislature he agreed to a number of measures for African political advancement. The outcome was the 1961 constitution which conferred 'a remarkable degree of self-government' in external affairs and confirmed the trend towards virtual internal self-government.[6] None the less Westminster retained 'the inalienable power ... to legislate'.[7] Nkomo and the nationalists repeatedly drew attention to this authority and urged the British government to assume full control in Salisbury. There was, however, a strong and stated convention that Westminster would not legislate on matters within the competence of the Legislative Assembly without the concurrence of the Rhodesian government. A number of Tory ministers interpreted this convention to mean that it would be 'constitutionally improper and impracticable' for the British government to enact a new constitution extending African political rights without first obtaining the approval of the Rhodesian government.[8] Whatever the legal position, no Tory cabinet would impose constitutional change upon Salisbury. On the other hand, the Tories rejected RF appeals to grant independence on the basis of the 1961 constitution and this view was strongly upheld by the incoming Labour Government after October 1964. Both parties insisted on the implementation of five principles before independence would be approved: unimpeded progress towards majority rule; guarantees against retrogressive constitutional amendment; an immediate improvement in African political status; progress towards ending racial discrimination; satisfaction on the part of the British government that any proposal was acceptable to the Rhodesian people as a whole.[9] It will be noted that the five principles fell short of requiring that majority rule precede independence. More important, insistence on these principles mattered less than the practical issue of whether the Labour Government would reverse the trend since 1923, assert its responsibility, and persuade or force Salisbury to proceed.

The test was UDI itself. All the published accounts indicate that Harold Wilson took extraordinary steps to forestall the rebellion. Richard Crossman said that the British Prime Minister was 'appalled' by the prospect of UDI and convinced himself that his personal intervention, including a trip to Salisbury, could save the situation.[10] Wilson regarded the Rhodesian crisis as his 'Cuba' and throughout 1965 initiated, presided over and closely followed an intensive round of negotiations. In his anxiety he went dangerously close to unconscionable concessions and was only saved from embarrassment by Mr Smith's desire to settle the issue once and for all. Crossman criticised his leader's otherwise laudable concern on the ground that preoccupation with prevention meant that he neglected to prepare a cure when UDI occurred.[11] A more serious and specific charge is that by publicly ruling out the use of force, both before and after UDI, Mr Wilson committed what Kenneth Kaunda of Zambia called 'one of the greatest blunders any government could make'.[12] Some members of Wilson's cabinet—including James Callaghan—did press for 'stronger measures' and were overruled.[13]

The consequences of this decision were threefold. First, the Rhodesians knew from the very start that any British threats were limited to non-recognition and the introduction of economic sanctions, neither of which would be as immediately devastating as a military operation. Whether or how far the threat of force would have made the Rhodesian government more amenable during negotiations is hard to determine but undoubtedly Britain's bargaining position was considerably weakened. Secondly, by refusing to seize power in Salisbury, the British allowed the Rhodesian government to consolidate its power at the only time before the late 1970s when its ability to maintain law and order was in question. Finally, the act of rebellion provided a perfect excuse to deal with settlerdom; the refusal to use it reduced Britain's direct role in Rhodesian affairs to that of peacemaker, negotiator and messenger boy and, somewhat more dubiously, policeman and moral guardian. In 1965 Britain abdicated the role of 'imperial arbiter'.[14]

A number of factors explain why force was rejected.[15] When discussing African pressure for military intervention Crossman said it was an option which could not be taken:

> partly because it will split the country from top to bottom and partly because we haven't got the troops and if we had it would be geographically impossible to put them in.[16]

Public opinion was a major consideration, and public opinion plainly opposed a war against 'kith and kin'. There was the question of logistics and manpower, of the huge cost of mounting and sustaining such an operation, of the political problems of upholding law and order once the European government fell and the problems of maintaining troop loyalty when dealing with fellow whites and British subjects. Because some of the arguments were never tested it is difficult to judge their intrinsic worth, just as it is hard to determine which particular arguments weighed more heavily. What is evident from the Crossman diaries, Harold Wilson's own writings and press comment is that two kinds of argument took precedence. One was political—the fears of a public outcry, Labour's narrow majority in the House of Commons, the desire for a bipartisan policy—and it was his skill in handling the domestic politics of the Rhodesian crisis which so enhanced the Prime Minister's reputation at home in late 1965 and early 1966. The other argument was military. While on paper the British forces were vastly superior, the difficulties of launching an attack from Nairobi or Lusaka were clearly formidable. Once again Richard Crossman pinpointed the problem:

> We have no means of enforcing law and order on the rebels, whereas the rebels obviously have every means of maintaining law and order in defiance of us.[17]

The probability that these two arguments counted significantly against the use of force illustrates how Britain's freedom of action in dealing with the rebellion was limited. The same point applies to the introduction and enforcement of economic sanctions, a programme complicated by Britain's own contradictory interests and the failure of the international community to act in concert. The assumption was that an economic stranglehold would soon bring an end to UDI and, hopefully, lead to African political advance and eventually to majority rule. Some in 1966 challenged the assumption: Sir Edgar Whitehead argued that it was 'a basic error in British official thinking' to suppose that 'political and racial attitudes can be altered by economic pressure';[18] Ian Smith pointed out that 'the more we are attacked the more determined, indeed the more defiant, we become'.[19] The real problem, however, apart from misjudging the versatility of the Rhodesian economy and of its businessmen, was that, even supposing that an embargo could produce 'correct' political change, the British lacked the means and the will to impose watertight sanctions.

Almost immediately after UDI the British government introduced selective sanctions, prohibited oil imports into Rhodesia and progressively extended the trade boycott. Invited by Britain to intervene, the Security Council of the United Nations approved selected mandatory sanctions in December 1966 and comprehensive mandatory sanctions in May 1968. By the end of the 1960s an extensive boycott was allegedly in force. Yet without the co-operation of Portugal and South Africa no sanctions policy could be properly effective, and South Africa's consistent stand since 1965 of maintaining normal trade relations with Rhodesia enabled the colony to retain existing links and open new ones with sanction-breaking countries and firms. The obvious solution was to extend the embargo to include South Africa itself, and it was equally obvious that a naval blockade of the entire region would have been expensive, complicated and, without the total support of the entire Western world, impossible to maintain. In any case, British ministers had no intention of instituting an economic war against South Africa. Richard Crossman argued in the cabinet that to do so 'may split the Commonwealth or commit economic suicide'.[20] In one sense he exaggerated the importance of the South African connection as British exports to the white *laager* accounted for less than four per cent annually of the total export figure during the late 1960s. On the other hand, British investment amounted to ten per cent of total overseas investment, while the Labour Government, despite a ban on arm sales, actively involved itself in trade promotion in South Africa. Anthony Crosland, as President of the Board of Trade, insisted that political differences over apartheid 'should not be allowed to affect the expansion of our mutual trade'.[21] Nor did they: between 1969 and 1971 British exports to South Africa rose by 50 per cent while the Heath Tory Government of 1970 extended the Crosland proposition to include the sale of arms. Labour's return to power in 1974 did signal a new and cooler outlook, notwithstanding the continuing development of trade relations. By then, sensitivity about the British economy was lessened by expanded trade contacts with the rest of black Africa and offset by a greater awareness of the implications of any association with Pretoria. Nevertheless, until the mid-1970s the overriding fear was that a blockade of South Africa would harm Britain's ailing economy and—to give the argument more respectability—hurt South Africa's black population as well as push South Africa and Rhodesia closer together. The arguments of the time were openly stated and perfectly understandable. Their effect was equally clear: the whole elaborate system of economic sanctions had its fatal flaw in southern Africa itself, and both the unscrupulous and the ostensibly honourable exploited this weakness with relative impunity.[22]

Successive British governments were not prepared to sacrifice perceived national interests for the sake of ending UDI. Neither, it seems, were they unambiguous in their role of moral policeman. The Bingham Report, for example, raised serious doubts about the determination of both the Labour and Tory administrations to close every avenue for Rhodesia's oil supplies.[23] If sincerity of intention is not in dispute, then dedication in action most certainly is. The 1965 order banning oil imports, followed by the formation of the Beira patrol to blockade Mozambique's main port facility supplying oil direct to Rhodesia, represented swift and decisive action against Rhodesia's oil sources. Yet the Bingham Report indicates that Rhodesia's oil consumption actually doubled between 1965 and 1978, despite stringent rationing after 1974. It now transpires that a vital source of fuel was established in 1968 whereby the

Shell and BP subsidiaries in South Africa supplied oil to the customers of the French company of Total in return for Total meeting contracts inside Rhodesia. This arrangement expired in 1971 when Shell and BP in South Africa supplied oil to Rhodesian buyers from stocks delivered in Lourenço Marques (now Maputo) by Shell Mozambique. The question is how much did the Labour and Tory Governments know of these sanction-busting arrangements. Evidently George Thomson, Minister without Portfolio, knew all the details of the Total agreement in February 1969 and there is now some argument between himself and his former Prime Minister about whether the Overseas Policy Committee, chaired by Harold Wilson, was also informed. It does seem odd that such fundamental breaches of sanctions could, over a period of some eight years, escape the notice of three Prime Ministers, five Foreign Secretaries and nine Energy Ministers who in 'ignorance' gave assurances about British compliance with sanctions. In November 1978 another Foreign Secretary, Dr David Owen, explained this apparent laxity in terms of four factors preventing British ministers from closing the oil route to Salisbury: Portugal and South Africa created huge gaps in any proposed blockade; attempts to close the gaps would involve 'economic confrontation with South Africa'; the other Western powers were reluctant to put pressure on the oil companies and, in any case, there were legal difficulties in dealing with international companies and with British subsidiaries abroad; the British government was unwilling to act alone and thereby attempt to enforce unworkable policies. In his view there was no 'complicity, deceit or double dealing', only 'honest men of successive governments struggling with massive political problems'.[24] Honest or deceitful, it hardly matters. Dr Owen's defence, and the negligence revealed in the Bingham Report, plainly demonstrate the essential pragmatism of British policy and how, in the face of practical difficulties, British ministers could be less than intrepid policemen. The Beira patrol was dramatic but it became irrelevant; the arrangement with Total was deceptive but effective as well. It is not surprising, therefore, that when Rhodesia faced a serious fuel crisis from the mid-1970s the cause was the sharp rise in oil prices and not the oil embargo.

The 'stick' failed. British policy, with its UN support, never threatened to bring Mr Smith 'to his knees'. Rather, it was Zambia which came closer to bankruptcy while the Rhodesian economy, in many ways, actually expanded.[25] From 1965 to 1974 the Gross

Domestic Product had risen by 83 per cent in real terms, industrial output nearly doubled and mining output tripled, the range of goods produced inside the country trebled, there was a 60 per cent jump in exports and a 50 per cent increase in foreign investment and, in the same period, inflation averaged only 3.5 per cent per annum and white immigration leapt ahead of emigration. While every year the prophets of doom forecast imminent collapse, and leading Rhodesian businessmen professed alarm about 'the already marked deterioration of the economic situation'[26] and warned of the long-term consequences of economic sanctions, most white Rhodesians believed they were winning the 'economic war' and applauded their Prime Minister in his frequent denunciations of the 'jeremiahs' and 'leftists' who spread pessimism and despondency. Certainly there were problems, which were evident to any detached observer long before the downturn of the mid-1970s. Economic expansion had not absorbed all the eligible Africans into the workforce nor improved their relative wage position; the immediate necessity of providing full employment for skilled white workers and upholding their standard of living stored up serious political problems for the future; the tobacco industry was badly buffeted by sanctions, replacement parts were hard to obtain, export returns were subject to high charges imposed by overseas middlemen and, despite the improved rate of foreign investment, Rhodesia could not gain sufficient access to capital markets to exploit its natural advantages or keep pace with population growth. Meanwhile, businessmen complained bitterly about petty government regulations and about 'irrational racial prejudice' which restrained 'natural progress' in the country by ignoring the African market to satisfy the demands of the small white community.[27] The mistake, however, was to interpret these murmurings and setbacks as evidence that sanctions would soon achieve their objective. From 1965 until the mid-1970s there was no such possibility.

There were two main reasons why this was so. First, so long as the loopholes remained, the principal *political* effect of the embargoes was to unite the white population behind the Smith Government. Instead of encouraging the opposition, the 'economic war' converted all but a handful into stout 'patriots'. Even as they grumbled about the exchange regulations, petrol rationing and shoddy local substitutes, white Rhodesians took delight in morale-boosting coups like the purchase of three Boeing aircraft in 1973 and all those visible signs of 'victory' including multi-storey buildings in

Salisbury, new tourist hotels at Victoria Falls and Kariba, the European and Japanese cars on the roads and locally-built machinery on the farms. Instead of abandoning the RF they voted consistently and overwhelmingly for 'Good Old Smithy',[28] they endorsed the 1969 constitution which offered the Africans only the distant hope of parity with the whites in the parliament, and they dismissed the small white opposition parties as irrelevant and 'un-Rhodesian'. Like the Prime Minister himself they turned viciously and crudely on those who dared to criticise or question white Rhodesia's future. In 1967 one businessman, conservative by nature, complained sadly to the chairman of the RF that to be 'anti-isolationist', to favour a settlement, was to risk accusations of being 'anti-Government' and even 'unpatriotic'.[29] Given this atmosphere it was inherently unlikely that the local business community—fondly expected by many British officials to lead a revolt against Mr Smith—would do more than press privately for renewed negotiations between the two governments. Between 1967 and 1969 one organisation, the Forum, consisting of the less significant managers of foreign capital and mainly of local manufacturers and financiers, frequently saw Mr Smith and visiting British political figures. At no stage did they go further than seek a common meeting-ground between the two governments; they never threatened the Rhodesian government with a boycott of their own indispensable and brilliantly-conceived operations for breaking sanctions; they roundly denounced any British proposal stipulating that the RF Government or Ian Smith himself should stand aside as a condition of organising a settlement. The expectation or hope, therefore, that sanctions would induce or enforce a return to 'Whiteheadism' and the 1961 constitution never had any basis in reality.

The second reason why sanctions failed politically was that the British government applied the 'carrot' as well as the 'stick'. This may be a harsh judgement, easy enough to make in retrospect, particularly at a time when it is fashionable to depict Harold Wilson as concerned only 'with every short-run occurrence of political importance' and when more decisive action from the mid-1970s has precipitated the decline of white Rhodesia. None the less, Labour's tactics after the failure of the 'quick kill'[30] of 1965-6 were based on two false premises: that the 'stick' would break the white monolith inside Rhodesia, and that the 'carrot' would induce Mr Smith to discard his right-wing and agree to significant if not revolutionary concessions for the sake of a settlement. The latter assumption presupposed that the Prime Minister was a moderate, shackled to extreme racialists in the cabinet and in the extra-parliamentary executive. In part the assumption made sense. The fact that Ian Smith was prepared to negotiate surely indicated a willingness to compromise; better than most he knew of the long-term consequences of sanctions; he appeared to give every encouragement to the Forum in seeking business and farming support for a settlement within the broad scope of the five British principles; he kept talking in public about wanting the 'first prize'. It was also true that the cabinet, the parliamentary caucus and, especially, the party organisation were stacked with 'hard-core isolationists' who regarded the British connection as expendable and who were afraid of what their leader might give away when cornered in the wardroom of a British cruiser somewhere near Gibraltar. Finally, it was confidently and justifiably expected that from 1965 Mr Smith could 'sell' anything reasonable to the white electorate. He was so impeccably Rhodesian; if it was alright for 'Smithy' then it must be alright for Rhodesia. Unfortunately these very persuasive arguments overlooked Ian Smith's consistent and deeply-felt conviction that white supremacy was a desirable end in itself. If at times he complained of the strength of his right-wing and expressed concern about splitting the white community, the realisation that he himself was totally committed to the retention of white Rhodesia and would never compromise on its essentials, seems not to have penetrated British thinking until the 1970s, or was overborne by a certain residual credulity that the Rhodesian Prime Minister was a realist and a man of integrity. On this basis Labour and Tory ministers bargained with Mr Smith about constitutional technicalities. They succeeded only in convincing him that the issue was not the straightforward one of majority rule but a modified and legalised version of the status quo.[31]

It is difficult to see how the British proposals for a settlement—the *Tiger* and *Fearless* constitutions of 1966 and 1968, and the Anglo-Rhodesian agreement of 1971—can be regarded as substantial advances towards majority rule.[32] Admittedly, in theory, African rule would eventually have emerged. Yet all three sets of proposals relied ultimately on a new spirit prevailing in Salisbury, and African critics of the various schemes were understandably sceptical about any change of outlook within the RF. Admittedly, too, at the Commonwealth Conference in September 1966 the British government was virtually forced into acknowledging the principle of NIBMAR (no independence before majority African rule)[33] and, in theory, NIBMAR symbolised basic and irreconcilable differences between the Labour Government and Mr Smith. Yet judging by Richard Crossman's account of the cabinet meeting of 10 September 1966 Wilson himself was especially reluctant to support NIBMAR.[34] To concede the principle, in the face of Commonwealth pressure, would be to turn British policy 'upside down'. In Wilson's view, such a step 'would end the chance of negotiations and throw the white Rhodesians into the arms of South Africa'. George Brown, as Foreign Secretary, then reminded the Prime Minister that it was agreed not to mention NIBMAR only 'because it was tactically unwise to do so during our negotiations with Smith ... we never thought that NIBMAR was not the prevailing principle on which our policy was based'. If George Brown was right on the matter of fundamental principle then all those 'soundings' taken in Salisbury before 1970 and all the adroit manipulation of legal terminology were a waste of time because Ian Smith would not, and could not, countenance NIBMAR. Alternatively, had the negotiations with Smith been meaningful and produced an agreement, then the British cabinet faced a split within its own ranks and a revolt from its backbench. The simple fact remains, however, that NIBMAR was not a condition for an agreement in 1966 or in 1968 and was clearly disregarded by the Tories in 1971.

The Rhodesian cabinet may not have liked the *Tiger* or *Fearless* terms but, as both Wilson and Brown indicated in September 1966, the British government, for tactical reasons, put forward proposals which did at least provide a continuing basis for discussion. In keeping the lines of communication open London was no doubt relying on the impact of sanctions and judgements about Smith's desire for a settlement. Looking back, the Rhodesians were unwise not to accept that, in an imperfect world, an indefinite period of a modified version of white rule was better than a few years' grace for a system which could, conceivably, collapse overnight and in total bloodshed. Similarly, on reflection, the British government's offers, for all the horrendous possibilities envisaged by the far right in Salisbury, give the distinct impression that the principal objective was disengagement and, if necessary, disengagement at the expense of majority rule in the foreseeable future.

After 1970 the Tories, who also alienated black Africa in other ways, pushed disengagement still further by signing the Anglo-Rhodesian agreement of 1971. Arguably, the agreement diluted the

British commitment on each of the first four original principles. Under the fifth, requiring the Rhodesian people as a whole to accept any settlement, the Pearce Commission was appointed to test opinion inside Rhodesia. In 1972 the Commission reported a massive 'NO' among the six per cent of Africans consulted.[35] In accepting the Commission's finding, that the settlement was indeed rejected by the people as a whole, Sir Alec Douglas-Home told the House of Commons that it was now up to the Rhodesians to reach a settlement among themselves. He urged Mr Smith to negotiate with Bishop Muzorewa and the African National Council which had been formed to oppose the 1971 agreement. The irony of this proposal was that just when international intervention promised some satisfaction to the white Rhodesians their Prime Minister was being asked to seek, instead, a Rhodesian solution and to talk with those he dismissed as unrepresentative.

The Douglas-Home speech marked the end of an important phase in Anglo-Rhodesian relations. From this point Britain's role in the Rhodesian conflict ceased to be that of a principal party, and of spokesman for Rhodesian African interests, and became one of mediator trying to bring the nationalists and the white rulers to the same negotiating table. As a principal party Britain's record was by no means an unmitigated disaster. There were occasions, it is true, when only white intransigence or the African 'NO' in 1972 saved the Labour and Tory Governments from circumventing or abandoning the first four principles. On the other hand the test of acceptability proved a useful safeguard for African interests and the honour of the British government. Besides, no British minister came near to accepting UDI or the 1969 constitution and, for all the bitter attacks from the African countries in the Commonwealth and from the OAU (Organisation of African Unity) and the demands that force be used to bring down the 'Smith regime', it should be remembered that the rejection of these two attempts to cement white supremacy amounted to a serious blow to the ambitions of the European community. In any event, no British government could afford to regard the Rhodesian problem as purely a matter of implementing certain moral principles. According to Dr Owen on 7 November 1978, both the Labour and the Tory administrations had to balance a range of considerations: the need to weigh every punitive act with renewed prospects for a settlement; Britain's relations with the Commonwealth and with the international community; the problems created by the economic crises after 1967; concern for the 'extensive commercial and investment interests built up over many years in South Africa, and for South Africa's willingness to exercise a moderating influence on the regime'; the lack of enthusiasm among major allies for sanctions.[36] The key punitive act was to impose and police sanctions. The chosen methods were inadequate and inadvertently strengthened white resistance. In the end, all Dr Owen could say in reply to such charges was to deny that the operation had been a 'waste of time' and a 'farce', even though sanctions had not brought about majority rule. After all, he claimed, sanctions were 'a clear demonstration of a national and international resolve not to accept UDI'. The reply may sound lame, but acceptance was what white Rhodesia both wanted and needed. And insofar as the answer was lame, the reason was simply that in circumstances where Britain could not forsake other interests, and expect support if she did so, white Rhodesia was able to sustain the rebellion.

III

It was soon apparent that sanctions would not administer a 'quick kill' and, in isolation, would not end UDI for a long time. It was also clear to those nationalists who had escaped the clampdown in Rhodesia in 1964 that constitutional protest was impracticable. For them the main hope seemed to lie in the prosecution of a guerrilla war.[37] Initially the odds against success were long. A bare handful of Africans, given rudimentary training in the Soviet Union, China or Ghana, were ranged against security forces which had the advantage of better equipment and training, whose senior officers were veterans of the counter-insurgency operation in Malaya and which were backed by an armoury of repressive legislation and an extensive intelligence network of paid African informers. Perhaps the one disability facing the security forces was their lack of co-ordination,[38] a deficiency soon remedied after the guerrilla incursions began in 1966. Indeed the military had little difficulty in containing guerrilla activity between 1966 and 1969—especially given South African police assistance after 1967—and were to a degree overconfident about their capacity to deal with a 'scruffy lot'[39] of black insurgents. Even when the situation changed in 1972-3 the security forces repeatedly assured the government and the public that the situation was well in hand. In March 1976, for instance, during or just before the mass incursions in the Eastern Highlands, Major Brian Barrett-Hamilton told a passing-out parade that there were 'not enough (guerrillas) to go around ... so please get yours early'.[40] One reason for confidence was, and is, the public quarrelling and the power struggles within the nationalist movement: the splits within and between ZAPU and ZANU in the early 1970s, the internecine war of 1974-5, the factionalism within and between the sections of the Patriotic Front. Tribalism, personal ambitions, ideological divisions, all militated against unity in the 1960s and 1970s and diverted attention from what was supposedly the main objective. Nevertheless the ill-conceived tactics of the 1960s were replaced in the 1970s by more sophisticated methods of guerrilla warfare, the quality of weapons improved considerably and so, in time, did the knowledge of how to use them. The guerrillas also became much more adept in persuading the local tribesmen to support their cause. As a result, after 1976, breezy remarks about 'cowardly ters' and confident predictions of 'victory' were belied by a succession of guerrilla triumphs. Some were of enormous psychological importance in weakening white morale, like the killings on the outskirts of Salisbury in January 1978. Others simply underlined the central fact that in 1978 no area in Rhodesia outside of the urban centres was 'safe', that the African rural population was no longer 'reliable' and that ordinary travel on the major roads was unwise during daylight as well as after dark and wise only in convoy. The war is neither won nor lost but the 'Rhodesian way of life' has become much less attractive.

The question to be examined now is how far intervention by the socialist countries is responsible for the improved guerrilla performance, and how much influence they aim to achieve, and do achieve, with the guerrillas. But first, to see the question in perspective, it is necessary to look at the relationship between the liberation movement and the OAU.

Originally and in principle throughout the entire conflict, the OAU insisted that it was Britain's responsibility to end the rebellion and to effect changes inside Rhodesia. Immediately after UDI an abortive and embarrassing attempt was made to pressure Britain into using force by issuing an ultimatum threatening to break diplomatic relations with London. In the event only nine states did so.[41] Despite this disaster the OAU kept up pressure on Britain and at the United Nations, urging the extension of sanctions, exposing the 'hypocrisy' of Western nations and denouncing any wavering in negotiations with the 'illegal and fascist regime'. Several times the 'Zimbabwe patriots' were called upon 'to take matters into their own hands' with the proviso that liberation movements should always wage their own war receiving only moral and material assistance from member states.[42] Violence was not the only option. Under the Lusaka Manifesto, approved by the OAU in 1969, it was agreed to discourage violence, provided that the white states of southern Africa entered into meaningful talks leading to majority rule.[43] A meeting of East and Central African states in Mogadishu in 1971 was more impatient and said there was nothing left 'except armed struggle'[44] while the solemn Declaration of 1973 saw armed struggle as 'the main form of action'.[45] In the meantime the OAU Liberation Committee, inaugurated under the OAU Charter of 1963 which directed the body 'to eradicate all forms of colonialism in Africa', channelled aid to liberation movements, sought to impose an oil embargo on southern Africa and generally acted as an accrediting agency for the multifarious organisations claiming to be the true representatives of nationalism in their territories. The Committee had its own problems: by 1969 half the member states had not paid their contributions, allegations were made of Tanzanian dominance, and the Committee itself was subject to a three-year OAU investigation because of complaints about inefficiency and the misuse of funds. Yet a large part of its annual budget of more than £2 million in the early 1970s did reach the liberation movements, although until 1974-5 the bulk went to the Portuguese territories. The Committee also tried, in a fairly hopeless situation, to unite the several factions of Rhodesian African nationalism, its only notable success being the short-lived unity of 1974-5 during the period of southern African detente.[46]

The OAU interest in the Rhodesian conflict had two important implications for intervention on the part of the socialist countries. First, it provided a useful cover of legitimacy; the Soviet Union and its allies as well as China could rightly claim to be assisting general African aspirations. Secondly, the OAU and its representatives of more recent years—the front-line presidents of Zambia, Botswana, Tanzania, Mozambique and, to a lesser extent, Angola—insist that apart from British involvement the Rhodesian conflict is an African affair and that all aid to guerrillas should be channelled through the OAU.[47] To this degree, and particularly in the case of the Soviet Union, direct intervention is circumscribed by the need not to antagonise the African states.

The question of motive is not an easy one to answer. A conservative commentator argued recently that a 'new Soviet imperialism' is abroad, a scheme invented by the ruling clique in Moscow to divert attention from domestic crises by seeking outlets through overseas expansion.[48] The thesis is no less attractive than Lenin's explanation for the imperialism of Western capitalism. What is clear is that both the Russians and the Chinese sought to outbid the West in Africa and that for most of the 1960s failed dismally. The Russians proved to be particularly crude and counter-productive in their relations with emerging Africa and had great trouble comprehending the eccentric behaviour of those states who appeared to be 'progressive'. Their best move was to support federal Nigeria throughout the civil war, and during the early and mid-1970s they achieved remarkable success in siding with the Dergue in Ethiopia and the MPLA in Angola. It is harder to explain Soviet-Ugandan friendship in ideological terms although support for President Amin may indicate that the Russians now follow the Chinese practice of not requiring African regimes to exhibit a deep ideological commitment or to implement programmes of scientific socialism. No such dexterity is required to support the liberation movements of southern Africa: they are anti-colonialist, anti-racist and, politically, anti-Western.

From the Rhodesian point of view Russian involvement in southern Africa exemplifies the Soviet plan of world domination and the strangulation of the West. In February 1976, in one of several similar statements, P.K. van der Byl, then Minister of Defence and Foreign Affairs, said Rhodesians, 'black and white', were 'fighting Communist expansionism, which is using the medium of black terrorist groups'.[49] The assumed objective is Soviet domination of southern Africa, thereby depriving the West of vital strategic materials and threatening the sea lanes around the Cape. It is a persuasive argument, much favoured by white southern Africans and their supporters overseas. But it also contains several flaws: without direct military intervention by the communists, South Africa, if not Rhodesia, is unlikely to fall, and such intervention would risk a global war; southern Africa is not yet of sufficient strategic importance to warrant a confrontation between the superpowers; the current Soviet objective seems rather to be one of seizing the advantage where the West is caught between its material ties in southern Africa and the need to placate African opinion. Above all, the argument misses the point that a principal Soviet aim in Africa, including support for the Rhodesian guerrillas, is to outmanoeuvre 'the Mao Tse Tung group'.[50] The Sino-Soviet split is a central factor in Moscow's aid to President Neto in Angola, to China's support for the unlikely President Mobutu in Zaire and in Soviet backing for Joshua Nkomo and increased assistance to the ZANU forces in Mozambique.

Soviet and Chinese aid to the Rhodesian guerrillas was not substantial in the 1960s. Obsolete weapons and inappropriate advice were in many ways a positive disadvantage. It became a different story in the 1970s. Soviet, Chinese, East German and Cuban instructors are now active in Angola, Zambia, Mozambique and Tanzania although the precise disposition remains unclear. So far there is no evidence of communist combat troops in action inside Rhodesia. This position could change in the future. For despite the reluctance of the front-line presidents to introduce foreign forces to 'solve' the Rhodesian problem, Kenneth Kaunda periodically warns the West that Cuban forces may have to perform the role they did in Angola and Ethiopia.[51]

Where there is substantial and present evidence of communist support is in the area of military supplies, much of the information regarding such supplies admittedly emanating from the Rhodesian government.[52] The government claims, for instance, that in its raid into Chimoio in November 1977 the 'conservative' figure of twelve tons of Soviet and Chinese equipment was captured. Another seven tons were collected in one of the Zambian raids in 1978. An arsenal in Salisbury acts as a kind of showpiece for communist equipment: there are Soviet AK-47 assault rifles, light machine-guns and pistols, the Chinese 60-MM mortars, 40-MM calibre rocket-launchers, fragmentation and percussion hand-grenades, anti-personnel mines and the devastating TM-46 and 48 anti-vehicle mines which cause havoc on the dirt roads of rural Rhodesia. Neighbouring regular African armies are believed to possess Soviet missiles which, in the case of Zambia, now supported by more modern British weapons, could hamper if not deter those highly successful Rhodesian airborne strikes against guerrilla bases. It is also widely believed that ZAPU forces loyal to Nkomo are now so well trained by the Cubans and supplied by the Soviets that they could destroy the ZANU army as well as drive the whites into city-based *laagers*.[53] Clearly the 'scruffy lot' have been transformed by communist aid.

The other question to consider is whether the Rhodesian guerrillas owe their revolutionary ideology to communist influence. Unfortunately there can be no simple answer; to some extent the guerrillas were radicalised by the failure of constitutional politics, by the hardships experienced under RF rule and by the failure of negotiations with Mr Smith; to some extent they were also bound to absorb the revolutionary ideology thrust on them by foreign or foreign-trained instructors. In the case of Joshua Nkomo it is difficult not to be sceptical. He was the great international traveller in the early 1960s when his fellow nationalists at home were languishing in gaol or detention, and when he did suffer long years in detention he showed signs of regarding the 'struggle' as a personal battle for holding the leadership and combatting ZANU. Then in 1976, amply supported, as he still is, by the international corporation Lonrho, he negotiated with Ian Smith on terms which make the present internal settlement look positively revolutionary. Now in 1978 'Good Old Josh', remembered with affection by European businessmen in Salisbury, still regarded by Mr Smith and the European business houses as someone who could be rescued from the Patriotic Front and installed in the transitional government, talks only the language of revolution and violence and of the eradication of all who compromise with the hated Smith. His conversion must be suspect; the supreme opportunist wants power and if Marxist terminology expresses the current convenience then Nkomo will conform.

Robert Mugabe is a different case. While not immune to personal ambition and while, like Nkomo, constantly threatened by power struggles within his own organisation, Mugabe, like the young radicals who support him, is at least consistent in proclaiming the revolutionary cause. One of their documents of late 1976 declared the objective of creating a Marxist state: the 'National Democratic Revolution' will be followed by the 'Socialist Revolution' and 'A Peoples [sic] Democratic Dictatorship'; parliamentary democracy based on one man one vote is 'bourgeois democracy' for the 'exploiting classes' and will be eliminated; all civil and military power will belong to the worker-peasant alliance; capitalist relations of production and private ownership of land will be destroyed and replaced by co-operatives and collectives.[54] Mugabe himself is regarded by white Rhodesia as a bloodthirsty hardliner,[55] notwithstanding his devout Catholicism and apparent readiness for most of 1978 to join all-party talks. The error would be to regard him as an empty vessel into which sinister communists have poured all the revolutionary ideas and phrases he now uses. Mugabe himself was a nationalist in the 1950s, his younger followers were drawn to him by what they saw as an unjust society inside Rhodesia. Outsiders have merely given them a place within the 'international struggle', helped them express their protest in shorthand slogans and confused as well as saturated the comrades with 'political lessons' which may win the peace but which could also get them killed beforehand by neglecting basic military training.[56]

Three points ought to be emphasised about the Sino-Soviet role in the Rhodesian conflict. First, in conjunction with sanctions, although more dramatically, the guerrilla war forced the Rhodesian government into negotiations with the African nationalists and undermined its ability to control the countryside; and the main reason for the guerrillas' achievement, apart from their own desire to 'liberate Zimbabwe', is that they are trained and supplied by the communist countries. Secondly, the Sino-Soviet dispute has both helped the guerrillas by making them beneficiaries of Soviet competitiveness and burdened them by aggravating existing divisions between ZAPU and ZANU. In 1976, for example, following fighting between ZAPU and ZANU guerrillas in Mozambique it was reported that 'Chinese military experts' attacked 'panic-stricken former ZAPU recruits'[57]. Despite increasing Soviet assistance to ZANU, the principal ally is still ZAPU and Nkomo has always gratefully acknowledged Eastern European support.[58] For his part Robert Mugabe no doubt pleased his hosts at a Peking banquet in 1977 with a thinly veiled attack on the Soviet presence in southern Africa:

> in contrast to the genuine assistance from the Chinese people the 'aid' rendered by social-imperialism is out of the ulterior motive by grabbing spheres of influence, contending for hegemony and fostering puppets... The people of Zimbabwe are facing menace [sic] from both Western imperialism and social-imperialism—and the menace from social-imperialism, in particular, is more insidious and dangerous.[59]

Thirdly, it would be a mistake to assume with Mugabe, or indeed about Mugabe himself, that any of the Patriotic Front nationalists are or will become so beholden to a communist power that they would be willing tools of communist expansionism in southern Africa. The danger, if there is one, lies more with the Soviets than the Chinese who are both more reticent and more understanding in dealing with African leaders. As Ambassador Young of the United States pointed out, when asked whether the Soviet Union had influence in southern Africa, direct or indirect dependence on arms supplies 'inevitably gives the Soviets some influence'; but 'they have a way of messing up just like we have a way of messing up. I think they do a better job of messing up than we do.'[60] For the present, Soviet objectives in southern Africa coincide with the aims of the liberation movements. Given their problems with President Neto of Angola and in the Horn of Africa, the Soviets cannot assume that the present affinity with ZAPU would restrain a future ZAPU President of Zimbabwe from behaving like any other independent African nationalist. The point was well made by President Obasanjo of Nigeria:

> To the Soviets I should like to say that having been invited to Africa in order to assist in the liberation struggle and the consolidation of national independence, they should not overstay their welcome. Africa is not about to throw off one colonial yoke for another.[61]

IV

In April 1974 there was a military coup in Portugal. The reverberations were felt throughout southern Africa except, momentarily, inside Rhodesia. Mr Smith was engaged in unhurried discussions with the African National Council, and the Bishop was prepared to accept his proposed package of wide-ranging social reforms and minimal political change. Sensing that at last the 'winds of change' were to blow south of the Zambesi, the Bishop's executive rejected the deal. Why, after all, accept a few more seats in a white-dominated parliament when the parliament itself would soon belong to them? The euphoria of mid-1974 was catching: the black Angolans and Mozambicans were not alone in seeing independence within their grasp.

Further south Mr Vorster was making a different set of calculations. Previously his foreign policy had presupposed the existence of white buffer-states stretched across South Africa's northern borders. In 1974 he recognised that the best he could hope for was a friendly relationship with moderate black neighbours. To achieve this required a speedy and peaceful transition to majority rule in Rhodesia and Namibia (South West Africa): the alternative was 'too ghastly to contemplate'. North of the Zambesi, President Kaunda, starting from different premises, reached similar conclusions: majority rule was now closer in southern Africa and the choice lay between an intensified armed struggle and an immediate but peaceful transfer of power. Between them Vorster and Kaunda successfully levered the white and black Rhodesians into considering the possibility of negotiation. The immediate results of this southern African detente[62] were a ceasefire, the short-lived unity of most of African nationalism, the withdrawal of South African forces from Rhodesia and the abortive talks between Mr Smith and the nationalists at Victoria Falls in April 1975. The longer-term effects included the wider recognition of South Africa and the front-line states in future discussions about Rhodesia. Hitherto South Africa's role was seen in Africa simply as a prop for white Rhodesia; now its own fears of 'liberation' could be exploited by encouraging the National Party Government to pressure Mr Smith into making substantial concessions. On the other side, the changed scene of 1974 brought together the black states of south-central Africa to perform what Colin Legum so aptly described as the role of 'ringmasters' in the Rhodesian conflict.[63]

A sense of urgency developed in southern Africa in the years after 1974. Angola and Mozambique became independent, the civil war in Angola brought in the superpowers and, in particular, the Soviet Union; the armed struggle in Rhodesia intensified as the guerrillas now utilised the 'sanctuary' of Mozambique; the situation in Namibia seemed at last to be moving. Some things, however, continued as before. That other Rhodesian war—the fratricidal conflict among the guerrillas—merely entered new cycles. For a brief moment Joshua Nkomo got away from it all and tried to negotiate a settlement with Smith in early 1976. White Rhodesians hardly took any notice. Judging by the local press they were much more interested in killing 'ters' and denouncing communists, and in debating those heady issues of Rhodesia's lamentable performance in Currie Cup cricket and whether garbage cans in Salisbury should be collected from inside or outside the front gate. For white Rhodesians, as always, the note of urgency had to be impressed from outside. On 22 March 1976, just after the Smith-Nkomo talks broke down, James Callaghan, the new British Prime Minister, announced tough preconditions for renewed settlement talks: agreement on the principle of majority rule, majority rule elections within eighteen months to two years, no independence before majority rule, no drawn-out negotiations.[64] A month later, in Lusaka, Dr Henry Kissinger endorsed Callaghan's strong stand. America would give 'unrelenting opposition' to the Rhodesian government and support moves for an independent Zimbabwe.[65]

The American intervention began another phase in the 'internationalisation' of the Rhodesian conflict and highlighted the new departure in American policy towards Africa. Following the Kennedy era, the America of the Vietnam war regarded Africa with 'benign neglect'.[66] Dr Kissinger himself seemed to oscillate between contempt, disillusionment and indifference. In January 1975 President Mobutu of Zaire described US policy in Africa as one of '*status quo* and *fait accompli*';[67] a position clearly taken in the National Security Memorandum 39 of 1970 in which Dr Kissinger endorsed the option accepting and to a degree supporting the white regimes of southern Africa;[68] and a position reflected in the Byrd amendment of 1971 which permitted the United States to import Rhodesian chrome in defiance of UN sanctions. Debates within the administration and Congress during the Nixon years pointed to deep divisions over the question of supporting the economic embargo on Rhodesia. On one side were those who argued that all embargoes were immoral and ineffective and that, in the case of chrome, the importation of high quality Rhodesian ore and ferrochrome relieved the United States from dependence on the Soviet Union for supplies of these strategic materials. On the other side were those who saw the Byrd amendment as 'the most serious blow to the credibility of our African policy' and, by 1975, as unnecessary anyway because of existing stockpiles and technological innovations in American industry.[69]

By 1975-6, however, the whole issue was overshadowed by another turn of events in southern Africa: the Angolan civil war, the Russian and Cuban intervention following the ill-fated South African invasion of Angola and the humiliating rebuffs to State Department efforts to build a barrier against Soviet intrusion. For the Ford administration the Byrd amendment was now an acute embarrassment; and Senator Clark was relieved to discover that repeal 'would do what is politically and morally right without any economic sacrifice'.[70] The political question was now one of halting Soviet advance in southern Africa, and to this end Dr Kissinger jettisoned the 1970 option and set about wooing the front-line presidents by offering Mr Smith's head 'on a platter'.[71] Capitalising on South Africa's desire for a peaceful resolution of the Rhodesian conflict, and on its need for friends and allies at a time when the Soweto riots had created some awkwardness, the Secretary of State enlisted Mr Vorster's aid in forcing the Rhodesian Prime Minister into his apparent surrender of September 1976. Informed that he could no longer count on any American or South African assistance Mr Smith agreed to the Kissinger package, a refined version of the Callaghan plan of 22 March, and publicly committed himself to majority rule and the formation of an interim government. It seemed at last that international intervention, stimulated by superpower competition, could resolve the issue. But, for one, Julius Nyerere of Tanzania remained sceptical: 'decades of history cannot be wiped out by a single speech and a few months of individualistic one-man diplomacy'.[72]

The Tanzanian President was right to be dubious about the Kissinger whirlwind. But the real problem was not American sincerity or persistence. As in the 1960s, the difficulty was to clinch any deal with Ian Smith, a problem now aggravated by a deep and destructive split within Rhodesian African nationalism. Unless the Americans, in conjunction with the British, were prepared to enter the conflict as participants—to intervene militarily—then the white Rhodesians could effectively play upon the divisions between the nationalists, create or aggravate differences among the front-line presidents, and outlast even more Western political leaders simply by ignoring accusations that they are fighting the forces of history. Yet the Anglo-Americans had, and have, no intention of sending forces into Rhodesia, at least for the purpose of determining who will win and who will lose. Nor do the neighbouring African states regard such a venture as the test of sincerity in supporting black majority rule in Rhodesia. What really is at issue at the end of 1978 is whether by exertion of pressure from every quarter, and on all the primary and secondary participants, it is still possible to solve the Rhodesian problem without direct superpower involvement. At the moment the superpowers, each with particular interests to advance, are standing off. The Soviet Union would probably be satisfied so long as the ultimate victor remains friendly and keeps up the pressure on South Africa; the United States could certainly tolerate a radical regime so long as it produces that kind of stability which provides neither the occasion for, nor the cause of, global tension. Yet in view of the strategies being pursued by both black and white Rhodesians, the affected aloofness of the Soviet Union and the desperate efforts of the Anglo-Americans to remain aloof may not survive circumstances of real instability.

Since 1976 there have been a succession of Anglo-American initiatives all aimed at 'resolution' through the 'political sphere' rather than the 'military field' and at avoiding situations of superpower rivalry. The central assumption is that Africans should solve their own problems, assisted if necessary by the 'developed' societies. The desirable end is majority rule and an end to what the Carter administration sees as racial and social injustice in southern Africa.[73] In practical terms this Anglo-American approach in 1977-8 meant four things: short of their own military intervention, bringing every conceivable pressure to bear on the Rhodesian government; complete backing for the front-line presidents; persuading, or attempting to persuade, all parties to meet around the same negotiating table; rejecting any proposed settlement which excluded significant parties to the conflict. On these grounds the British tried hard at Geneva in 1976-7 to hold that unreal conference together even though it was plain that Mr Smith had recovered his poise since his meeting with Dr Kissinger, or else was merely being his devious and divisive self, and that the nationalists were as much concerned to argue with each other about their right to speak for the people of Zimbabwe. On the same grounds the Anglo-Americans rejected Mr Smith's internal settlement of 3 March 1978. It was exclusive rather than inclusive and there were strong suspicions of any agreement which appeared, even if only temporarily, to retain the white control of the armed forces, the police, the civil service and, indeed, of the government itself. Besides, the front-line states rejected the settlement, and so did the Patriotic Front, and that was the end of the matter.[74] Instead, the Anglo-Americans have persisted in trying to sell the plan they launched in September 1977: an immediate surrender of power by the Rhodesian government and a return to legality, an orderly transition to majority rule in the shortest possible time, a UN presence and a UN force during the transition, the establishment by the British government of an administration to conduct elections before independence, a constitution which guaranteed democracy, human rights and an independent judiciary, a development fund to revive the economy. Variations were introduced to meet particular objections but, so far, have failed to bring the parties together.[75] One reason is that the whites and now the blacks in Salisbury fear that the Patriotic Front fully intends to seize power whatever is decided, and Smith himself is deeply concerned about suggestions either of incorporating 'terrorists' into the military structure or simply handing over to the guerrillas the role of maintaining law and order. There is also the strong conviction in Salisbury that for all their vaunted impartiality Dr Owen and Andrew Young are no more than 'stooges' of the Patriotic Front.[76] On the other side there are doubts about Mr Smith's real commitment to a transfer of power and continued postponements of dates for elections and for independence, in part the result of guerrilla activity, have obviously strengthened this belief. So, faced with an atmosphere of mutual suspicion and a basic reluctance by the white leadership in Salisbury and by the guerrillas to find common ground, the Anglo-American initiatives, more persistent than those of the British government in the 1960s, continue to founder for want of any real rapport or of any real winner in the current war. By deliberately choosing to support an 'African' or 'Rhodesian' solution the Anglo-Americans are not primary or secondary participants.[77] Rather they alternate the roles of courier and mediator. As the former they are highly efficient, as the latter they are continually frustrated.

Three factors seem to militate against their attempts to promote negotiations for a peaceful transfer of power. First, a number of incidents in the region—often too inconvenient to suggest sheer coincidence—tear the parties apart just when progress is being made. The murder of missionaries, Rhodesian security force raids into Mozambique and Zambia, the shooting down of a civilian airliner: events like these serve to harden white attitudes or persuade the guerrillas that the war must be prosecuted until the very end. Collectively, incidents of this kind, and continuing uncertainty about who really does control rural Rhodesia—at least uncertainty in the minds of the protagonists—mean that neither side is ready for a final decision at the negotiating table.

A second and more important factor is that the nationalists are now fundamentally split between those who with Ndabaningi Sithole and Bishop Muzorewa are firmly identified with the internal government, and those inside and outside Rhodesia, including the front-line presidents, who regard the Patriotic Front as the legitimate representatives of Zimbabwean nationalism. This division is not the only one. Sithole and Muzorewa are competing for power and influence inside the country, just as they seek to outbid each other for international and African support. They were deeply antagonistic at the time of the settlement talks and their parties are currently engaged in a popularity contest among potential African voters as well as in building the private armies they may need in the event of independence.[78] At the same time both are in a sense prisoners of the interim agreement. Cynically, one could argue that

Ian Smith has now so tamed them, that these 'black Smiths' have no choice but to follow his every ruse to delay independence. The only disadvantage of this 'tactic' is that in losing credibility among Africans, and in failing to fulfil their promise to end the guerrilla war, Sithole and Muzorewa are more lame than tame.

Perhaps for this reason Mr Smith renewed his contacts with Joshua Nkomo in August-September 1978. A vital clue to understanding Ian Smith is that he rarely enters any discussions with a clearly-formulated plan; he waits for others to make offers, or he merely shops around hoping for something to turn up.[79] This attitude makes him difficult to pin down, but also means that he is highly flexible within the general objective of doing all he can to preserve white control and influence within Rhodesia. It also means that he is very adept at exploiting the 'weaknesses' of his opponents; and, in particular, Nkomo's ambitions to lead an independent Zimbabwe and President Kaunda's urgent need for a settlement. And there is plenty of scope for his inclination to play one side off against the other. The front-line presidents found it harder in 1978 to maintain their unity of 1976,[80] the struggles between the wings of the Patriotic Front showed no signs of abating, the disagreements between the fighters and the politicians continued, the brave words which followed the raids into Zambia in October 1978 did not disguise the fact that, for the moment, the Rhodesian forces can not only hurt the guerrillas but remind their hosts of the costs of sanctuary including the threats to internal order. Above all, in 1978, it was patently clear that the divisions within African nationalism made it easier for Mr Smith to tighten his grip on the interim government and postpone that awful day when Christianity and Western Civilisation must pack up and leave south-central Africa.

The whites are in no doubt that the choice is between Civilisation and Chaos. It is remarkable that in spite of soaring defence costs,[81] the loss and disruption of life, and their disillusionment about the transitional government—either that it has failed or that it exists at all—they remain behind in sufficient numbers[82] to hold the line and to frustrate the Anglo-Americans, the front-line presidents and the Patriotic Front. One reason the whites do stay is that they are not allowed to take very much with them; another is the blind hope that 'Good Old Smithy' still has something up his sleeve; a further consideration is that the armed forces, with their predominantly black component, cannot be beaten and could possibly win. Whatever the reason, the presence of something over 200,000 Europeans in Rhodesia, and their refusal to let go, is the third and most significant factor in the failure to reach a settlement in the Rhodesian conflict. If no one cause can explain either the emergence or the perpetuation of the armed struggle, the one constant and most decisive influence has been white determination to resist African political advance and delay until the last minute African inheritance of the state created by Cecil Rhodes's Column of 1890.

V

In two respects the great powers have thwarted the aims of white Rhodesians; they denied them a guaranteed white supremacy by rejecting UDI and the 1969 constitution; and they denied them a favourable compromise by rejecting the internal settlement of 1978. On the other hand, it is arguable that a *Tiger* constitution, even supposing that Africans could be persuaded to pass it on the test of acceptability, would ultimately have been challenged and subjected to an unceasing guerrilla war. The point is that the final arbiters of the Rhodesian question remain the blacks themselves. In the shorter term, however, the white Rhodesians have been the effective masters, at least within Rhodesia itself. Confronted by the durability of white Rhodesia, the great powers tried every expedient without becoming directly involved. The danger now is that unless the Rhodesians can solve their own problems, and to the satisfaction of the 'ringmasters', then the South Africans and the West and the Soviet Union—reluctantly or otherwise—may find themselves intervening directly. And the greatest irony of all is that Mr Smith, the proponent of the 'Rhodesian solution', is the one who feels he has most to gain by such an involvement.[83]

Notes

The writer would like to thank Barbara Payne and Nick Warner for their research assistance.

1. The argument of this paragraph is based on Mr Smith's parliamentary speeches since 1964, his several attempts since 1972 to reach a 'settlement' with, or promote, the chiefs and the disreputable leaders of small and discredited African political parties, statements made after the publication of the Anglo-American proposals, during the internal settlement talks and throughout 1978 and on interviews with past and present officials of the Rhodesian Front conducted in Salisbury early in 1978.

2. The Foreign Office was accused of deliberately delaying the departure of the Pearce Commission, appointed to test popular opinion on the 1971 Anglo-Rhode-

sian agreement, allegedly to create time for the African opposition to organise. Interview: Lt Col W.M. Knox, Salisbury, 16 February 1978.

3. Colin Legum, 'The Soviet Union, China and the West in Southern Africa', *Foreign Affairs*, vol. 54, no. 4 (July 1976), p. 745.

4. For two excellent African accounts of nationalist feeling and protest, both personal and general, see N. Shamuyarira, *Crisis in Rhodesia* (Transatlantic Arts, New York, 1965) and L. Vambe, *From Rhodesia to Zimbabwe* (Heinemann, London, 1976). See also R. Cary and D. Mitchell (eds.), *African Nationalist Leaders in Rhodesia: Who's Who* (Books of Rhodesia, Bulawayo, 1977).

5. Useful studies of the lead-up to UDI include C. Leys, *European Politics in Southern Rhodesia* (Clarendon Press, Oxford, 1959); J. Barber, *Rhodesia: The Road to Rebellion* (published for the Institute of Race Relations by Oxford University Press, London, 1967); L.W. Bowman, *Politics in Rhodesia: White Power in an African State* (Harvard University Press, Cambridge, Mass., 1973).

6. C. Palley, *The Constitutional History and Law of Southern Rhodesia, 1885-1965* (Clarendon Press, Oxford, 1966), p. 413.

7. Ibid., p. 702. The speaker was Duncan Sandys, Secretary of State for Commonwealth Relations, 23 March 1961.

8. Ibid., p. 707. Duncan Sandys, 8 November 1961.

9. E. Windrich (ed.), *The Rhodesian Problem: A Documentary Record, 1923-1973* (Routledge and Kegan Paul, London, 1975), pp. 205-6. Mr Wilson added a sixth principle in early 1966: the need to ensure that, regardless of race, there is no oppression of the majority by the minority or of the minority by the majority.

10. Richard Crossman, *The Diaries of a Cabinet Minister, Volume One, 1964-1966* (2 vols., H. Hamilton and J. Cape, London, 1975), p. 378. For Wilson's own account see Harold Wilson, *The Labour Government, 1964-1970: A Personal Record*, (Weidenfeld and Nicolson, London, 1971).

11. Crossman, *Diaries*, vol. 1, p. 378.

12. Quoted in R.C. Good, *U.D.I.: The International Politics of the Rhodesian Rebellion* (Faber and Faber, London, 1973), p. 63.

13. Crossman, *Diaries*, vol. 1, p. 406.

14. Dennis Austin, quoted in Good, *U.D.I.*, p. 312.

15. For extended discussions of this question see ibid., pp. 55-65 and M. Loney, *Rhodesia: White Racism and Imperial Response* (Penguin, London, 1975), pp. 138-46.

16. Crossman, *Diaries*, vol. 1, p. 407.

17. Ibid., p. 393.

18. Good, *U.D.I.*, p. 73.

19. Ibid., p. 111.

20. Richard Crossman, *The Diaries of a Cabinet Minister, Volume Two, 1966-1968* (2 vols., H. Hamilton and J. Cape, London, 1976), p. 91. For an extended discussion of the British-South African connection see Loney, *Rhodesia*, pp. 151-5, and R. First, J. Steele and C. Grundy, *The South African Connection: Western Investment in Apartheid* (Harper and Row, New York, 1973).

21. *Africa Contemporary Record* (*ACR*), 1968-9, p. 24.

22. In 1978 the United Nations published a list of 593 Western firms (444 of them British) alleged to have broken sanctions after 1965 including the major international companies engaged in mining, tobacco and the oil industry. *Africa Research Bulletin* (*ARB*), 1978, Economic, Financial and Technical Series (E, F and T), 4809 B-C.

23. *Report on the Supply of Petroleum and Petroleum Products to Rhodesia*, by T.H. Bingham and S.M. Gray, presented 22 August 1978. For extracts and discussion see *ARB*, 1978, Political, Social and Cultural Series (P, S and C), 4997C-4998C and *ARB*, 1978, E, F and T, 4808B-4809B.

24. London Press Service: Verbatim Press Service, 128/78.

25. *ARB*, 1978, E, F and T, 4773A-4775C. Much of this report is based on an article published in the *Financial Times*, 27 June 1978. See also the Rhodesia entries in *ACR*; L.H. Gann, 'Rhodesia and the Prophets', *African Affairs*, vol. 71, no. 283 (April 1972), pp. 125-43; M. Bratton, 'Structural Transformation in Zimbabwe: Comparative Notes from the Neo-Colonialism of Kenya', *Journal of Modern African Studies*, vol. 15, no. 4 (December 1977), pp. 591-611. A Rhodesian boot-manufacturer attributed Rhodesia's 'success' to 'dear old Britain'; he claimed that 'necessity is the mother of invention, and we've not only survived international pressures but we've made capital out of them'. *New York Times*, 8 May 1977.

26. E.S. Newson, Chairman of the Rhodesian Iron and Steel Corporation, *Rhodesia Herald*, 27 November 1968. This article started a controversy in which Mr Smith distinguished himself with some of his most sneering remarks about the Rhodesian business community.

27. Interview: Sir Ewan Campbell, Chairman of the Standard Bank of Rhodesia, Salisbury, 16 February 1978.

28. The RF share of the vote at general elections was as follows: 1962, 55 per cent; 1965, 78 per cent; 1970, 77 per cent; 1974, 76 per cent; 1977, 85 per cent.

29. Record of Statement by L.K.S. Wilson to Lt Col W.M. Knox, 26 April 1967: Forum Papers held by B. O'Connell in Salisbury. Wilson was a prominent figure in the tobacco industry. The Forum Papers include invaluable material for the study of Anglo-Rhodesian relations as seen by Rhodesian businessmen in the late 1960s, and also verbatim reports and summaries of talks between Mr Smith and the members of Forum.

30. This phrase was attributed to Harold Wilson. Good, *U.D.I.*, p. 113. The phrase referring to short-term occurrences was certainly his. Ibid., p. 297.

31. Much of the material for the above paragraph is drawn from interviews with past and present officials of the RF, the Forum Papers which contain statements by visiting British ministers, and from the works by Wilson, Crossman, Good and Bowman.

32. For the details and a general discussion of the 1966, 1968 and 1971 constitutions and proposals see the relevant years of *ACR* and Good, *U.D.I*, Chs 7, 10 and 11. The obstacle in 1966 was really the British government's insistence on 'a return to legality' (the prior abandonment of UDI) and in 1968 an argument over external safeguards which the Rhodesians felt would give them only a second-class independence. The franchise proposals extending the number of African voters caused misgivings in Rhodesia but their cautious nature caused even more concern among the African states and pro-African groups in London.

33. Good, *U.D.I.*, Ch. 7.

34. Crossman, *Diaries*, vol. 2, pp. 29-30.

35. *ARB*, 1972, P, S and C, 2480Aff. This issue also includes the speech by Sir Alec Douglas-Home and Mr Smith's response to the report.

36. London Press Service. In 1976 the United States Treasury argued that unilateral extension of the American enforcement of sanctions would be unfair to American business and that the US should not do more than other nations were prepared to do. In other words, unilateral action would be ineffective and was not obligatory, and common action was not possible. See Response by the Department of the Treasury to Additional Written Questions submitted by Congressman Diggs, Chairman, Subcommittee on International Resources, Food and Energy, 10 September 1976.

37. For accounts of the war see A.R. Wilkinson, 'Insurgency in Rhodesia, 1957-1973: An Account and Assessment', *Adelphi Papers*, no. 100 (1973) and Kees Maxey, *The Fight for Zimbabwe: The Armed Conflict in Southern Rhodesia since U.D.I.* (Collins, London, 1975).

38. Interview: Nick Warner with Major-General R.R.J. (Sam) Putterill, Juliasdale, 10 December 1977.

39. *Citizen*, 28 October 1966.
40. *Rhodesia Herald*, 14 March 1976.
41. Good, *U.D.I.*, pp. 101-5.
42. *ARB*, 1971, P, S, and C, 2294B; *ACR*, 1972-3, A49-50, C143-5.
43. Ibid., 1969-70, C41ff.
44. Ibid., 1971-2, C18-19.
45. Ibid., 1973-4, C7-8.
46. Ibid., 1974-5, A24.
47. Ibid., 1976-7, A53.
48. Julian Amery, 'The Crisis in Southern Africa: Policy Options for London and Washington', *South Africa*, vol. 8, no. 4 (April 1978), pp. 197-208, 229-39.
49. *ARB*, 1976, P, S and C, 3939B, and ibid., 1977, 4376C.
50. *ACR*, 1968-9, p. 42.
51. *ARB*, 1978, E, F and T, 4676A.
52. The evidence which follows is drawn from Rhodesia Government: Fact Paper, 2/78, pp. 5-7.
53. One of the most earnest supporters of the first part of this proposition is the Rhodesian government, and the point is made as well in the Weekly Background Briefings prepared by the Rhodesian Ministry of Foreign Affairs. For support of the general point about the training of the ZAPU forces, see issues of *ARB*, 1978, P, S and C, 4939C-4940A. The present ZAPU forces go under the name of ZIPRA and those of ZANU under ZANLA.
54. This document is purported to have been written by the Zimbabwe Action Committee.
55. The point is often made in the Fact Papers and the Weekly Background Briefings issued by the Rhodesian Ministry of Foreign Affairs. For a more rounded judgement, see *ACR*, 1976-7, A17-18.
56. Entries from a diary dated 12-21 July 1976, seemingly authentic, and apparently kept by a guerrilla killed by the Rhodesian security forces, indicate that the training programmes in one camp in Mozambique involved more intensive study of the political thoughts of Chairman Mao than of particular military skills.
57. *Zimbabwe Review*, vol. 5, no. 5 (1976).
58. *ARB*, 1977, P, S and C, 4376B.
59. Summary of World Broadcasts, Second Series, FE35543, 22 June 1977. Quoting this speech in Fact Paper 2/78 the Rhodesian Ministry of Foreign Affairs substituted 'Soviet Union' for 'social-imperialism'.
60. Hearing before the Subcommittee on Africa of the Committee on Foreign Relations, House of Representatives, 7 September 1977.
61. *West Africa*, 24 July 1978.
62. For the build-up of the detente exercise see *ARB*, 1974, P, S and C, 3387C-3391A and 3420B-3422C.
63. *ACR*, 1976-7, A10.
64. *ARB*, 1976, P, C and S, 3971C-3972A.
65. Ibid., 4004A.
66. American attitudes towards Africa and southern Africa are discussed in *ACR*, 1974-5, A87-101.
67. Ibid., A99.
68. Ibid., A99-101.
69. See, for example, Full Committee Consideration of the H. Con. Res. 1287, Committee of the House of Representatives, 23 July 1975, and *Resources in Rhodesia: Implications for US Policy*, Committee of the House of Representatives, April 1976.
70. Subcommittee on African Affairs of the Senate Committee on Foreign Relations, 10 February 1977.
71. This phrase was in fact said to have been used by Mr Smith when he returned to discussions with Dr Kissinger after the Secretary of State had brutally

summarised the reasons why white Rhodesia had to surrender. 'All I have to offer is my own head on a platter.' *ACR*, 1976-7, A35.

72. J.K. Nyerere, 'America and Southern Africa', *Foreign Affairs*, vol. 55, no. 4 (July 1977), p. 673.

73. See the statement by Philip Habib, Under-Secretary for Political Affairs, Department of State, Hearing before the Subcommittee on Africa of the Committee on International Relations, House of Representatives, 3 March 1977, pp. 2ff, and the statements by Ambassador Young and Richard Morse, Assistant Secretary for African Affairs, Department of State, before the same subcommittee on 7 September 1977.

74. See the speech by Dr Owen in the House of Commons on 7 November 1978 giving the Foreign Secretary's reasons for rejecting the settlement, his emphasis on the importance of Britain being able to retain a negotiating position, and the arguments he offered which he said showed that the British government had been wise in rejecting the temptation to support the agreement of 3 March and to end economic sanctions. London Press Service.

75. *ARB*, 1977, P, S and C, 4571C-4574B. For a variation in late 1978, see ibid., 1978, 5034A-B.

76. This view is strongly emphasised in the Weekly Background Briefings of the Rhodesian Ministry of Foreign Affairs.

77. See R.C. Good in Hearings before the Subcommittee on African Affairs of the Senate Committee on Foreign Relations, 9 July 1975, p. 126.

78. The antagonism was especially obvious in the internal settlement talks, judging by the minutes made available by the Sithole group. Press reports in London and the Weekly Background Briefings indicate that both Sithole and Muzorewa are worried about their lack of a military power-base.

79. Interview: Des Frost, former chairman of the RF, Salisbury, 12 January 1978. Frost was an opponent of Smith's plans to 'sell out' in early 1978 but, allowing for his bitterness, his criticism that Smith never really had clear ideas of his own and perhaps no ideas of any kind, can be supported in the Forum Papers and in the British and African accounts of past negotiations.

80. *ACR*, 1976-7, A10-13. Tension emerged after President Kaunda re-opened the border with Rhodesia in October 1978, argued to be necessary by Zambia to relieve the country from its serious economic plight. *ARB*, 1978, P, S and C, 5036A-B.

81. The escalation of defence costs, and the implications, can be followed in the *ACR*. The internal government recently tried to control the rising costs, no doubt hoping that the war would slow down or that the West would enter. *ARB*, 1978, P, S and C, 4773A ff.

82. There are various estimates of the size of the 'permanent' white population ranging from 180,000 to 250,000 at the end of 1978. For migration trends see *ARB*, 1978, E, F and T, 4775A.

83. He has been repeatedly assured by the Anglo-Americans that he is wrong to assume that they will help to bail him out, but the argument used by P.K. van der Byl in March 1977 still guides the thinking of the whites in the transitional government: if 'Russian territorial gains' in Africa were not halted they could lead to a third world war: 'The free world must come to its senses very quickly indeed and help the pro-Western countries in Africa who are under threat and attack.' *ARB*, 1977, P, S and C, 4376C.

8 South Africa

D.J. GOLDSWORTHY

I

South Africa differs in important ways from most of the other countries and regions examined in this volume. In South Africa it is not (yet) a matter of internal war with each 'side' supported by foreign allies. Nor is South Africa party to an international war with the warring states supported, again, by outside powers. Rather, the situation is one in which domestic, regional, continental and global factors interact to produce conflict in a diversity of forms, ranging from anomic protest to armed confrontation, and in which the social landscape is shadowed by the dark prospect of much greater conflicts to come. It is a situation whose long-term significance has worldwide ramifications. For all the great antonyms of our age—rich against poor, West against East, white against black—find simultaneous and increasingly sharp expression in southern Africa; and within the region, South Africa is their ultimate point of convergence.

There is indeed a sense in which all the issues of the region turn ultimately on the nature of South Africa's domestic policy dilemmas, economic, political and above all racial. It is not possible to say by what mix of internal and international conflict these dilemmas will eventually be resolved. But in any interim analysis such as the present one, it seems essential to begin with a sketch of South Africa's domestic conflict potential and to broaden out from there. Thus South Africa's internal dispensation—the system; its supports; the challenges to it—will constitute our first level of analysis.

The second level is the regional one. Southern Africa, the ten countries south of Zaire and Tanzania, which until 1974 knew a brittle kind of regional stability, has become, since the collapse of Portuguese colonialism one of the most critically destabilised regions of the world. There has been a major civil war in Angola. There has been a continuing government-versus-guerrilla struggle in Rhodesia, a struggle whose effects have been directly felt in Mozambique, Zambia and Botswana as well. On a lesser scale there has also been guerrilla fighting in Namibia. All of these conflicts have had deep implications for South Africa, and in each of them it has intervened. For South Africa's interest in a (re)stabilised region is high indeed; arguably the maintenance of the domestic social system, the growth of the economy, perhaps even the survival of the state, are all at stake. Of course South Africa is by far the most powerful state in the region with a certain capacity of its own to impose the local solutions it prefers and veto those it dislikes: something which has lately been fairly apparent, for example, in relation to Namibia. Yet the domestic, regional and international constraints on South Africa's local freedom of action are formidable too, and analysis must take account of them.

And third, the region is of increasing strategic and economic importance globally. As such it has become an arena of competitive intervention by the two superpowers, especially (once again) since the turning-point year of 1974. Yet this is no mere bipolar conflict. Britain's historic interest in the area remains the deepest of any power's, its economic stake the greatest; and in recent years France, West Germany and China have all taken a growing interest and part in the region's affairs.

The following discussion will attempt to consider all these areas of actual and potential conflict and their interrelations. But at the outset it must be noted that the obstacles to producing a logically clear-cut analysis are very great. Broadly speaking, one may conceive the overall problem as a contest between two long-standing international coalitions, ranged for and against white South Africa. Each coalition embraces not only national actors but also subnational (for example, the externally-based liberation movements) and supra-national (for example, the OAU, the UN and the institutions of international capital). This seems clear enough. But these coalitions are not very stable; different actors tend to drift in and out of them according to immediate questions at issue, or build short-term sub-alliances across the divide (South Africa and Zambia), or temporarily oppose their own partners (South Africa versus Rhodesia), or even manage—as the Western powers do—to play long-running roles in both coalitions at once. It is a dynamic situation in which the nature of the game is adaptation to a very swiftly changing environment. What tends to follow is that, although the most fundamental objectives of the major actors may not change much, the particular policies they pursue often seem to embody 'reversals', 'contradictions', 'hypocrisies'. South Africa builds aparheid at home yet treats it as an unacceptable solution for Rhodesia. Mozambique has a treaty relationship with the Soviet Union and rhetorically denounces the South African system, yet it co-operates closely with (and helps buttress) that system by supplying it with important goods such as hydro-electric power and migrant labour. Zambia sponsors the violent liberation of Zimbabwe (through Nkomo's army), yet re-opens its border to trade with Rhodesia. The countries of the region pull apart, yet are tied together; they seek to collude, yet are torn apart. In short, there is no easy way of predicating any country's policies upon its supposed interests, for in a situation of such many-layered complexity it is more than likely that its own interests will be in dynamic tension with each other and hence give rise to policy 'contradictions'.

It may be not unfair to suggest, then, that those who think they understand the southern African situation must have been misinformed. What is certainly true is that any understanding of things attained at some particular times cannot be expected to serve indefinitely. To today's reader, the sheer datedness of analyses written in, say, 1976 (the year of Kissinger diplomacy in southern Africa) is perhaps their most striking characteristic. So mobile is the situation that analyses such as the present one can seldom aim to do more than outline the more enduring sources of conflict and speculate about the broadest of trends.

II

The power and prosperity of South Africa's 'white' political economy needs no stressing. What is of interest here, since this is primarily a discussion of conflict and conflict potential, is the sets of factors which severally sustain and threaten the South African system, and the tensions between them.

Let us consider first the system's external supports. It is easy, perhaps, for an outsider to gain the impression of a 'fortress South Africa', a powerfully self-sustaining system in large measure independent (and defiant) of the rest of the world. In practice, South Africa's military power and economic success have been underwritten to a very high degree by the world outside. Historically South Africa developed on a classic African export-import pattern, selling raw materials—notably gold—to the Western world and importing finished goods and technology. Then in the sixties came a boom decade of expansion from which South Africa emerged as the world's fifteenth-biggest trading nation and a ranking industrial power. This development was based upon heavy foreign investment and massive imports of high technology, was nurtured by an interventionist state through a whole array of acronymic parastatal corporations—IDC, ISCOR, SASOL, ESCOM, ARMSCOR and others[1]—and was paid for, largely, in gold. The capital investment came mainly from West Germany, Britain and the United States; much of the technology came from a Gaullist France eager to stockpile gold bullion as a base on which to build the franc's independence of the dollar. The oil which fuelled South Africa's growth came almost entirely from Iran, which in turn gained a stake in the system through its minority share of South Africa's main refinery. Along with the double-digit growth rates came a vast increase in South Africa's defence capabilities. Once again France was a key provider in the take-off decade, though there was also a considerable contribution from a sister 'isolated' state, Israel.[2]

Foreign—and for that matter domestic—investment was highly profitable in large part because of the apartheid system, with all that it implied by way of very cheap, non-unionised and tightly regulated labour. So significant was apartheid's role, indeed, that it could be regarded as a principal internal support of the system, with the labour market providing the venue where external and internal factors interacted to ensure profit maximisation. At the same time, economic growth did create an embryonic black middle-class which, it was hoped, would be supportive in other ways by expanding the market for consumer goods, by helping to divide the black population and by acting as a buffer between rich whites and poor blacks. Various leaders of this class also assumed political leadership in the Bantustans. These Black Homelands not only represented the philosophy of separate development taken to its logical conclusion; in more immediate political-economic terms their existence served to confirm the migratory (and hence more exploitable) status of the overwhelming black majority which lived and worked in what could now be *legally* defined as White South Africa.

The building of this whole system was, on the whole, a joint Afrikaner-English achievement. It is conventional to see these two communities as historically at odds, and indeed there are large elements of truth in the stereotypes: the Afrikaner community inward-looking, tightly bound together by language, church, Broederbond and destiny, obsessed with survival, determined to maintain supremacy over all other communities (Africans, Coloureds, Asians, English) through control of the state; the English more urban, cosmopolitan, liberal, socially loose-knit, sophisticated in business and finance. But the point here is that the great boom of the sixties worked to the high material advantage of both communities, and derived a good deal of its momentum from the fact that Afrikaner state and English business community worked effectively together in the joint interest. The result was a steady erosion of English support for the liberal parliamentary opposition and the establishment of a much more nearly united front in defence of shared achievements.

We have sketched, then, the ways in which the edifice of white power and prosperity rests upon three particular supports: economic input from outside, the apartheid system, and the growing solidarity-complementarity of the two white communities.

But just how firm are these supports?

It is fairly clear that the third one at least is unlikely to give way; rather, the greater the sense of threat to the South African system, the stronger the defensive Afrikaner-English coalition is likely to become. With the other two, however, the situation is much more problematic. By their very nature, both of these have their obverse sides: they create not only 'security' for the edifice but also forms of vulnerability. In stronger words, there are certain major contradictions in the system and a high degree of conflict potential; moreover, it is a conflict potential which the system seems almost wilfully to institutionalise.

In developing this point it is necessary first to stress the obvious. Domestically the apartheid system, even as it helps generate prosperity at the top of the social structure, generates explosive social pressures at the base. The human miseries of apartheid have been described and documented in many places.[3] Apartheid systematically and inequitably discriminates between races in terms of the human fundamentals: access to education, employment, housing, the dignities of family life, the enjoyment of meaningful civil and political rights. The social response to such repression, much of the time, is apathy and defeatism. But not always; and when protests do occur, the system is seen as doubly repressive. For having created the conditions which are being protested against, it moves to stifle protest by the most ruthless of means.

The Sharpeville massacre of 1960 appears now as the earliest significant demonstration of this point in the post-1948 era of systematic apartheid. Then in 1976 came the much more wide-sweeping urban violence initiated by the schoolchildren and unemployed youth of Soweto. The Soweto rising ignited a chain combustion that lasted for months on end, spread to other cities, engaged urban black workers (with jobs to lose) as well as the unemployed, led to many deaths and necessitated a massive containment action by the state. If this was not a revolution it was no mere urban jacquerie either; a 1905, perhaps, in Johnson's term[4]. What it demonstrated was the inexhaustibility of black anger. What it left behind was the certainty that 'Sowetos' will happen again.

This in spite of the fact that the South African state is almost certainly militarily capable of 'containing' further such uprisings—or even more highly organised urban and rural guerrilla operations—for a long time to come. Johnson's careful analysis of the revolt potential of each major section of the black population—the urban employed and unemployed, the rural employed and unemployed, the youth, the Bantustan populations—rings sombrely true in its conclusion that no domestic African group or combination of groups has the capacity to sustain a militarily effective campaign against the armed might of the state in the foreseeable future.[5]

But the point remains that uprisings, protests, acts of sabotage and the like will happen again, because the pressures which produced the 1976 events remain as before. Indeed they will intensify, because the problem is in large measure a function of the apartheid system itself and because the black population locked within the system is growing rapidly. And if 'containment' remains the foreseeable outcome in a purely military sense, the question must nevertheless go on looming larger: what are the *costs* of containment?

Obviously the social and human costs are, virtually by definition, very high indeed. But here it is worth making a point in more literally economic terms, since it is the economic costs of the operation that will, in the long run, be felt most directly by the white community.

Since the mid-seventies the state's expenditure on police, intelligence and the military has soared, and there seems no end to the escalation. Already by 1976 'defence' accounted for 25 per cent of the whole national budget. How much of this reflected South Africa's sense of external threat and how much related to internal security cannot really be estimated, for there are large areas of actual and potential overlap; suffice it that the domestic component is very substantial and is increasing, and that all such expenditure cuts heavily into the funds available for social investment and for directly productive purposes. This in turn must contribute to further depression of the living standards of the rapidly increasing black population, and hence to further deepening of the initial problems. Ultimately there must be some undermining of white prosperity itself. Harry Oppenheimer, South Africa's principal industrialist, put this point very succinctly one month before Soweto exploded: 'The economic growth required for our prosperity and indeed for our social and political stability is hardly compatible with such rapidly increasing defence expenditure.'[6]

At what point the costs of coping with 'unrest' might begin to seem intolerably high to the white community cannot be predicted. That point might well be a long way off yet, for the resources of the state are massive and so is the will to dominate. But what can be said is that the costs must seem proportionately very much higher today than they would have done if comparable unrest had occurred in the sixties. For in the seventies the boom ended. The South African economy ran into severe difficulties, thereby putting a much greater strain on the system's capacity to pay its social costs in the very period in which they began to soar.

This economic malaise must now be considered in some detail, for it provides the key to understanding South Africa's dilemma in a much more systematic way. It is at this point, too, that we need to reintroduce the external factors into our analysis, with the aim of showing how the external and the internal have interacted to intensify the dilemma—and to augment the already high potential for future conflict.

As Oppenheimer's words implied, it is essential to the survival of the system in its present form that the economy should continue to grow at a high rate. To maintain white standards, to maintain defence capacity, to prevent huge increases in black unemployment, a growth rate of something like 5.5 per cent per annum would seem to be required.[7] But since the early seventies growth rates have fallen critically short of that level; in 1975 real GDP growth slumped to only 2.2 per cent.

Why? To some extent South Africa was afflicted by global problems not of its (or any other single country's) making, and beyond any one country's capacity to control: worldwide inflation, the trade recession, the international monetary crisis. But there were other ways in which foreign factors combined with intrinsically South African domestic factors to produce especially severe economic consequences for the republic. The freeing of gold from its fixed dollar price naturally affected South Africa, as the world's leading gold producer, more directly than any other country; and though the short-term effects were beneficial, by the mid-seventies there had developed a long-term downward trend in the price of gold with the result that the proportion of foreign exchange brought in by gold sales fell steeply from 37 per cent in 1974 to only 23 per cent in 1976. The quadrupling of the price of oil came at the very time when South Africa had begun a large-scale programme of oil stockpiling; oil imports which in 1973 had cost R190 million were by 1975 costing R1,100 million. It was in this same period of dwindling foreign reserves that South Africa was multiplying its defence expenditures, with much of this money being spent abroad: spending rose from R462 million in 1973 to R948 million in 1975 and R1,650 million in 1977. And the events of Soweto and after compounded the crisis by triggering off an outflow of capital at the rate of some R100 million a month from mid-1976 to late 1977, in spite of restrictive monetary measures. These events also had a clear deterrent effect on new foreign investment; as a major American report put it, 'South Africa is a less secure investment in 1976 than it was in 1974'.[8]

And meanwhile, an economic problem that was truly unique to South Africa was also becoming more and more apparent in this era. Apartheid itself was emerging as economically counter-productive, not just because of the costs of repression but because of its own intrinsic logic. The profitability of the manufacturing economy had been built very largely on the cheapness of black labour; yet that same cheapness placed a decisive domestic limit on the possibilities for growth. Apartheid, by rigidly excluding the bulk of the population from the benefits of capitalist expansion, created its own barriers to that expansion, restricting the internal sources of savings and capital, restricting the supply of skilled labour, above all restricting the size of the domestic market. These self-imposed limitations on domestic growth potential have naturally increased South Africa's dependence on its overseas connections; yet ironically, these same market limitations have apparently increased the post-Soweto reluctance of overseas firms to invest in new projects.

In these interweaving ways, then, foreign economic inputs and the domestic apartheid system were serving more and more in the seventies to undermine the same economy they had done so much to build up in the sixties. 'Supports' were becoming 'threats'. The indicators were capital shortage, recession, high inflation, two devaluations of the Rand, heavy unemployment, and a fall in the GDP growth rate to a point where, taking black population increases into account, there was virtually no growth at all per capita through the mid-seventies.

Faced with these ever starker realities, South Africa was in desperate need of new remedies. And from the vantage point of the late seventies, it is possible to discern two in particular that were tried. One was a drive—still continuing—to tap the foreign loans market as never before, with American, Swiss and West German banks as the principal creditors. This drive has certainly brought in a great deal of new loan capital and alleviated various short-term difficulties. But the totals raised have amounted to nowhere near the levels sought and the loans have come at exceptionally high interest rates.[9] Such incurring of larger and larger debts can hardly be regarded as a genuine 'remedy'; in many ways it simply augments the underlying problem.

The other, a strikingly bold move in the circumstances, has been an all-out effort to enlist black Africa itself as South Africa's market. There had been earlier commercial overtures to black Africa, along with cautious attempts at 'dialogue' with potentially sympathetic conservative states such as the Ivory Coast, but in the early seventies this so-called 'outward' policy hardened into an unprecedently determined drive for trade relations with the continent at large. There were certain under-the-counter successes; by one account some two dozen black African states were doing at least some trading with South Africa by 1976.[10] But in fact the total volume of trade remained very much smaller than Pretoria had hoped for, and it now seems clear that perhaps the most critical of all the reversals in South African economic policy in the seventies has been the general refusal of black Africa to trade with her on a large scale. Had South Africa been able to flood the African continental market with goods, she might well have had no trade deficit, would be far less dependent on foreign investors and lenders, far less dependent on gold, would still boast a powerfully expanding manufacturing sector and would have a much decreased unemployment problem. Instead, the enforced contraction of manufactured output has pushed her back to concentrating once again on production of raw materials for the West, with all that this implies in terms of 'dependence' and constricted opportunities for development. Arguably, then, black Africa's refusal to respond to the 'outward' policy can be seen as contributing directly to the continuing build-up of explosive social pressures at home.

But black Africa's refusal, of course, is itself related directly to South Africa's unacceptable domestic race policies. Were these policies to be abandoned, the trade barriers would presumably be unlocked and South Africa might well become—as it has long dreamed of being—the 'workshop of Africa'.

Thus the central dilemma confronting white South Africa is surely becoming very plain. Apartheid now threatens the prosperity it helped to build. Apartheid, it may be said, is a product of both economics and ideology. For a time it served both kinds of imperative very effectively. But recently the conjunction has ceased to hold firm; economics and ideology have tended to pull in different directions. Whereas the ideology apparently remains much as before, economic rationality suggests an increasingly strong case for basic change. No doubt a dismantling of the apartheid system, and the whole associated apparatus of job reservation, wage discrimination and so on, would bring costs of its own, including steep short-term falls in the profits hitherto dependent upon rock-bottom wage rates. But in the longer run the spread of skills and capital and the expansion of markets—internal and more especially external—should more than compensate for this, while increasing profitability should in turn serve to attract more domestic and foreign investment. At the same time the cost of repression, currently spiralling ever higher, could be expected to fall. And in the still longer term the improvement in black living standards could be expected to have the historically demonstrable effect of curbing the population growth rate.

And yet there is no indication whatever that a decisive move away from economic apartheid is being regarded as a real policy option. Certainly there have been cosmetic changes in 'petty apartheid', partly in the hopes of persuading foreign opinion that conditions are becoming more liberal, more open, more stable. But fundamental change is simply not on the agenda. Ideology, it would appear, reigns triumphant over economic rationality. In other words, the point has certainly not been reached where the systemic costs are regarded as too high. It follows that the existing socio-economic pressures must go on building up, and that the whites will go on defending their place in the sun by repression, not by reform. Until this situation changes it is hard to foresee other than a deeply bitter future for South Africa: a continuing cycle of 'Sowetos' and 'containments'.

In short, external and internal factors blend to produce a situation of enormous domestic conflict potential.

The question now becomes: at what stage, if any, are outside actors likely to intervene in this unhappy process? More generally, what are the prospects of South Africa becoming involved in wider conflicts embracing other countries? Once these questions are asked, it becomes necessary to broaden the analysis beyond the borders of South Africa. We must first seek to see South Africa more clearly in the context of its region, and to take account of the additional dimensions of conflict which are thereby brought into focus; and then go on to consider the interests and policies of the major powers which are involving themselves more and more deeply in the region's troubled affairs.

III

Southern Africa is a vast and diverse region comprising South Africa, Namibia, Zimbabwe-Rhodesia, Malawi, Botswana, Lesotho, Swaziland, Angola, Mozambique and Zambia. To these ten names the South African government (but no other government in the world at present) would add those of the Bantustans: Transkei, Bophuthatswana and various others in the making. Several of these countries are mineral-rich: not only South Africa with its huge reserves of gold, uranium, diamonds, chromite, manganese, platinum, coal and other minerals, but also Namibia with copper, zinc, uranium and possibly off-shore oil, Zambia with copper, Botswana with copper-nickel, Angola with iron ore, diamonds, manganese and proven oil reserves. But of course South Africa is by far the most advanced and powerful state in the region by almost any measurable criteria: not just mineral production but also industrial production, food production, military strength, technological sophistication, size of professional and tertiary sectors, communications facilities and so on. The single most telling statistic, perhaps, is that South Africa is responsible for 70 per cent of the combined GDPs of the whole region.[11]

How far do these South African strengths translate into 'domination' of the region? It is not difficult to demonstrate that each of the countries named is in some degree dependent on South Africa. In some cases, indeed, the somewhat overworked notion of a metropolis-satellite relationship can quite justifiably be applied. Namibia, for example, has long been a directly administered dependency of South Africa's, initially under League of Nations and UN mandate and since 1966 in defiance of the UN's revocation of that mandate. Rhodesia, which in almost every sense except the juridically literal one could be regarded as a South African colony, had its UDI sustained from the outset by South Africa, both in the sanction-breaking supply of fuels and import-export routes and in the provision of military assistance against guerrilla activities. Botswana and Lesotho, Swaziland and Malawi, all desperately poor, landlocked countries, would have scant hope of economic survival were it not for their export of labour to South Africa, principally to work in the mines. Mozambique's similar—though less complete—dependence on labour export has already been mentioned. In Angola, South African capital still plays a part in certain long-established joint enterprises (principally mining and prospecting) with French and US capital. Zambia's copper-mining industry depends crucially on South African technology, skills and finance, provided chiefly by the Anglo-American Corporation which dominates mining in both countries. Indeed, Anglo-American may be seen as the major institution of South African capital abroad: a true conglomerate, heavily involved not only in mining but in a whole multitude of enterprises throughout the region (and beyond).

The power of South Africa as local metropolis is also felt in more general ways through multilateral institutions and arrangements. This power operates for example, through the Rand Currency Area, under which South African currency and money markets have functioned as regional institutions for Namibia, Botswana, Lesotho and Swaziland; through the participation of these same countries in the Southern African Customs Union; through technical co-operation (between technological unequals) in such matters as telecommunications, water supply, and power generation; and through the workings of a railway network which radiates out from the Rand conurbation—the very heart of South African power—into Namibia, Botswana, Lesotho, Rhodesia, Zambia and even Mozambique.

In these sorts of ways, economists and industrialists at least might well regard southern Africa as a genuinely interdependent 'region', capable of becoming quite closely integrated to general economic advantage with South Africa acting as prime supplier of capital, technology, goods and overall leadership in economic policy. Once again Harry Oppenheimer has provided an admirably pointed statement:

> We in the Anglo-American Corporation Group have long had important interests in virtually every country in this vast area and are therefore perhaps more conscious than most of the high costs of division and strife, and of the benefits which would flow to all its peoples from a relaxation of tension and cooperation on a regional basis.[12]

Of course such co-operation would also be of the highest geopolitical significance for South Africa, in effect helping to buttress her security much as the 'buffer states' (as they used to be called in their days of white rule) used to do. Understandably, then, the task of converting those former 'buffer' states into something approximating 'client' states has been for some years one of South Africa's major foreign-policy objectives, finding expression in 'dialogue', in 'detente' and in an overall flexibility on regional matters which contrasts very strikingly indeed with the rigidities at home.

Yet success has been rather elusive. The simple but overwhelming barrier to comprehensive 'integration' of the region, with South Africa as the acknowledged core state, has been, once again, black Africa's refusal to transact more than the necessary minimum of business—in a word, survival business—with South Africa. The stumbling block remains the same: South Africa's internal race policies. Certainly there have been occasional exercises in detente between South Africa and such front-line states as Zambia, Mozambique and Botswana. But the point is that the two sides have understood the purpose of detente in quite different terms. Whereas South Africa conceived detente as an alternative to confrontation, a device for buying time, respectability, status and ultimately acceptance, black Africa, acting more or less in the spirit of the Lusaka Declaration of 1969, has seen it as an additional opening through which to *pursue* confrontation: a means of keeping the issue of South Africa's policies constantly *on* the agenda. South Africa seeks order: black Africa, change. The fact that leaders of the two sides, Vorster and Kaunda in particular, have in recent times met and talked, and have even sketched out possible deals for the future of a territory such as Zimbabwe, does not alter the point that basic views about the optimum long-term distribution of power and benefits in the region remain in opposition. Hence supposed clients have in general pursued a regional diplomacy that shows a considerable independence of the wishes of their supposed patron, Botswana's being perhaps the clearest example. Nor has detente altered the repeatedly demonstrated readiness of black African states to forego potential economic advantage in the political cause; to pay, in Richard Hall's phrase, 'the high price of principles'. The refusal to enter into full-scale trade relations has already been noted. More dramatically visible cases in recent years have been Zambia's self-severance from the southern African railway system from 1973 until late in 1978 and Mozambique's maintenance of its border closure with Rhodesia since March 1976. And as Shaw points out, even for the smallest and most dependent states 'formal cooperation with South Africa is an increasingly controversial policy ... as their choices gradually increase with the independence of Mozambique and Angola; indeed, their control over crucial flows of labour, water, and other resources may enhance their bargaining power'.[13] Notably, in 1974 Malawi withdrew its labour from the mines after an air accident in which 74 returning Malawian miners were killed; and by 1976 there were active moves by some of the member states to withdraw from both the Rand Currency Area and the Southern African Customs Union.

Thus the historic pattern of regional linkages is increasingly overlaid by a newer pattern of regional disengagements, expressive of the enduring antagonism which the black states feel towards the South African regime. South Africa's inability to secure full-scale integration even in the most functional of areas reflects the fact that the relaxation of tension for which Oppenheimer called is not in sight at present, and is most unlikely to be attained in future—this side of major changes inside South Africa. In this respect South Africa's environment is decreasingly a supportive one, neither as stable nor as malleable as Pretoria would wish; certainly not an environment in which Pretoria can go on hoping for external solutions to its internal problems.

Moreover, and here we come to matters absolutely central to the analysis, the region has lately become rife with armed conflicts whose implications for the republic run very deep. For although these have all been essentially internal struggles in countries beyond South Africa's border, all have revolved around the crucial issue of 'who is to rule'; all have at some stage involved black-white confrontation; and all have attracted foreign participation in forms far from congenial to Pretoria's interests. Collectively they have generated an aura of crisis which represents the most critical way in which South Africa's environment has become destabilised. To these conflicts and their consequences we must now turn.

The turning point, as has been sufficiently stressed already, came with the Portuguese revolution of April 1974. This event followed (and in large measure arose from) nearly thirteen years of bitter armed struggle in Angola and Mozambique between guerrilla liberation armies and Portugal's mainly conscripted armed forces. South Africa had taken no direct part in these conflicts, believing apparently that the Portuguese were unlikely to be defeated so long as they could rely (as they did) on indirect American support through the NATO relationship. But in Rhodesia and Namibia, the other theatres of guerrilla operations in the region, South Africa did intervene. Though the operations were on a much lesser scale in these countries, South Africa's sense of commitment was very much higher. Namibia was of course her 'own' territory, and counter-insurgency operations reflected therefore Pretoria's direct concern for law and order. As for Rhodesia, the kith-and-kin argument mattered very much to the South African electorate; South African strategists tended to see Rhodesia as the republic's own forward-defence zone; and in general, there was a perception of Rhodesia as a domino whose fall must not be permitted. Hence in the late sixties and early seventies South Africa not only sustained Rhodesia through her 'trial by sanctions' but also contributed personnel and equipment to her military defence against the small groups of guerrillas operating mainly out of the 'liberated' areas of Mozambique. Of course the South African government was always anxious for a settlement in Rhodesia, but not nearly so anxious as to subject the Smith regime to the kinds of material economic pressures which Britain was asking it to apply. Broadly speaking, Pretoria worked on the assumption that the regional military situation could be kept under control—barring any sudden disasters.

Nothing could have been either more sudden or more disastrous than the Portuguese collapse. It led within months to the installation of the Soviet-leaning FRELIMO regime in Mozambique. This in turn led to steep escalation of the Rhodesian conflict. Portuguese withdrawal unleashed too the internal war for the succession between the MPLA, the FNLA and UNITA, the three rival liberationist movements in Angola. South Africa watched these developments with all the more dismay in that this was the very period when the economic difficulties at home were making the establishment of closer and more stable economic relations with neighbour states seem such an important policy priority. Instead, not only was the prospect of closer relations being shot to ribbons on African battlefields, the same destabilisation was forcing Pretoria to divert ever greater resources into its own military build-up, thereby intensifying its economic problems in ways already noted.

By late 1974 the South African government had arrived at the 'realistic' conclusion that in Rhodesia at least, the solution would have to be African majority rule in the fairly near future. This was the period of the first face-to-face negotiations between Vorster and Kaunda, for here was one of the issues on which, for the time being, they were in agreement. It was also the period of Vorster's insistence to Smith that Nkomo, Sithole and the other detained African leaders—most of them, it was hoped, 'moderates'—must be released and brought into discussions; an idea which Smith himself was now ready to accept. And though Vorster was still restrained by domestic political considerations from applying the pressures which would count most, in particular an oil blockade, he did make South Africa's new policy emphasis very clear when in 1975 he withdrew South African military personnel from Rhodesia even as the fighting intensified.

By mid-1975, however, it was the situation in Angola that had become the most urgent. For the intervention Pretoria dreaded most—a Soviet one—had become a visible reality. The background to Soviet support of the MPLA will be touched on in the next section. What matters here is the South African government's reaction. The measure of its concern is that, for the first time ever, it took the drastic step of committing a regular armed force to an African war. The initial armed penetration of southern Angola in July 1975 was intended only, it was claimed, to protect the Cunene Dam installations on the Namibia-Angola border. If so, the purpose soon changed fundamentally. For in October and November the South African 'Zulu' column, operating in tactical alliance with UNITA, proceeded to sweep half the length of the country to within shooting distance of the capital, Luanda.

The real stimulus for this South African penetration and subsequent advance, it would appear, lay in Pretoria's understanding that Dr Kissinger had asked for it and had promised full American co-operation.[14] Apparently this was to take the form of American sponsorship of a simultaneous southward thrust by the FNLA (which already enjoyed various forms of support from America, France, Zaire and, for good measure, China) so as to crush the MPLA in a pincer. It is history that there was no such outcome;

that there was no massive American-backed descent from the north; that the supply of Russian materiel and (from November 1975) Cuban troops gave the MPLA such superiority in the field that by February 1976 it was in control of most of the country and the South African force had been obliged to withdraw to the Namibian border. The result was the confirmation in power of a second Soviet-leaning government within the space of a year, a development sealed by the signing of Soviet-Angolan and Soviet-Mozambican treaties of friendship and co-operation in October 1976 and April 1977 respectively.

Understandably, South Africa was both furious at the American 'betrayal' and deeply alarmed at the speed of these changes. Yet Pretoria's capacity for flexible adaptation in regional matters was very soon in evidence once again. Clearly the Vorster Government saw it as all the more imperative in the new circumstances to push for African majority rule in Rhodesia and, also, now in Namibia: that is, the two territories for which South Africa had the most directly 'metropolitan' responsibilities. In the installation of moderate African regimes while time still availed, it seemed, lay the best chance of preventing further armed conflict and the spread of radical influence under Soviet auspices.

Thus it was that in September 1976 Ian Smith was at last brought to concede the principle of majority rule for Rhodesia. It was a concession stemming most directly from the threats and inducements brought to bear by Dr Kissinger, but Kissinger's effort was most materially aided by the Vorster Government which showed itself prepared for the first time covertly to impede the flow of Rhodesian exports and imports through South Africa. The outcome, after intricate negotiations, was the establishment of the 'internal agreement' Rhodesian regime of March 1978 led by Smith, Muzorewa, Sithole and Chirau. Though this major shift did not, after all, bring an end to the guerrilla war—which by late 1978 was being prosecuted more actively than ever by the leaders who remained outside the agreement, Mugabe and Nkomo—it did set Rhodesia on the path to the kind of settlement which South Africa had come so keenly to desire: namely, one designed to establish in office the most 'moderate'—albeit embattled and mutually suspicious—of the available African leaders. What remained unresolved was the question of whether, and how far, Pretoria might need to become militarily committed in any further settling of accounts between Zimbabwe's various African leaders and their respective armed forces.

In Namibia, South Africa as the occupying power has felt able to take a much tougher line. Her concern to secure an acceptable settlement—meaning the installation of a government which would shut out the part-radicalised SWAPO movement, along with retention of the economically and militarily strategic Walvis Bay as a South African enclave—was manifested in the final defiant decision of Mr Vorster's premiership that South Africa would administer the territory's independence elections unilaterally rather than accede to the plan for UN supervision. It was a decision that brought South Africa directly into diplomatic conflict with the Western powers, committed as they were to the principle of UN control over the transfer of power and, more especially, to the participation of SWAPO in the process. How this difference would be resolved remained unclear as of November 1978, the time of writing; though there were signs that the Botha cabinet was looking for some kind of intermediate ground on which to do business with the United States in particular.

And here it is appropriate to proceed to the third and final stage of the analysis, namely consideration of the interests and interventions of the great powers.

IV

Prior to the dramatic intrusion of the Soviet Union in 1975, the pattern of great-power interests and influence in Southern Africa had seemed relatively firm and unchanging. It was, without question, a Western sphere. The mesh of Western interests in the region, especially in South Africa, had grown complex and very extensive indeed in the post-war era, as a few figures will indicate.

Firstly, there was trade. In 1972 Britain, the EEC six, the United States and Japan between them provided South Africa with 72 per cent of its imports and bought 67 per cent of its exports (excluding gold).

Secondly, there was capital investment. The value of British direct investment, taking governmental and private investment together, stood at about US$5.8 billion in 1977. West German and United States investment each amounted to some $1.7 billions, having grown rapidly in the later sixties—that is, the high period of South Africa's ecnomic take-off, which their investments both fuelled and profited by. South Africa, it was perfectly accurate to say, was the regional agent of Western capitalism, so that Western corporations were no less interested than South Africa's own in the problems of achieving regional stability and market penetration.

Thirdly, there was the republic's significance as a supplier of strategic minerals to the West, a significance that can be demonstrated most succinctly in tabular form.[15]

Table 8.1: *Percentage of Non-Communist World Resources in Southern Africa*

Asbestos	100*
Amosite	100*
Chromite	74*
Platinum	70*
Gold	70
Manganese	60
Uranium Oxide	30

* Denotes US totally dependent on foreign sources of supply.

It would probably be wrong to see such figures—as some have done—as indicating an absolutely critical Western dependence upon South African minerals. In the long run the US and Western Europe could probably find adequate replacement resources for virtually all important minerals if South Africa were 'lost' to the West.[16] The factor that nevertheless gave South Africa its extraordinary importance was the sheer concentration of so many key resources in one country, a concentration probably matched only by that in the USSR.

Fourthly, there was the significance of the Cape of Good Hope as a trade route, especially for Western Europe. By the early seventies some 70 per cent of Europe's strategic raw materials were being shipped via this route, including in particular 80 per cent of its oil. America's direct dependence on the route was less, but according to some projections would increase; for example, some analysts have suggested that up to 25 per cent of America's imported oil supplies might be coming round the Cape in the eighties.[17]

And fifthly, there was the added military importance to the West of the same route (and of South Africa's shore-based naval facilities) arising out of the increasing Soviet naval activity in the Indian Ocean.

It was a pattern of very tangible interests in South Africa which the Western powers showed every intention of maintaining and defending, notwithstanding the frequency of their public condemnations of South Africa's internal race policies. The consistent use by the Western powers of their Security Council vetoes to forestall UN plans for international economic sanctions against South Africa was evidence enough of this.

Certainly the United States—the Western 'leader' and the great power of major interest for this discussion—avoided any visibly activist role in southern Africa. But a role there was. From 1969 to 1975 it was the role laid down as Option Two in Kissinger's secret policy document on southern Africa, NSC Study Memorandum 39 of 1969 (the 'Tar-Baby Option', as it became generally known when this document was subsequently leaked and published in full[18]). Option Two was built on certain premisses: that US interests in the region were 'important' rather than 'vital', and that the US must not be seen to be publicly supportive of apartheid. But it embodied also the crucial *realpolitik* calculation that 'The whites are here to stay and the only way that constructive change can come about is through them. There is no hope for the blacks to gain the political rights they seek through violence, which will only lead to chaos and increased opportunities for the communists.' What was advocated was a 'selective relaxation of our stance toward the white regimes', thereby encouraging 'some modification of their current racial and colonial policies ... Our tangible interests form a basis for our contacts in the region and these can be maintained at an acceptable political cost.'

The belief that such an approach might induce 'modification' stood in odd contrast with the document's later assertion that 'The current thrust of South African domestic policy does not involve any basic change in the racial segregation system... There is virtually no evidence that change might be forthcoming in these South African policies as a result of any approaches on our part.' But beneath this apparent doublethink what mattered was that Option Two dictated a strategy (never officially stated as such) of recognising, dealing with, and discreetly supporting the established power-holders in Southern Africa. Tar-Baby was principally designed, of course, to serve American interests rather than to preserve white rule as such, but in the circumstances the latter was seen as a necessary corollary of the former. America's continuing indirect support for Portugal's African wars in return for use of the Portuguese Azores as an Atlantic airbase,[19] for example, was fully consonant with Option Two. So was the Byrd amendment which exempted chromite from the US embargo on Rhodesian goods, a Congressional initiative which no doubt enjoyed Kissinger's private approval.

So we come once again to the Portuguese revolution, and to the consequential event which impelled an exceedingly rapid American reappraisal: the Russian arrival on the scene.

Here it is necessary to consider for a moment the general contours of Soviet policy in Africa. Assessments vary, but the consensus among professional Western analysts would appear to be that the stepping-up of Soviet activity in 1975 did not represent some *qualitative* change of policy, an attempt to apply some new 'grand design' to the continent. Since the early sixties, the era of black African independence, the USSR has quite consistently pursued the kinds of policies that could readily be deduced from its known interests, and the Angola-Mozambique penetrations were simply an opportunistic extension of these.

Summarily, the USSR has sought diplomatic and economic relations with as many states as possible. Where circumstances have seemed propitious (as for a time in Ghana) it has sought to export its development model. In a few strategically chosen countries (as for a time, Somalia) it has sought to establish servicing facilities for its navy. In others, where opportunity has presented itself (as for example in Libya, Uganda and Ethiopia) it has acted as an arms supplier. It has also equipped and trained selected liberation movements in exile (for example Nkomo's ZAPU). By all these means at its disposal—propaganda, diplomacy, aid, trade, the provision of weaponry—it has sought to build itself an influence in Africa countering that of the Chinese and undermining that of the West.

Of course the Soviet Union is a newcomer to Africa. For a long time Africa policy ranked relatively low among its priorities, even its Third World priorities; after all, Africa is out on the periphery of the Moscow-centred map, and the USSR has never had either historic connections with or entrenched economic interests in the continent to match those of the West. But by the same token it has had little to lose there and perhaps much to gain. Not only has the USSR had no great historic stakes to defend; by further contrast with the West, it is virtually free of the dilemmas inherent in having to do business with both 'black' and 'white' Africa. In short, it can aim to support whichever groups seem most likely both to favour its interests and to succeed in local conflicts. That is why the ideas of 'opportunity' and 'opportunism' pervade the foregoing summary account of Soviet policy. For the essence of that policy, to repeat, has not been to apply any preconceived overall design. It is simply to await, and then try to exploit, opportunities for the expansion of influence.[20]

Since 1960 the major openings for Soviet opportunism have occurred in the dislocatory circumstances of war. It is a matter of record that the Soviet Union has consistently intervened, if with mixed results, in black Africa's major wars—that is, wars involving large and potentially important countries: the Congolese civil war of 1960-1, the Nigerian civil war of 1967-70, the late-seventies war in the Horn of Africa, the Angolan civil war. The first of these interventions brought sharp reverses; the second, a certain (but far from dominant) influence in Nigeria. The outcome of the third remains indeterminate. But with the fourth, the Soviet Union hit the jackpot. Virtually at a stroke, the Russians stole a huge march on both the Chinese and the Americans, established potential access for themselves to major mineral and other resources, secured potential facilities for the Soviet navy, and won themselves a political voice they had never had before in the affairs of the southern African region.

There was nothing fore-ordained about this success. 'Jackpot' is a most appropriate image because the Soviet intervention was not just opportunistic; it was a gamble. It was, after all, an intervention at an enormous distance from Moscow, in unfamiliar territory, in a region of established Western interest and influence, adjacent to an ocean—the South Atlantic—dominated by Western seapower, on behalf of a liberation movement which as of early 1975 controlled only one seaport and one large airfield in the country. Well after the build-up of Soviet equipment and Cuban manpower began, the risks must still have seemed very palpable, since Kissinger had quickly responded with a build-up of aid in cash and kind to the FNLA channelled through Zaire. But by the end of the year the gamble had come off. Among the very important turning-points was the decision in December 1975 by the US Congress—the post-Vietnam, post-Watergate, Democrat-controlled Congress—that it would not authorise any further US aid to either the FNLA or UNITA. Arguably it was this decision, as much as any other, that left the South African force exposed and unsupported in mid-country, and opened the way to the MPLA's victory two months later.[21]

No doubt it is possible to overstate the extent of the Soviet triumph. In neither Angola nor Mozambique, hindsight suggests, has the Soviet Union established itself in complete 'dominance'. Mozambique is still tied economically to South Africa and the Soviet Union has not sought materially to change this situation; indeed it seems to have accepted the South African connection as the best available means of rebuilding Mozambique's war-shattered economy. In Angola, the exploitation of oil remains in the hands of the Gulf Oil Corporation, which pays handsome royalties to the MPLA Government and from time to time has had its installations *guarded* by the Cubans; moreover, the Angolan government has lately been exploring the prospects for new trade and aid arrangements with the US. Perhaps these might be regarded as further examples of the 'contradictions' this paper began by mentioning, though there is nothing very contradictory about the desire of even a revolutionary government to sell its goods in the most lucrative market. All that being said, however, the generalisation must stand: Angola and Mozambique did represent very significant net gains for the Soviet Union at the expense of its great-power rivals.[22]

Dr Kissinger's diplomacy, as he himself liked to proclaim, was essentially Metternichian. He did have a grand design, and it was conceived in classic balance-of-power terms. The basic objective was to secure peace and defend Western interests by preventing any unregulated change in the extant balance between the major powers (meaning the superpowers plus Western Europe, Japan and China). In general, his efforts were directed towards achieving detente between the powers and ensuring that they sought neither to annex each other's established spheres of influence nor to contest for control of the Third World. If for most of his term in office he took no great interest in southern Africa, it was because he regarded it as a region where the balance did not seem greatly threatened; it was an area of established Western influence which needed only to be maintained as such.

To Kissinger, then, the Soviet intervention in Angola represented a direct and shocking violation of the rules. The Soviets' ensuing success posed a high threat to the Metternichian order, and of course the Western interests which it secured. It became necessary to move very fast. Suddenly Rhodesia looked perilously like 'the next domino', and Namibia the one after that. Thus southern Africa became the prime focus of Kissinger's attention during 1976, his last year in office.

His most fundamental aim was to ensure the security of South

Africa, where the West's deeper interests were concentrated. To do that he had to restore stability in the region. To do that he had to promote a controlled decolonisation of Rhodesia and Namibia, installing moderate African leaderships while short-circuiting the kinds of armed struggle that gave the Soviets their best chance for further intervention. It was a strategic assessment which closely matched Vorster's own, and which brought the two of them into a significant working alliance. Not that Kissinger was taking any chances. Pretoria, he knew, was still bitter at Washington's 'betrayal' of the South African force in Angola. Further, there remained a chance that Vorster might back down, as he had done before, when it came to the crucial matter of squeezing white Rhodesia. But Kissinger had quite a deal of leverage available to him; notably, in the event of South Africa failing to see reason, the US was in a position to manipulate IMF gold-auctions to keep the price depressed.[23]

At any rate, it was the year of shuttle diplomacy in southern Africa; of Kissinger's Lusaka speech declaring US support for the principle of majority rule; of the Kissinger Plan, that amalgam of threats and bribes which finally won Ian Smith's concession of this principle for Rhodesia; and of the all-party Geneva talks which, although abortive in their wider purpose of giving effect to the Kissinger Plan, did open the way to the 'internal settlement' of March 1978. But at the end of the year Gerald Ford lost office, and so did Henry Kissinger.

It was possible in that era to speak without much confusion of the Kissinger policy for southern Africa. Since then it has become necessary to speak of the Carter-Mondale-Brzezinski-Young policies, and to learn to recognise the periodic alternation of 'liberal' and 'conservative' ascendancies in policy-making. Indeed, a more detailed account than the present one would have to chart a quite considerable twisting and turning along the way.[24] Nevertheless, it is possible to distil certain broad themes and tendencies.

The new administration's successor to NSSM 39 was Policy Review Memorandum 4, prepared under Brzezinski's supervision immediately after Carter's inauguration. The central argument among PRM 4's drafters was whether to maintain Kissinger's emphasis on pursuing settlements in Rhodesia and Namibia with South Africa's co-operation before directing attention to South Africa itself, or to confront South Africa immediately without waiting for solutions elsewhere. President Carter was persuaded by the liberals (led by Andrew Young) to adopt the second view, and in March 1977 signed a confidential presidential directive to guide policy on southern Africa. This directive emphasised that southern African problems should be regarded as urgent; that the US should remain committed to peaceful solutions, since guerrilla warfare could be exploited by the Soviet Union in its own interests; and that the US should work co-operatively with European allies and African states to find solutions. With regard to South Africa, the directive stressed that the US must take a more critical line against apartheid or risk jeopardising its relations with the Third World. Further, it would have to take visible steps to scale down its relations with South Africa if the whites persisted in refusing to contemplate any sharing of power with the blacks. In a phrase, selective relaxation was out; selective hardening was in.

These guidelines have found expression in policy in several ways. The first significant indication of the administration's attitude came within days of Carter's directive, in the form of heavy—and successful—lobbying of the new Congress to repeal the Byrd amendment. At about the same time, the administration sponsored a 'Statement of Principles' in relation to the operations of US firms in South Africa, stressing for example the desirability of moving away from discriminating employment practices. Several major corporations fairly promptly announced their acceptance of these principles.

Two months later, in May 1977, Vice-President Mondale officially warned South Africa to move away from apartheid or suffer deterioration in its relations with the United States. A range of possible measures was publicly spelt out: withdrawal of US military attaches from South Africa, cutting of links between the two countries' intelligence agencies, tightening of American visa requirements for South Africans, limiting of export-import bank guarantees on loans to South Africa and suspension of tax credits for US corporations in South Africa. In his Notre Dame speech in the same month, Carter made it clear that America's commitment to majority rule applied to South Africa no less than to other countries in the region, a point on which Kissinger had been rather less specific. Generally, there was a new rhetorical emphasis on judging and condemning South Africa by human rights criteria, again something Kissinger had avoided doing (he used to argue that moralistic lecturing was no concern of his, and would in any case serve only to harden white attitudes). Not that the administration's moral judgements have been wholly disinterested; Andrew Young has been quoted as pointing out (perhaps for the benefit of the domestic American audience) that 'if we don't take an interest in human rights in Southern Africa, we can't count on Nigeria to supply oil'.[25]

This remark points to a complementary aspect of the administration's policy, its stress on achieving good relations with Nigeria. In its own right, Nigeria has to be seen as the emerging power of black Africa. It is also a major oil-supplier to the US; so large is the flow, indeed, that the volume of US-Nigerian trade has become something like double the volume of US-South African trade. Alliance with Nigeria is therefore 'natural', and it is almost necessarily a diplomatic alliance against South Africa since Nigeria's considerable diplomatic weight is increasingly being committed to the broader African campaign against the white South.

At the same time there has been an ostensible veering away from Metternichian preoccupations. In relation to Rhodesia and Namibia, the crisis states of southern Africa, this had led to a public emphasis on 'non-intervention' and an insistence that southern Africa must resolve its 'own' problem. This is not to say that Washington lacks policy prescriptions for the region. It insists, for example—and this is perhaps its principal point of difference from Pretoria in relation to current disputes—that settlements in Rhodesia and Namibia must include, not exclude, the Patriotic Front and SWAPO respectively. Whereas South Africa appears to regard the inclusion of such groups as necessarily subversive of moderate solutions, the current US view appears to be that any solution which excludes them will be inherently unworkable. This line of argument, it may be assumed, reflects Washington's current thinking on the broader problems of minimising anti-Western influence; thinking which, in accordance with the presidential directive, obviously goes on, for all Washington's public stress on non-intervention. No doubt that very stress reflects an assessment that for the time being there is little likelihood of any major new aggression in the region by the Russians or Cubans (or Chinese). Nevertheless there is clearly room for minor initiatives by these parties, and their further cultivation of liberation movements in exile would appear to be, as PRM 4 recognised, their most likely current course of action. By late 1978, in fact, the Soviets were visibly mounting support programmes for both Nkomo, their favourite Zimbabwean son of long standing, and Mugabe, hitherto backed mainly by the

Chinese; a classic hedging-of-bets operation designed to ensure a Soviet role whichever partner emerges ascendant from the future breakdown of the Nkomo-Mugabe marriage of convenience. Presumably, this is precisely the kind of development which the US is anxious to counter by bringing such movements in from exile.

The administration's belief that a radical movement incorporated is preferable to a radical movement at large has so far been pressed mainly by diplomatic means; through the UN, through tours by Young and Vance, or face to face with Ian Smith in Washington. Yet perhaps there is a little more to the administration's efforts than that. Quietly, and surely significantly, it has taken to budgeting quite substantial sums for what is termed 'Security Supporting Assistance' in the southern African region. This is a category of aid to be used at the President's discretion 'to promote economic or political stability' of the kind previously poured into Indo-China and after that the Middle East. In 1978 some $115 million of such security aid was budgeted for spending in Botswana, Lesotho, Swaziland, Zambia and Zaire, five states bordering on the radical states of Angola and Mozambique and the crisis states of Rhodesia and Namibia. The basic purpose, it must be supposed, is to help bolster the relatively non-radical governments of these countries in the cause of creating an overall regional environment in which the containmnt of radical movements will be a less difficult task.[26]

But there is another very important thing that 'non-intervention' has effectively come to mean, something which takes us back to South Africa again (while falling compatibly into place with the point just made). In practice, the government has come to appear scarcely more inclined under Carter than it was under Nixon and Ford to take concrete punitive measures against South Africa. Notwithstanding the warning notes sounded early in Carter's term, the government's anti-South Africa moves since that time have been made almost entirely at the level of expressive or symbolic politics. This might even be said of America's vote for the Security Council resolution of November 1977 which imposed a mandatory international arms embargo on South Africa. The US has officially maintained just such an embargo for fifteen years, so the vote represented no new commitment. But neither did it put an end to America's provision of dual-purpose equipment such as C-126 aircraft, which the South African police and armed forces have put to visibly heavy use during recent crises. And this leads to the more general point; in broad economic-cum-technological terms, the relationship would appear to be 'business as usual'. The reality behind non-intervention is a pattern of economic engagement with the South African system that has been maintained with minimal disturbance through the change of administration. (We saw earlier that the pattern has been affected by events *inside* South Africa, such as Soweto, but that is a different point.)

Why this broad continuity? No doubt domestic considerations have played some part. It may be presumed that US firms with a stake in South Africa have pressed the administration to keep their interests in mind. Signing the government-sponsored 'Statement of Principles' was all very well, but corporations can hardly be expected to do other than oppose more punitive measures against business interests such as those adumbrated by Mondale. The administration may also be feeling uneasily conscious of having run some way ahead of domestic (and Congressional) opinion with its expressed attitudes.

And yet it is hard to see the administration's general maintenance of 'business as usual' as simply a response to domestic pressures. The contemporary situation is one in which, for example, the US maintains technical nuclear collaboration with South Africa (officially in order to be able to influence it to sign the Non-Proliferation Treaty); in which new American bank loans are helping to tide South Africa through its present economic crisis (though by no means all American banks are willing to deal with South Africa); and in which the government unequivocally refuses to countenance substantive withdrawal from normal investment and commercial relations. Ambassador Young, again, has made this last point clear to UN and African audiences on several occasions. Moreover, the US continues to block any UN efforts to mount economic sanctions campaigns against South Africa, as was seen again in late 1978 when the idea of sanctions came back into serious consideration over the Namibia issue.

Disengagement and sanctions, the administration has argued, are not the way to produce the internal changes in South Africa that all desire. Reform is more likely to follow from internal socio-economic change, partly of an 'automatic' kind: the spread of the market, the growth of a black middle-class, black consumerism, perhaps assisted by periodic non-violent boycotts. Ambassador Young has explicitly argued along these lines,[27] and of course such prescriptions are very reminiscent of the way in which the black middle-class, of which he is a representative, has developed in the United States. But in the South African environment it remains surely an unrealistic argument. Not only does it take wholly inadequate account of what was referred to earlier as the 'inexhaustibility of black anger'; it is subject to a very great practical difficulty that was also touched on earlier. The point is that, even assuming the viability of a 'market' solution, it cannot begin to work effectively until *after* formal apartheid is dismantled. To argue otherwise is to put the cart before the horse. Closer to home, it is to ignore the fact that in the US there has at least been no *legal* impediment to the growth of a substantial black middle-class.

We are left, in brief, with the image of an American administration extremely unwilling to commit real political or economic power to the cause of securing the kinds of changes in South Africa which it claims to seek. It is hard to avoid the conclusion that this administration basically espouses a 'pragmatic' view which is not much more or less than an up-dated version of Tar-Baby. To wit: however deplorable South Africa's race policies may be, it would be foolish in the present circumstances to act in ways which might jeopardise the strength and stability of the South African state, or which might impede the revival of the South African economy. Given the recent and current crises in the area, the strength of South Africa appears even more than before to be the prime guarantor of the West's regional interests. And of course, dealing with South Africa remains an important generator of profits for American enterprises; not a minor consideration in this era of economic embattlement for the United States.

V

Yet such a relationship need not necessarily entail permanent American support for white rule. The phrase 'in the present circumstances' in the previous paragraph is important. The primary factor remains America's perception of its interests; white rule remains not a primary factor but a contingent one. What must be kept fully in mind in all future discussions is the Rhodesian precedent. Certainly the American policy on Rhodesia in 1976 and after reflected Washington's concern to reduce the threats to stability in South Africa's environment; something from which Pretoria could rightly take comfort. But at the same time, it showed that if American interests warranted it, white rule as such could be regarded as expendable. Ultimately what matters from the American (and more broadly, the Western) point of view is political-economic stability, not the colour of a regime's skin. There is thus no necessary reason to doubt that in changed circumstances the option of applying full-scale pressure in order to install a 'safe' African leadership in power in South Africa (beginning, perhaps, with Kissinger-style pressure on the price of gold) might come to seem a strategically preferable option for the US and its major allies.

To be sure, the US would almost certainly not seek to act in such a 'decolonising' role in South Africa unless the Pretoria regime appeared in any case close to collapse and the door seemed wide open for intervention by anti-Western powers. Yet forces which might bring things to such a pass do potentially exist, and it is by no means being unrealistic to speculate about them. Notwithstanding all that has been said about the power of the South African state, it is quite plausible to hypothesise (for example) truly massive internal disorder arising from the conditions analysed earlier, *in combination with* a general economic crisis, *in combination with* large-scale, Soviet-equipped guerrilla attacks launched from Mozambique, *in combination with* a change of regime in Iran that forced South Africa back on to its stockpiled oil reserves; in short, a crisis for Pretoria of quite unprecedented severity, and a situation of potential chaos in which the Western powers might well feel impelled to intervene with a pre-emptive transfer of power.

This then is one possible scenario, and not an intrinsically implausible one. But so many are the variables that a very large number of scenarios, pointing to many different outcomes ranging from the regressive to the revolutionary, could quite readily be constructed by anyone prepared to make the effort. One writer, for example, has ingeniously correlated three hypothetical political futures—pro-apartheid, liberal and revolutionary—with three hypothetical economic futures—'continued dependence', a 'New International Economic Order' and 'collective self-reliance'—to produce a matrix embodying nine distinct scenarios for southern Africa.[28] He is prudent enough, however, to refer to all these as possibilities rather than probabilities; and given all the complexities and contradictions which this paper has explored, there is every reason to echo his prudence. One may well consider it probable, indeed more than probable (as the present writer does), that eventually an Azanian state will emerge. Thankfully, it is no part of this paper's brief to engage in fine and detailed speculation about the permutations of the whens and hows.

That being said, there is one particular projection which does deserve comment at this point: not one dealing with the emergence of Azania but one concerning conflict potential, which is very much within the paper's brief. This is the most dire projection of all, the doomsday projection. So critical is the unfolding situation in South(ern) Africa, it is often enough argued, that there is an acute danger of the superpowers being drawn eventually into direct, large-scale, armed conflict with each other. To pretend otherwise, to shy away from thinking the unthinkable, is an evasion: an evasion of one's analytic and human responsibilities. If a plausible scenario of escalation is required, consider the following. Azanian guerrillas attack South African targets and retreat to sanctuaries in Mozambique; South African forces penetrate Mozambique to destroy the sanctuaries; guerrilla (or Mozambican) forces retaliate by firing Soviet missiles at South African cities or other major targets; South Africa invades Mozambique and engages in direct conflict with the Mozambican army reinforced by Cuban troops; the Soviet Union invokes its treaty obligations to Mozambique and underwrites a full-scale counter-invasion of South Africa; the Western powers come to South Africa's defence; general war ensues.

No one can deny that it might happen. Nevertheless, it is possible to counter-argue with some confidence that such an escalation would be most unlikely to enter its cataclysmic final stages. The principal ground of the argument is that the Soviet Union would have very good reasons indeed not to press things so far.

For a start, and whatever its windfall gains in 1975-6, it remains much the lesser power in the region. It could not contemplate so major an operation as an attack on South Africa without a very substantial prior build-up of its forces, and that would be likely only to provoke a counter-build-up, under Western auspices, of South Africa's already formidable military capacity. Nor could the Soviet Union credibly threaten to use nuclear weaponry, in that its objective must be to defeat the white army, not to decimate the black population; apart from which, the usual arguments about nuclear deterrence apply with all the more force in that South Africa must by now be presumed to have its own nuclear weapons which could be used against other countries in the event of war.

In theory, the incentive for an invasion is there. Quite apart from 'liberating the black population', a Soviet capture of South Africa by military means would give it massive new power *vis-à-vis* its global rivals since it would gain near-monopolistic control of several important mineral resources together with control over a sea route vital to the West. But that, in the end, is precisely the main reason why an attack seems out of the question. So palpable are the West's interests in South Africa that the Soviet Union simply could not afford to assume that the West would be prepared to see the country 'fall' rather than intervene and risk world war. In the last analysis, of course, no one can know for certain whether the West would go to war to save South Africa. But the probability is so very high that the risk is almost entirely on the Soviet Union's side. It is a risk of a completely different order from the one the Russians got away with in Angola; one that it seems virtually inconceivable they would take.

A much more likely projection of the South African conflict—and this can serve as a very general conclusion to the whole discussion—is that it will develop into a long-drawn attritionist struggle in which the central issue, as in Angola, Rhodesia and Namibia, will be the contest for local power among local groups, some of them based in neighbouring countries; and in which the role of the superpowers, as in Angola, Rhodesia and Namibia, will largely be one of sponsoring different groups with the aim of securing long-term influence with any successor regime. The choosing of whom to sponsor could become an increasingly difficult business, especially for the Western powers, which might well find it necessary for wider political, economic and diplomatic reasons to support both white interests and black at the same time. And the task is likely to become all the more complex in that the struggle will not necessarily remain a straightforward matter of white against black. There is no reason to doubt that competition between rival liberation movements for the succession will grow in intensity as time goes by, just as it did in Angola, Rhodesia and Namibia; for black South Africa is nothing if not highly differentiated, both in its socio-economic structures and in its socio-economic interests. Thus further problems of choice may arise. It is noticeable that the Soviet Union already supports the ANC, the more overtly radical of the main Azanian liberation movements, in preference to the PAC. China prefers the PAC, largely for anti-Soviet reasons. The US too finds the PAC more acceptable (Young had a close relationship with its late leader, Robert Sobukwe). These particular alignments may not endure indefinitely, but they do illustrate enduring points. They provide yet another indication of the multiple dimensions of internal conflict in South(ern) Africa, and they reveal again the determination of the great powers to find the right horse to back—and to be in at the finish.

It is not self-evident, of course, that any great power will achieve dominance over a future Azanian state. Azania could well be a state of considerable institutional strength and relative autonomy, a state capable of reconciling many of the historic Western connections with newer ties to the non-Western world. But to repeat: how and when the South African conflict will resolve itself, no one can pretend to know. The one thing that can be said with a sense—a tragic sense—of near-inevitability is that there will be strife and human suffering on an enormous scale before the agony runs its course. It would be good to be proven wrong on this, but unrealistic to expect to be.

Notes

1. Industrial Development Corporation, Iron and Steel Corporation, South African Coal, Oil and Gas Corporation, Electricity Supply Commission, Armaments Development and Manufacturing Corporation.

2. The most comprehensive guide to foreign involvement in the South African economy is John Suckling, Ruth Weiss and Duncan Innes, *Foreign Investment in South Africa: The Economic Factor: Study Project on External Investment in South Africa and Namibia (South-West Africa)* (distributed by Africa Publications Trust, London, 1975). A brief, more up-to-date account is Kenneth Good, 'South Africa's Links with the World Economy', *World Review*, vol. 17, no. 2 (June 1978), pp. 39-52.

3. Among recent descriptive and analytical (and critical) accounts may be cited R.W. Johnson, *How Long Will South Africa Survive?* (Macmillan, London, 1977), pp. 179-91; Donald Woods, *Biko* (Paddington Press, New York, 1978); and a series of booklets published by the International Defence and Aid fund, including Hilda Bernstein, *For their Triumphs and For their Tears: Women in Apartheid South Africa* (1975), Freda Troup, *Forbidden Pastures: Education under Apartheid* (1976), and Barbara Rogers, *Divide and Rule: South Africa's Bantustans* (1976).

4. Johnson, *South Africa*, p. 294.

5. Ibid., pp. 295-303.

6. Chairman's Statement, Anglo-American Corporation of South Africa Ltd, May 1976; quoted in Timothy M. Shaw, 'The International Politics of Southern Africa: Change or Continue?', *Issue*, vol. 7, no. 1 (Spring 1977), p. 21.

7. 'Who cares About Foreign Investment?', *Financial Mail* (Johannesburg), 25 November 1977.

8. *US Corporate Interests in Africa*. Report to the Committee on Foreign Relations, US Senate, January 1978, p. 45; quoted in Jennifer Davis, 'U.S. Dollars in South Africa: Context and Consequence', *Issue*, vol. 7, no. 4 (Winter 1977), p. 20.

9. Good, 'South Africa's Links', p. 44.

10. *Australian*, 14 July 1976.

11. For further statistics see G.M.E. Leistner, 'Southern African Community of Interests—A South African Viewpoint', *South African Journal of African Affairs*, vol. 6, nos, 1-2 (1976), p. 25.

12. Chairman's Statement, Anglo-American Corporation of South Africa Ltd, May 1975; quoted in Shaw, 'International Politics'. For Oppenheimer's thoughts developed at length, see his article 'Prospects for Change in Southern Africa', *South African International*, vol. 8, no. 3 (January 1978), pp. 117-26.

13. Shaw, 'International Politics', p. 24.

14. See Johnson, *South Africa*, pp. 147-55.

15. Adapted from Peter Vanneman and Martin James, 'The Soviet Intervention in Angola: Intentions and Implications', *Strategic Review* (Summer 1976), p. 96. These are 'southern' African figures, but in every case South Africa has the lion's share.

16. Report by Charles Rivers Associates to US Department of Commerce, summarised in *Financial Times* (London), 30 December 1976.

17. See, for example, R. Murapa, 'A Global Perspective of the Political Economy of the U.S. Policy Toward Southern Africa', *Journal of Southern African Affairs*, vol. 2, no. 1 (January 1977), p. 94. The possibilities, however, are many. For example, the recent confirmation of the vast extent of Mexico's oil deposits (some four times the size of America's own remaining reserves) changes the picture. By systematically exploiting those deposits, along with those of (say) Canada, Venezuela, Nigeria and Angola, the US could presumably reduce its dependence on Middle Eastern oil (and the Cape route) considerably.

18. Barry Cohen and Mohammed A. El-Khawas, *The Kissinger Study of Southern Africa* (Spokesman Books, London, 1975). 'Tar-Baby', because the policy was seen as making it extremely difficult for the US to disengage itself from the white regimes.

19. This arrangement is explained in detail in William Minter, *Portuguese Africa and the West* (Monthly Review Press, New York, 1973), Ch. 5.

20. This summary draws mainly on David E. Albright, 'Soviet Policy (in Africa)', *Problems of Communism*, vol. 27, no. 1 (January-February 1978), pp. 20-39.

21. This turning point is analysed at length in K.U. Menon, 'The Impotence of Power: United States Policy Towards the Angolan Civil War 1975-1976', unpublished MA thesis, Monash University, 1977.

22. The present account is concerned mainly with Soviet-American rivalry, but it is worth noting that the Soviets' initial (i.e. pre-1975) support for the MPLA was stimulated mainly by alarm at the progress China appeared to be making in the country through support of the FNLA and UNITA. See Colin Legum, 'The Soviet Union, China and the West in Southern Africa', *Foreign Affairs*, vol. 54 (July 1976), pp. 745-62.

23. By Johnson's account, this pressure tactic had already been used more than once in the years since the dollar had come off the gold standard. See Johnson, *South Africa*, pp. 216-20, 234-42.

24. As does, for example, the factual chronology by R. Deutsch, 'Carter's African Record', *Africa Report*, vol. 23, no. 2 (March-April 1978), pp. 47-51.

25. *Africa Confidential*, vol. 18, no. 17 (19 August 1977), p. 2.

26. See Edgar Lockwood, 'The Future of the Carter Policy Toward Southern Africa', *Issue*, vol. 7, no. 4 (Winter 1977), p. 13.

27. Speech to South African businessmen in Johannesburg, 21 May 1977, cited in Lockwood, 'Carter Policy', pp. 12, 14.

28. P. Thandika Mkandawire, 'Reflections on Some Future Scenarios for Southern Africa', *Journal of Southern African Affairs*, vol. 2, no. 4 (October 1977), pp. 427-39.

9 The Roots of Conflict

MOHAMMED AYOOB

I

As T.B. Millar has pointed out in his introductory essay in this volume, all conflict is, to some extent, intervention. But what makes great-power intervention in conflicts around the Third World a distinct category of analysis is the existence of a number of factors which gives such intervention a unique character.

This uniqueness, however, does not depend primarily on the geographical remoteness of the great-power intervenors from the actual arena of conflict, although such physical distance does form a part of this intervention syndrome. It depends to a much greater extent on the total relationship between the Third World on the one hand and the great powers on the other, all of whom, with the exception of China, form a part of the 'industrial North' (as contrasted with the 'developing South'). This relationship, in all its manifestations—military, economic and political—displays the great inequality in power, again in all its manifestations, including the economic and the political, between the great powers of the North (and particularly the superpowers) on the one hand and the countries of the Third World on the other. This inequality is, in fact, quantitatively so great that it tends to take on a qualitative dimension as well. This is particularly true of the Third World's relationship not only with the two superpowers, the US and the USSR, but also in its relationship with the economic giants, West Germany and Japan as well as the countries of the EEC collectively. It is this inequality which renders the Third World—or large parts of it—so open to permeation on the part of the great powers—militarily, economically and politically—and thus renders the Third World's aspiration for autonomy from these managers of the international system so difficult to achieve.

This disequilibrium in power is the most dramatic manifestation of the hierarchical nature of the post-Second World War international order (with the two superpowers at the apex of this order). It is a reflection of the relative rigidity of the pattern of power-distribution within the system that the hierarchy that emerged at the end of World War II has by and large remained intact and the countries of the Third World, despite the euphoria following formal decolonisation in the 1950s and 1960s, have by and large remained, although with certain relatively significant exceptions, at the bottom of the international pecking order.

Possibly the only successful major attempt to break out of this rigid hierarchical order was made by the People's Republic of China which was able to mobilise its domestic resources in such a fashion as to demonstrably improve its standing within the international hierarchy. However, the fact that it had to do so in the teeth of opposition by the dominant powers—the US in the 1950s and 1960s and the Soviet Union in the 1960s and 1970s—is a significant demonstration of the superpowers' interest in preserving the hierarchical order and in deterring potential challengers from undertaking the Herculean task of challenging the fundamental assumptions on which this order has been based. It is only when a country like China breaks the 'power barrier' that it is reluctantly accepted as a junior partner in the global management enterprise. The recent attempts by the OPEC members, while apparently dramatic in the short run, and while somewhat successful in improving the bargaining status of these countries, have not been able to make any major dent in the existing hierarchy of power, mainly because of their single-product economies and their dependence in economic and military terms on the superpowers and/or the industrialised countries of Europe. The fragile nature of many of their political structures (as was demonstrated by the fall of the Shah of Iran) further detracts from their ability to present a coherent challenge to the existing power structure and to demonstrate their autonomy from the managers of the international system. Therefore, although the great powers are forced to take some of the OPEC members' susceptibilities into account while the energy shortages last and while technological developments are unable to find economically viable alternatives to oil, in the long run their above-mentioned weaknesses preclude the OPEC countries from seriously challenging the entrenched power-hierarchy in the international system. Already, even in the economic sphere, where they are supposed to carry some clout, certain measures like the recycling of petro-dollars into Western economies, has seriously hampered their capacity, potential or actual, to challenge the major industrialised countries.

Great-power intervention in Third World conflicts, therefore, is a part of this global inequality of power and when one analyses particular cases of such involvement, one must not lose sight of the total picture of which this one instance forms a part. For it is only if one understands the totality of these relationships that each particular part falls into place; and it is this totality of global relationships which is manifested in a major fashion in great-power interventions in Third World conflicts, thus making such conflicts, as well as the accompanying intervention, a distinct category of study and analysis and sets them apart from other types of conflict and other cases of intervention.

One must, even at the risk of diversion, say a few words here about the concept of the 'Third World' itself. Without going into a detailed discussion and debate about the conceptual validity or otherwise of this term and the various characteristics which add up to make a country part of the Third World, I would only like to point out at this stage that this concept is one that encompasses in its totality the *feeling* of deprivation, both in terms of the recent past as well as the current situation, among a large section of the world's population *vis-à-vis* the privileged few (in relative numerical terms). Although there are concrete indicators—economic, military and technological—which bear out this thesis of deprivation and colonial and neo-colonial exploitation,[1] I would only like to emphasize here the *perceptual* aspect of this phenomenon. As all perceptive students of the field realise, in international relations, perceptions, whether they do or do not coincide with reality, are infinitely more important than reality itself. What binds the Third World together—in an emotional and psychological sense—is the perception of having been at the 'receiving end' for the last 300 to 400 years, i.e. at the 'receiving end' economically, militarily, politically and (possibly above all) technologically. It is this perception and the corresponding desire to change this state of affairs and to regain a degree of autonomy within the basically hierarchical international system that gives a certain amount of unity to the Third World—despite its diverse nature and its own internal problems—particularly *vis-à-vis* the dominant powers within the international system. And it is this interplay of the Third World's quest for autonomy on the one hand with the great powers' desire to control and manage the international system on the other that provides possibly *the* major contradiction within the international system as it is organised today.

It is in this context that a study of regional conflicts in the Third World and great-power interventions therein becomes both relevant and important. This is so because these regional conflicts provide the dominant powers with a major excuse and instrument to intervene in Third World affairs, thereby further undermining its incipient autonomy.

In addition, they also perform two very important functions for the great powers, as two perceptive Third World scholars, Sisir Gupta and Ali Mazrui, have so eloquently pointed out. The first, to quote Gupta, emerges out of

> the very stability of the global power balance and the determination of the Great Powers to avoid a confrontation [which] makes them prone to seek lower levels of conflict and less dangerous ways of conducting their rivalries, which, in effect, means a concerted attempt to confine their conflicts to problems that impinge on them less directly and to localize them in such areas as are far removed from the areas where their vital interests are involved. To fight out their battles in the Third World is one way of ensuring that their own worlds are not touched by their conflicts and that they retain a greater measure of option to escalate and de-escalate their conflicts according to the needs of their relationships.[2]

In addition to performing the task of providing outlets for competition and low-level conflict-involvement for the major (and particularly the super) powers, regional conflicts also provide the opportunity for the great powers, who also happen to be the major arms manufacturers and suppliers around the globe, to sell as well as test their weapon systems, thereby not merely solving some of their balance of payment problems, particularly in relation to the oil-rich countries, but also keeping track of their own and their adversaries' technological advancement at least in the field of destructive agents. Such conflicts and the accompanying (and, quite often, preceding) supply of large-scale arms to Third World countries also reinforces the structure of dependency within the international system by forcing developing countries and their increasingly nervous elites to sink even deeper into the morass of economic and military dependence upon the super and great powers. Despite occasional demonstrations of autonomy on the part of certain Third World countries *vis-à-vis* their great-power military and political patrons, e.g. Somalia in 1977 and Iran in 1979, and despite the existence of a few centres of relative self-reliance in the Third World, e.g. India, Vietnam and, at times, Egypt and Indonesia, by and large this dependency has led to the further consolidation of the hierarchical nature of the international system and, in fact, to the emergence of a neo-imperial order.

As Ali Mazrui has pointed out so forcefully:

> There has certainly been a change from the old days of Pax Britannica. Whereas the old imperial motto was 'Disarm the natives and facilitate control', the new imperial cunning has translated it into 'Arm the natives and consolidate dependency'. While the British and the French once regarded it as important to stop 'tribal warfare', they now regard it as profitable to modernize 'tribal warfare'—with lethal weapons.[3]

If one puts Gupta's and Mazrui's arguments together one would arrive at a deeper understanding of the major rationale for great-power involvement/intervention in Third World conflicts. This is not to say that there are no other specific reasons which are peculiar to each conflict. Obviously there are many such reasons of a particular rather than a general nature. They include: defence of client regimes, lip-service to particular ideologies, assistance to particularly useful outposts (both in terms of protecting regional interests and appeasing powerful domestic constituencies), attempts to assure the supply of strategic raw materials, from gold to oil. These and many other specific motivations can be attributed to great power decisions to intervene in a particular conflict or regional confrontation. But, in the absence of the two overarching factors pointed out by Gupta and Mazrui, they do not provide the complete answer to the question: why do great powers intervene in regional conflicts around the Third World?

II

Now, a word about regional conflicts. Obviously, although great powers intervene in and exacerbate these conflicts, it can be argued that they do not create or produce all these conflicts. However, if one adds to current great power activity the role played by the European metropolitan powers during the heyday of colonialism and their contribution to the creation of conflict-prone situations around the Third World, one would come to the conclusion that external agents (whether in the form of the former imperial powers or the present-day dominant powers) have been responsible in substantial measure for the existence of regional conflicts in the Third World today and quite often possibly more than the regional actors themselves. While this does not mean that the intrinsically local and regional roots of such conflict should be neglected in the study of regional conflicts (and the contributions to this volume have more than adequately dealt with these factors), it does give considerable weight to the Third World argument that these conflict-prone situations have been deliberately created and encouraged by the dominant powers, both during colonial times and currently, in order to keep the Third World divided and, therefore, weak.

But deliberate or not, this certainly seems to have been the outcome of colonial strategies and their reinforcement and/or continuation by the dominant powers after World War II and during and after the process of formal decolonisation. This contention is also borne out by the case studies we have assembled in this volume. There is not a single case study among the seven that have been analysed here that demonstrates the primacy of exclusively indigenous factors, although such factors are present invariably in almost all cases, in the areas under discussion. The two that come closest to doing so are those relating to South Asia and the Horn of Africa. But even in these instances, the role of external powers, particularly of the great European powers of the colonial days, is crucial. As S.D. Muni has asserted in his chapter on South Asia, while Hindu-Muslim antagonism might have been a fact of Indian political life (although many would argue that prior to British imperial rule, intra-elite conflicts in India were not viewed in such simplistic terms), the almost 200 years of direct British rule, the attempts to rewrite Indian history during that period, and the peculiar communally-based evolution of Indian political life since the early years of the twentieth century which received constant British encouragement from the time of the Aga Khan's 'command performance' of 1906, created a situation which was radically and qualitatively different from the preceding period. It was in the interest of the British imperial masters that intra-elite conflict, always a part of Indian political life, be depicted in communal terms and that it should revolve around Hindu-Muslim issues. It can be reasonably argued that it was this subtle method of 'divide and rule' that left such an indelible mark on the evolution of the subcontinent's political life that it led not only to the division of

India in 1947 but to the continuing hostility between the two successor states—India and Pakistan.

While this factor does not explain all aspects of the South Asian conflict, and while one can also argue that the Hindu and Muslim elites of the subcontinent were not merely puppets incapable of thinking for themselves, it does explain a great deal and is a thesis that requires much greater study and appreciation than it has received. Muni's contention that after 1947 external powers—but primarily Britain and the US—built upon the experiences of the past to continue to exacerbate tensions between India and Pakistan also has considerable explanatory power and provides the missing link between the Hindu-Muslim-British colonial triangle and the India-Pakistan-Great Powers triangle of the post-1947 period.

As far as the Horn of Africa is concerned, while in my chapter on the Horn I have traced the evolution of the Somali-Ethiopian conflict to the attempts on the part of the Christian Amharic rulers of Abyssinia to dominate the largely Muslim population of the Somali lowlands, the dispute in its present form is, once again, the result of the intrusion of European colonial forces into that area. Had the British, the French and the Italians not got into the act of appropriating Somali territories in the late nineteenth century, possibly there would have been little or no provocation for Emperor Menelik of Abyssinia to follow suit and claim large portions of Somali-inhabited territory as part of his empire. Moreover, had the three European powers not accepted the Abyssinian claims in order to protect and legitimise their own colonial possessions on the Somali coast, Abyssinian title to Somali territory, always very thin on the ground, could not have been translated into effective subjugation and occupation after World War II which, in turn, triggered off a Somali reaction which was most dramatically manifested in the Ogaden war of 1977 but whose last chapter has still to be written. The exacerbation of this conflict by the involvement of the superpowers has been documented in my chapter, and when one stands back and takes a dispassionate look at the situation in the Horn one is struck by the remarkable continuity of great power policies in that troubled region. It was first Britain and then the US which had guaranteed the territorial integrity of the Ethiopian Empire. Now it is the turn of the Soviet Union to perform the same role.

At the other end of the spectrum of our case studies are the two very obvious cases of European colonisation which have led to conflict in one case (Rhodesia) and an extremely conflict-prone situation in another (South Africa). The external European factor in the creation of these conflicts is so evident that it does not need any dilation. Both Rhodesia and South Africa are manifestations of the settler-colonial phenomenon which in southern Africa has mounted colonialism's rearguard action. The transformation of Rhodesia into Zimbabwe is proceeding apace, although at considerable human and material cost, as this volume goes to the press. South Africa, isolated within its own *laager*, now provides for students of conflict an almost 'ideal type' situation for study and analysis, a situation where all possible components of conflict—domestic, regional and international—are concentrated and in large measure. When South Africa blows up, as it finally will, it will become *the* conflict of the 1980s before which all other major preoccupations of today's conflict-managers will pale into insignificance. It will also possibly be the bloodiest conflict that the world has seen since the end of the Second World War.

In both these conflicts, however, where the European settler factor obviously predominates, this is not the only externally injected factor. The support extended to the white settler regimes, particularly of South Africa, by the great powers of the West, and particularly by the US until Washington's reassessment of its interests in southern Africa following the Portuguese revolution of 1974 and the subsequent decolonisation of Mozambique and Angola, has resulted in the exacerbation of the conflict by hardening white attitudes and by giving the settler regimes a false sense of security. These policies have also provided the Soviet Union with the opportunity (which is bound to increase as South African intransigence increases in the 1980s) to fish in the troubled African waters at minimum cost and risk to itself. D.J. Goldsworthy and I.R. Hancock have dealt very ably with these propositions and there is nothing more than I can add at this stage to their conclusions.

The Indo-China conflict, encompassing as it does not merely Vietnam and Kampuchea but also China and (at one remove) the Soviet Union, is an extremely complex development, not least because Marxist rhetoric has run wild among all participants. However, if one cuts through all this rhetoric, as J.L.S. Girling has done, and gets to the bare bones of the conflict one will find an intermeshing of various rivalries and conflicts—between Vietnam and Kampuchea, between Vietnam and China, between China and the Soviet Union—which has largely determined the course of events in Indo-China. Once again, although many analysts make a big song and dance about the centuries-old hostility between Vietnam and Kampuchea and look upon it as the 'trigger factor' in the conflict, to a detached observer this seems like putting the cart before the horse—and for a number of reasons. First, it ignores almost totally the entire French colonial experience that Indo-China underwent and the distortions that it introduced in the inter-state relationship within that region. It also ignores the disastrous 15-year American involvement—that is, disastrous for the people of Indo-China. This was, again, basically a continuation of France's colonial war and an attempt to deny Hanoi the role of challenging the foreign imperial power by the creation of various puppet regimes to keep it in check. Superimposed on this were the Soviet-US, the Sino-US and the Sino-Soviet rivalries which immensely complicated the situation.

Since the US withdrawal from Indo-China happened to coincide with the Sino-US rapprochement, the stage was almost set for the beginning of a new phase with a new delineation of forces in that part of the world—the Soviets supporting Vietnam and China, with the blessing of the US, bent upon putting Hanoi in its place. Kampuchea and its Pol Pot regime were caught up in this web of conflicts partly because they had no choice and partly due to the lack of required political wisdom on Phnom Penh's part. In this conflict, therefore, the involvement of the two communist great powers and their attempts to use Indo-Chinese actors as proxies have combined both with the existence of regional antagonisms and the history of French colonial and American imperial exploits to create a situation which excludes a tidy solution.

III

We now come to the last two conflicts, in Cyprus and in the Middle East, about both of which there have been continuing debates relating to the primacy of domestic versus external factors in creating these conflicts and in determining their course.

Once again, if one delves into the history of the origin of these two problems one would come to the conclusion that the colonial experience under European rule (both Cyprus and Palestine were British possessions, one a Crown Colony the other a League of Nations Mandate) has determined, to a very large extent, the contours of the present problems and the consequent conflicts between regional adversaries.

While it is true that Cyprus had been a part of the Ottoman Empire and that the Turkish presence there dates to its pre-British experience of Ottoman imperial rule, British imperial interests and London's attempts to preserve its strategic foothold in Cyprus even at the time of the island's independence (in fact, as a price for the granting of such independence), as has been pointed out in the chapter by John Zarocostas, tended to compound the island's problems. When NATO, and particularly the US, got into the act, thus giving a global dimension to the dispute, the island's internal problem was almost totally lost in the web of larger regional and global issues. An accord between the two Cypriot communities *per se* was treated as a very low priority issue by the bigwigs of NATO, particularly the US, especially as compared to the intramural problem the Greek-Turkish conflict posed for NATO and in relation to the effect the escalation of such conflict in the close proximity of the USSR would have had for the global balance of power between Washington and Moscow. Thus, not only was the Cyprus problem to a large extent the creation of British colonialism, its solution has been greatly impeded by the intrusion of great power interests into the issue which have virtually changed the problem beyond recognition.

The origins of the Arab-Israeli conflict, very much like those of Cyprus, also tend to get lost in the current discussion of the problem and of its regional and global implications. But, even more clearly than the Cyprus issue, this problem was almost exclusively created by the great European powers during the first half of the twentieth century. The common mistake, often deliberate but sometimes unwitting, committed by most analysts of this dispute is that they take 1948 as the starting point of the problem. The actual origins of the issue, however, go back at least to the Balfour Declaration of 1917, made on behalf of the British government, which promised a rather ill-defined 'national home' in Palestine to the Jews of Europe. They go back again to 1922 when the League of Nations awarded the mandate for Palestine to Britain which immediately came under Zionist pressure for the creation of the promised Jewish homeland.

The development of the Zionist entity in Palestine, which emerged finally in 1948 as the state of Israel, followed closely the usual pattern of the development first of a European settler community in an alien Asian environment and then of the imposition of a settler regime against the wishes of the indigenous majority. The only big difference in this case was that this regime, with invaluable external help, was able to change the indigenous majority of the country into a minority—an objective which few other settler regimes have been able to achieve in history and certainly no other has been able to achieve in the twentieth century.

As Maxime Rodinson has so ably argued, in this process of settler colonisation,

> the historical role of mother country for *Yishuv* was played by Europe as a whole, which unloaded into Palestine elements it considered undesirable, just as it sent convicts to colonize Australia or Guyana. Great Britain was the motor force in that by force of arms it conquered the territory to be occupied, set up an administration there, and imposed what it is accustomed to call law and order. In return it met with the anger of its 'colonists' [Jews in Palestine] when it thought it could limit their progress toward completely controlling the said territory.[4]

The declaration in 1948 of the establishment of the State of Israel, therefore, corresponds not so much to the emergence, say, of India as an independent state in 1947, as to Ian Smith's Unilateral Declaration of Independence (UDI) for white-ruled Rhodesia in 1965. It was an act aimed against the mother country, viz. Britain, because the latter no longer continued to serve settler interests. In fact from 1922 to the early 1940s, Britain had admirably performed the role of the mother country for the Jewish settlers. During this period of 20 years the Jewish population in Palestine under British aegis grew from eleven per cent (in 1922) to 31.5 per cent (in 1943) of the total population thus establishing the demographic base for a Zionist takeover. But when London woke up to the fact that it could no longer go on serving Zionist interests at the expense of its wider interests in the Arab world (just as it woke up to this fact in the early 1960s in Rhodesia), the colonists were ready to cut the umbilical cord which, in any case, had outlived its purpose. Therefore, if one looks at the problem in its proper historical perspective, it will be very difficult for one to deny that, 'The advancement and the success of the Zionist movement thus definitely occurred within the framework of European expansion into the countries belonging to what later came to be called the Third World.'[5]

The seeds of the Arab-Israeli conflict, therefore, were sown by a European colonial power for its own ends which related only partially to Palestine but were inextricably intertwined with its wider imperial objectives regarding the Suez Canal on the one hand and its Indian empire on the other. There is no need to go into any great detail here in the analysis of the course of the conflict since 1948 and its present multi-dimensional importance—a task which has been already very ably performed by Robert Springborg in his chapter on the Middle East. I would only like to emphasise, once again, the primacy accorded by the hegemonic powers in the current world order to their wider interests—global and sometimes even domestic, particularly in the case of the United States[6]—and the very subsidiary importance accorded to the resolution of the Middle East conflict for its own sake. Since such a resolution cannot be achieved short of finding a just solution to the Palestinian quest for a political identity, but since this does not suit the interests of the global managers, and particularly of the US, the Palestinian demand is continuously ignored in the various 'peace' attempts being made by the great powers. While this might help one or both of the superpowers to get around the issue in the short run, in the long run it is bound to create a much more explosive situation.

But, as the title of this volume suggests, the role of the great powers, and particularly the superpowers, in the international system has been primarily one of conflict-management and, quite often, of conflict-exacerbation, rather than helping in the resolution of regional conflicts. As long as such conflicts stop short of threatening the central power balance they are considered tolerable —even if in a constant simmering state—with short regional wars permitted as a means of letting off steam. When such conflicts occasionally approach the point where the central balance is in danger of being directly affected one way or another, as was the case in the Middle East war of 1973, attempts are made to 'manage' them and to increase further the 'immunity' of the central balance from peripheral issues, disputes and conflicts. As Sisir Gupta has argued in his essay already quoted above:

> Although the relations between the Super Powers have been stabilized, there has been a perceptible rise in the level of permissibility of chaos, conflict and violence in those regions of the world which are peripheral for the purposes of the central balance. The evident fact that conflicts and clashes among the states of these regions provide the Great Powers with a high

> degree of leverage on them and a great opportunity to increase their influence over the parties in such a conflict must be appearing to them as a matter of some advantage, though as *status quo* states they cannot but be interested in maintaining a minimum degree of stability even in the remote regions of the world.[7]

What is, however, even more disturbing than this 'permissibility' of chaos and conflict in the Third World, is the recent indication of a reversion on the part of the great powers to a modified and updated policy of gunboat diplomacy, viz. direct intervention in areas of the Third World where they see their interests (or those of their clients) threatened. One would have expected that with the end of America's disastrous intervention in Vietnam, the overtly interventionist phase in great power policy towards the Third World would have come to an end. But, apparently, old habits die very hard. We now see a new phase of this policy opening with Soviet intervention in the Horn of Africa (partially by Cuban proxy but also directly) and by the US reaction to recent events in Iran leading to the overthrow of the Shah and the end of the old regime. While up till now there has been no *direct* US intervention in the affairs of the Gulf which can be equated with Soviet intervention in the Horn, the new pattern of US naval deployment in the Indian Ocean-Persian Gulf region, the talk at the highest US decision-making level of the creation of the Fifth Fleet to patrol that area (admittedly speculative so far), and the serious consideration being given in Washington, according to Defense Secretary Harold Brown, to the augmentation of US interventionist capability in the Gulf and other strategic resource-rich regions of the Third World[8] is cause for great concern. This is because these superpower strategies are aimed not so much at neutralising advantages that might have accrued to their superpower adversary in a particular region, but are aimed essentially at denying Third World countries the autonomy to define their own political, social and economic futures and the strategies by which they should be achieved. The parallels between Soviet policy in the Horn, which I have discussed in some detail in my chapter on that region, and American policy in the Gulf are in this respect very illuminating.[9] Certain other interventions by European powers, primarily by the French, in parts of Africa are another manifestation of the same phenomenon and have been undertaken with the blessings of at least one superpower.

To conclude, therefore, we find that not only are the roots of regional conflicts in the Third World today traceable in substantial measure to the acts of omission and commission performed by the European colonial powers—the great powers and conflict-managers of earlier days—but that during and after the period of formal decolonisation they have been exacerbated by the policies, strategies and activities of those who currently hold great, and particularly super, power status. Not only have these antagonisms been allowed to fester because low-level peripheral tension suited the interests of the superpowers once the central balance had become stabilised, but, in fact, many of them were actively encouraged, particularly by means of arms transfer, by those who aspired to manage the post-World War international system. In addition, a new phase of gunboat diplomacy on the part of the great powers now threatens to erode if not completely destroy the incipient political autonomy of the Third World countries. It is ironic that while negotiations about a New International Economic Order are in progress, the International Political Order seems to be moving in a retrogressive direction which, if it is not reversed, will lead to increasing control of the Third World's political activities—conflictual or otherwise—by the managers of the international system and thus stifle all demands for political justice in the Third World —at the level of individual, social stratum, class, nation or region. This, in essence, would perpetuate global inequality in the guise of preserving world order—an order imposed and controlled by the big few (and particularly by the big two) for their own benefit.

Notes

1. There are a number of excellent studies on this subject including Mahbub ul Haq, *The Poverty Curtain* (Columbia University Press, New York, 1976).
2. Sisir Gupta, 'Great Power Relations, World Order and the Third World', *Foreign Affairs Reports*, vol. 27, nos. 7-8 (July-August 1978), p. 134.
3. Ali A. Mazrui, 'The Barrel of the Gun and the Barrel of Oil', *Alternatives*, vol. 3, no. 4 (May 1978), p. 474.
4. Maxime Rodinson, *Israel: A Colonial Settler State?* (Monad Press, New York, 1973), p. 86.
5. Ibid., p. 77.
6. For an interesting discussion of this latter connection, see Jane Rosen, 'US Middle East Policy Courtesy of the Jewish Lobby', *Guardian Weekly*, 25 September 1977, p. 9.
7. Gupta, *Great Power Relations*, p. 135.
8. *International Herald Tribune*, 4 January 1979.
9. For details of this comparison, see Mohammed Ayoob, 'The Super Powers and Regional "Stability": Parallel Responses to the Gulf and the Horn', *The World Today* (May 1979), pp. 197-205.

Contributors

Mohammed Ayoob, Senior Research Fellow, Department of International Relations, Research School of Pacific Studies, Australian National University.

J.L.S. Girling, Senior Fellow, Department of International Relations, Research School of Pacific Studies, Australian National University.

D.J. Goldsworthy, Reader, Department of Politics, Faculty of Economics and Politics, Monash University.

I.R. Hancock, Senior Lecturer, Department of History, School of General Studies, Australian National University.

T.B. Millar, Professorial Fellow, Department of International Relations, Research School of Pacific Studies, Australian National University.

S.D. Muni, Associate Professor, Centre for South and Southeast Asian Studies, School of International Studies Jawaharlal Nehru University, New Delhi.

Robert Springborg, Senior Lecturer, Department of Politics, School of History, Philosophy and Politics, Macquarie University.

John Zarocostas, Graduate Student, Department of Political Science, School of General Studies, Australian National University.

Index

For Product Safety Concerns and Information please contact our EU representative GPSR@taylorandfrancis.com Taylor & Francis Verlag GmbH, Kaufingerstraße 24, 80331 München, Germany